DRINK
THIS

DRINK THIS

THIS

WINE
MADE SIMPLE

DARA MOSKOWITZ GRUMDAHL

BALLANTINE BOOKS
NEW YORK

Published in the United States by Ballantine Books, an imprint of
The Random House Publishing Group, a division of Random House, Inc., New York.
Ballantine and colophon are registered trademarks of Random House, Inc.

Library of Congress Cataloging-in-Publication Data
Grumdahl, Dara Moskowitz.
Drink this : wine made simple / Dara Moskowitz Grumdahl.
p.   cm.
Includes index.
ISBN 978-0-345-51165-2
eBook ISBN 978-0-345-51722-7
1. Wine and wine making—Popular works.   2. Wine and
wine making—Miscellanea.   I. Title.
TP548.G78 2009
641.2'2—dc22   2009036047

Printed in the United States of America on acid-free paper

www.ballantinebooks.com

2 4 6 8 9 7 5 3 1

First Edition

FOR NATHAN

CONTENTS

INTRODUCTION

I've been a restaurant critic since 1997, a period of time that has neatly coincided with the rise of email. Ever since I started writing about food and wine, emails from readers have flowed toward me, sometimes in trickles and sometimes in floods. Some of the most simple questions readers asked, and nearly all of the deceptively complex ones, had to do with wine. This book was inspired by those brief, often brilliant questions.

Dear Dara,

Why is wine more confusing than poker? More confusing than football? More confusing than politics, rock and roll, Socrates, Moroccan cooking, or the stock market? Any of those you can get a basic familiarity with on Wikipedia in about twenty minutes. Not so wine. I've tried. I've also tried reading wine magazines, talking to sommeliers, and getting help from the dude at my wine store, who seems very nice but sounds insane: Do I like pepper in my wine? Does anyone? I've been at this on and off for years, so at this point, I

bet no, this will never make sense to me. Is there any
hope?

—Truly, truly, baffled

Dear Baffled—There is always hope.

I was not born into a wine family, I didn't start drinking wine with any regularity until my midtwenties, but now I've got so many wine writing awards that the heavy bronze medals are the first thing I reach for to use as weapons when I think I hear burglars in the night. No, actually, I don't, but I could, and it's that idea that keeps me feeling safe.

How did I go from zero wine experience to plenty? I entered the workforce during the first George Bush recession, and set about pursuing my dream of becoming a novelist. I earned less than $7,000 one of those first years out of college, working three jobs. Seriously. As a way of putting actual protein on my plate, I became a restaurant critic. At the time this was considered a particularly low-status job. At my Minneapolis-based newspaper real writers spoke truth to power, they didn't speak truth to lasagna.

Yet when I started writing about food I found it both comforting and exciting. I had gotten my first job when I was thirteen as a dishwasher in a Cape Cod restaurant kitchen, and had climbed the hierarchy of the back of the house fast enough that by the time I was eighteen I was working as the sous-chef in a busy Italian place and moonlighting as a part-time pastry chef at a bed-and-breakfast. I also spent time waitressing, both in New York City and later in Minneapolis.

I knew what food was supposed to be, and when it was failing. It pissed me off both as a consumer and as a former restaurant cook when lobster ravioli showed up full of broken lobster shells. It infuriated me as a former server when I'd be sitting at a table as a diner with an empty water glass *and* an empty wineglass while my server sat near the kitchen reading newspapers. Consequently, my columns were pretty gloves-off. I'd write things such as:

> There I was withered to my bones with dehydration. Tumbleweeds rattled around my water glass. My waiter had apparantly given up the profession and lit out for a better life. The floor manager was busy giving free drinks to another, louder table, to apologize to them for all the things they wanted that they couldn't have— like food, and for them wine, since no one thought to entrust the floor manager with the key to the tantalizing wine cellar. It had been a long hour since I placed an appetizer order, and I may as well have been waiting for a bus for all the fine dining I was doing. I felt like Pamela Anderson at a NAMBLA convention.

My column in the *Village Voice*–owned alternative weekly *City Pages* developed a following. Unexpectedly, for someone who was just in it for the protein, I grew to love food writing as much as I had loved cooking. However, the pay left a lot to be desired. The job was taking four to six days a week, between writing, going to meals worth writing about, going to meals not worth writing about, and so on, and I was taking home about $150 a week—plus food!— without health insurance. While I was doing something I loved, I needed to figure out a way to make a living at what I loved, or move on.

My boss at the time figured it out for me: He proposed that if I started writing about wine, that would fill enough pages to earn a living wage and health insurance.

Most wine critics do not come into wine writing this way. Most love wine, and then find their way to writing about it. I didn't love wine until I had been writing about it for a few years. I liked it, I loved particular things I tried, but I didn't have a warts-and-all love for it for quite a while. Mostly at first I found it overwhelming. What again was the difference between Bordeaux and Cabernet Sauvignon? What made a good wine list and a bad one? What was the right wine list for a Thai restaurant? Why did some Syrahs taste like jam and others like smoke? After all, wasn't this just the fermented juice of grapes? All apple ciders taste pretty similar, so why are two Rieslings so different?

Once I stopped feeling overwhelmed I did fall in love with the stuff, and I fell hard. Now I think it's the rarest of all substances, a magical point where art and nature intersect— like a Renaissance landscape painting, or a bronze flower. But in this case the intersection doesn't just sit there to be admired, it's poured right into you and makes you one with workers, thinkers, trees, wind, rain, and sunshine thousands of miles away. Wine is not merely the most marvelous drink on earth, but, considering that the key to making wine—the yeast—is found right on the grapes themselves, one of the great miracles and wonders of the natural world.

The path from being overwhelmed by wine to understanding it and being able to relax and enjoy its grace wasn't easy for me to find. It required a lot of reading, and a lot of tasting. However, since I needed to turn myself into a wine professional, fast, I quickly grew impatient with wine writing. Wine writers, God love them, are almost all burdened by knowing too much. They can't hear the words "Sauvignon Blanc" without bringing to mind the flint *terroir* of Sancerre or the mango-lime bouquet of Marlborough, and they live in such a wine-involved universe that they don't know that most of the other people in the country,

even well-educated people, have no idea what they're talking about.

Now that I know a lot about wine I realize this isn't as
weird or arrogant as I once thought—we all know culturally
specific things that we express in shorthand. For instance,
you meet a friend you haven't seen in a while in the airport:

"Hungry?" you ask.

"Nah, I grabbed a Reuben in the business-class lounge."

"How was it?"

"Better than you'd think."

Chances are, a better-than-you'd-think business-class-
lounge Reuben conjures up a fairly definite picture in your
mind. What is that picture?

There's an inch or so of corned beef (salted, long-cooked
beef brisket sliced across the grain), topped with sauerkraut (fermented shredded green cabbage in the German
tradition), Swiss cheese (a cultured, long-aged milk product
with a nutty, tangy taste), a pinkish dressing made with a
good portion of mayonnaise (a creamy emulsification of egg
yolks in vinegar and oil), and ketchup (a dark red concentrated spiced tomato paste). The sandwich [as a whole] is
hot; it is contained between slices of rye or pumpernickel
bread thick enough to prevent it from exploding; those
slices of bread have a fifty-fifty chance of containing small
caraway seeds; and so on. You likely know even more about
this business-class-lounge Reuben without anyone's telling
you anything about it—for instance, it probably came with
a pickle spear (cucumber brined in pickling spices, including allspice, cut in lengthwise quarters), and thin, deep-
fried, well-salted slices of a white variety of a root vegetable
that originated in the Andes served at room temperature
(potato chips). Finally, you know intuitively, without even
thinking about it, that this business-class-lounge Reuben
was not consumed with a nice big glass of grapefruit juice

but with a big Coke poured over a glass prefilled with plenty of ice.

How do you know all this? The same way wine writers know what they know: through half a dozen experiences of putting the thing-in-question in your mouth. You didn't set out to learn what Reubens were like—in delis, in cafeterias, in gas stations, in truck stops, made cold and wan, made vegetarian or low-fat or with turkey pastrami—over time, you just did. But what if you were presented with the task of teaching a visiting Chinese scholar about Reubens? You'd take her to taste half a dozen sandwiches, and then she'd know as much about them as most Americans, and if she fell in love with them she could try another dozen, and she'd know as much about them as most Americans.

That's my big secret. After long research I discovered that to understand wine you had to taste it.

Actually, though, that's harder than you'd think. Wine is a rushing river, hundreds of thousands of producers, millions of different bottlings. A single winery might make six different Pinot Noirs, four Chardonnays, and a dozen other wines, and then the vintages change every year. To try to learn what Sauvignon Blanc is, you can't taste *one* bottle. You might end up with some gourmet sandwich maker's chipotle-braised brisket Reuben, or a cold gas-station Reuben, and then what have you learned? Nothing useful.

You can, however, taste six Sauvignon Blancs and scramble to the top of the heap of understanding pretty quickly— if you have a good guide. Turning myself into that guide took some doing. And I was greatly aided by strangers. You see, back at the start, as I buried myself in reference books and maps, my only real consolation was that I was not alone. Readers trying to untangle wine emailed me constantly. They asked deceptively simple questions, questions like why couldn't they find the wines written up in *The Wall*

Street Journal in their local shop? Why was all the cheap wine Australian? Why did restaurants offer entirely different wines than stores did? Often their questions took weeks to answer, because the answers were hard to find, though I did find them by talking to wine distributors, sommeliers, and winemakers, and mining the Internet for bits of information on dull subjects such as Australian tax policy.

This experience convinced me that wine writing, wine education, wine shops—the whole world of wine, as I came to think of it—was not meeting the needs of average Americans. Americans are smarter than most wine writers give them credit for—for instance, they quickly grow scornful of national praise heaped on wine made in a ridiculously small batch of forty cases—but Americans are also, dare I say it, dumber.

I know this because *I* am dumber. I grew up in the post-geography era of American public education, when social studies and computer science were core elements of the curriculum and had pushed out most everything that had to do with Europe. If someone asks me where the Vosges Mountains are or who Eleanor of Aquitaine was, I need to stall them long enough to run to a computer and find out.

To my great chagrin, I discovered you do indeed need to know something about European history and geography to comprehend wine. You don't need to know a lot, but you do need to know a few key things. As I went along learning about wine, I kept stumbling upon more and more key things, and eventually came up with a sort of quick and dirty way to teach myself—a secret decoder ring, if you will.

I tried it out on my friends, I wrote about it for my newspaper, and before I knew it I had scored two back-to-back years of the biggest award in wine writing, the James Beard Award for wine writing in a newspaper. I felt like the

Cowardly Lion; all of a sudden I could clank around the house in my wine medals.

Just as the Cowardly Lion's medal gave him courage, mine gave me courage. Specifically it gave me the courage to tell you: You *can* learn about wine, fast. You *can* teach yourself everything you need to know to be happy in wine shops, wine bars, and restaurants, and you *can* do it in a way that makes sense to you.

There's only one caveat: You can't teach yourself *everything* about wine fast. There's a reason people study it for a lifetime. Think of it like learning to write. Every high school graduate in the country should be able to write a decent three-page paper, giving them general, and eternal, competence in the world of written communication. However, whether any given eighth-grader goes on to be Mark Twain or Toni Morrison is another story.

General, but also eternal, wine competence is what I'm offering you. For most of you, that will be enough. Good enough to get you through every restaurant visit, every Thanksgiving wine purchasing experience, and your local wine shop. For the rest of you, competence will not be enough, and this book will merely be the kickoff to a lifelong adventure.

So, is general competence what you're in the market for? If you are someone who stands in the wine shop and looks at all the Pinot Noirs and wonders which one you'll like, this book is for you. If you are someone who gets angry because Americans simplify Burgundy by talking about it in terms of its major grapes, such as Pinot Noir, this book is probably not for you.

Drink This is about simplification, the same way that the first book you'd get in your first French class would be about simplification—*because you have to start somewhere.* Don't underestimate the magic and power of starting somewhere. Trying to learn everything at once is the major thing that keeps people floundering around in the world of wine and never making sense of it.

Most people try to learn about wine by trying something here, something there, something else another time. This is like trying to learn the day's news by randomly plucking a hundred sentences from a hundred newspapers. In order to really learn something about wine you have to simplify, and start somewhere.

How simple can wine really get? This simple: Each and every wine on earth is made up of three and only three things—what we will call the Holy Trinity of wine:

1. Type of grapes.
2. Where the grapes were grown.
3. How the grapes were turned into wine.

That's all. Of course, you could write volumes on each of these three things, but these are the three basic things we'll consider for every wine being discussed from here on out.

Think of those three elements as the legs of a conceptual stool. The grapes are one leg; the individual characteristics of where they were grown, including the soil, the local earthworms, the morning fog, and a hundred more variables that the French, and many others, collectively call *terroir,* is another leg; and the hundreds of choices involved in wine-making are the third. Each of those elements is a leg of the stool, and the wine itself is the magical thing created when those three things come together. Let's take the quickest possible look at each of these elements of the Holy Trinity of wine.

The **grapes,** of course, can't be underestimated. No matter where you grow them, no matter how many winemaking tricks you deploy, you can't make Cabernet Sauvignon out of Chardonnay grapes. No more than you can make tangerine juice out of a grapefruit. That's why this book is arranged primarily by types of grape, known as varietals. I picked the nine varietals I judged would be most helpful to you, the ones that comprise most of the wine sold and consumed in America: Zinfandel, Sauvignon Blanc, Riesling, Chardonnay, Cabernet Sauvignon, Syrah, Sangiovese, Tempranillo, and Pinot Noir. (I had to leave out some important grapes for reasons of length.) Know these nine grapes and you'll have the keys to the universe at your fingertips.

Terroir, or where the grapes are grown, can encompass any number of things, from the rain to the soil type to the length of the days and nearby wild plants. The French, and most American critics, believe that *terroir* is the most important characteristic of any wine. You may find that you agree, or you may not.

Winemaking—or, as the French call it, *élevage,* that is, "raising" grape juice to the exalted status of wine—is the third consideration. This can encompass any number of things, from careful management of the grapes in the fields (for instance, by trimming away select leaves so that grape clusters are exposed to sunlight), to different fermentation techniques, to choices such as what varieties of grapes to use in a final blend or whether to age the wine in oak barrels.

You'll find, as you go through the chapters of this book, that for any individual wine, one leg of the stool may become preeminent: Pouilly Fumé, for instance, the French Sauvignon Blanc, must be discussed in terms of *terroir.* Why? Because it smells distinctly of "gunflint," which no other Sauvignon Blanc does, resulting from the rocks it is rooted in.

Other wines are less about *terroir* than about winemaking. A very buttery, creamy, ripe and rich Chardonnay, for instance, is many people's idea of heaven. As you will learn in the Chardonnay chapter, it would not exist without its various techniques of *élevage*.

In each varietal chapter you'll see how these three "legs," or elements, are manifest in each category of wines. You'll get advice on how to taste and contrast one bottle of the same varietal against another that showcases a different leg of the stool. This can be done either as a party with your friends or on your own, to get a sense of how you like each wine and what you'll want to try again in the future. And that is how you will learn wine fast—by breaking down the process and approaching it systematically.

Want some more advice on being systematic? Don't think about, don't drink, and don't shop for Syrah and Pinot Noir and Cabernet Sauvignon all at the same time. Walk into a wine shop thinking: This store sells Syrah and things that are invisible to me. Pick up a wine list thinking: This list includes Syrah and things that are invisible to me. If you do this, I promise you that within six or ten experiences Syrah will be known to you, the Syrah choices around you will seem sensible and obvious, and you will be able to move on to your next grape.

Most of this book is about simplifying the choices before you so you can make sense of them. The point of learning about wine is not to know everything about wine. The point of learning about wine is to enjoy life more. The way that you enjoy life more is to use what you have learned so that you can more easily find what you like.

The idea of "what you like" is actually more of a land mine than you might think. The phrase rolls easily off the tongue, but just what is "what you like"?

What you like is the only thing that matters. It's your taste.

The whole idea of taste is usually off-putting to new wine drinkers. They think there's a hierarchy of wine and everyone likes "the good stuff." Not true. The same rules hold for wine as for the rest of human taste: Some people like chocolate cake, and some people like apple pie. Some people like spicy Thai curries, and some people like homey chicken soup. Some like all of these but prefer curry and chocolate cake one week, and apple pie and chicken soup another. Wine is no different. The only difference is that when it comes to wine there are people at the top saying: My favorite chocolate cake, 98 points; Italian apple pie, 91 points.

Most people new to wine think critical scores are objective things, like a stamp of 18-karat versus 24-karat gold. Once you work through a couple of these chapters, you will come to see that they're really just some guy's opinion, and just because some guy tells you that he likes some particular chocolate cake, or Cabernet Sauvignon, is no reason to alter your behavior, any more than you would sit down in a restaurant chair and ask for the exact same meal that the guy at the next table is having. The reason you want what you want is because of your taste. The real problem that new wine drinkers have is simply that they don't know what their taste is, because they haven't tasted all the representative wine styles.

What is your taste? Who knows! Some people drink Riesling and feel their knees go weak, but Cabernet Sauvignon leaves them cold. Some people love stony Chablis but hate buttery Napa Valley Chardonnay, even though the two are made from the exact same grape, and some people feel just the opposite. All of these are defensible positions, all of these are critically relevant. And you will be buffeted on the

Conversations with Bigwigs: Bo Barrett

The Judgment of Paris was the 1976 blind tasting at which a panel of critics compared top French Burgundies and Bordeaux with American Chardonnays and Cabernet Sauvignons, and, to everyone's great shock, gave top honors to two American wines. Chateau Montelena's Chardonnay was the white wine winner. Bo Barrett was just a kid then, starting out at his family's winery (the winning winemaker was Mike Grgich). Subsequently he guided Montelena to becoming one of Napa Valley's preeminent wineries, married one of the world's greatest winemakers (100-point generator Heidi Barrett, mother of Screaming Eagle, the cult Cabernet that defined cult Cabernets for a generation, among other wines), and generally put himself in the center of American winemaking. But how does he see American winemaking? As emerging from a hundred-year slump:

Bad ideas in the United States take about a hundred years to go away. Slavery was outlawed in the 1860s, but it didn't really start to fade until the 1960s. Prohibition wiped out American wine, the culture, the industry, starting from about 1910 and of course going official from 1920 [until 1933], and now that we're heading to 2010 it's finally starting to fade. When we came out of Prohibition, the only people who cared about wine anymore were the upper crust—the government can do a lot of bad things when it wants to, and it was basically government that wiped out wine in people's daily lives. Before that, American wine had a big boom in the 1890s and good market acceptance because of the scarcity of European wines, due to phylloxera [the vine pest that wiped out most European vineyards, forcing them to be replanted on American rootstock]. But then the government wiped out the wine industry in one fell swoop, and when we came out of that it was right into the Depression, and then right into

World War II, so there wasn't really any time or money for things like wine.

Once the war ended, there was all this technology, fertilizer, things that came out of the war. It was the Age of Industrial Wine—from about 1946 to say 1965. All the technological advances were driven by the Gallos—refrigeration, stainless steel tanks, and so on. At the time, really the only handcrafted wines in America were Inglenook and BV Georges de Latour; everything else was in an industrial wine style and the products were not very good. Of course, during Prohibition there was one legal loophole: You were allowed to make two hundred gallons of wine per head of household, for personal consumption. So most of the smaller vineyards in California survived those years by growing [grape] varieties that could survive transcontinental shipping [for home winemaking], like Grenache, Alicante [Bouschet], Burger, and some Colombard. When we got here in 1972 we had to replant everything.

But by 1968 things were changing. Robert Mondavi moved down the road from us, and the handcrafted deal started to spread around. Twenty-five new wineries opened around here in 1972—we call it the class of '72—and that was the beginning of the real California wine boom. The Greatest Generation guys were starting to wind down from the jobs they got after the military (in my father's case he was an attorney, corporate and real estate law), and at the same time there was the granola-cruncher movement. Everyone wants to get back to the land. But once we started making handcrafted wine—it's the early '70s, we really think we're on to something, but now we can't sell it. Wine snobs? Trying to sell California wine in Boston? Forget it. No one wants California wine, you can't give it away.

Then there was the Judgment of Paris, the cover of *Time* magazine, and market acceptance was basically overnight. What we had to do for all these wine snobs was to overrun their positions with quality. But then we had to

make sure we didn't turn into snobs ourselves; it's important to go out in the vineyard and keep your feet on the
ground, literally. Everybody [in Napa Valley] recognizes we
don't have a monopoly on quality: the South Africans are
doing some great things, and of course everyone else.
When you went out in 1976 you could easily find bad
wines, but when you go out now, the quality of wine across
the board is better; it's really hard to find a defective wine
anymore. You almost don't need to know anything to
avoid really bad wine because the crappy stuff is no longer
being sold. At the other end of the scale, the bar is always
moving upward. The top successful wines we made in 1978
would be also-rans now, which is something a lot of people won't admit.

For most of us, snobbery is not an option, because
you're covered with mud, you're out in the fields with the
guy that drives the tractor, and it becomes ever more obvious that the more you learn about wine the more you realize you don't know. It's a craft and an art and a science, and
people that get that get it and those that don't think they
know everything. The magic words there are "get it"—there
are a lot of people who don't get it and just go through the
motions. In winemaking, you build on your experience. It's
like baseball: Hey, I know this guy and I think I can get him
with a high slider. Sometimes it works and sometimes he
hits it. It's dynamic. You're not totally in control. The people
who think they are are just fooling themselves.

confusing seas of everyone else's opinions until you find
that most important of all things: your own taste.

When you discover your taste, the whole world will open
up to you. You won't fall into that trap of thinking that 98-
point wines are the really good ones while 80-point ones
aren't. You will see that it's simply as if some wines are

chocolate cakes while others are steaks, smoked salmon, doughnuts, black coffee, hot dogs, cassoulet, and so on. When critics give out 98-point scores, what they're really saying is, "When I compare this steak to the greatest steak I can possibly conceive of, I give it 98 out of 100 points." They are not saying, "Eat nothing but steak."

Depending on your taste, your mood, the weather, what you're eating for dinner, or a million other variables, you are sometimes going to want a steak, and sometimes salmon or a doughnut. This book sits you down in front of, say, six guises of salmon. It says, "Here are salmon sushi, hot smoked salmon, cold smoked salmon, poached salmon, cedar-planked salmon, and pan-seared salmon. Taste them. Now you know what salmon tastes like. If you liked them all, congratulations, you like salmon. If you didn't like any of them, congratulations, you don't like salmon. If you were absolutely enchanted with the salmon sushi, congratulations, you now have something to tell people in wine shops and sommeliers for the rest of your life."

The reason that wine is hard to learn about is that you can read about it for six straight years and that experience will be but dust in the wind compared to tasting it. In wine, tasting is everything. It's the most important part of wine, end of story.

And that's what makes this book different from other wine books: It will guide you through tasting methodically and in context. After this introduction you'll find a chapter on the nuts and bolts of tasting wine. The next nine chapters focus on grape varietals. I chose these because they make the majority of the world's wine and fill the majority of the wine lists in American restaurants, and I arranged the book by varietal because I find it's the fastest way to make sense of the flavors and wines you find around you.

Just as there are different sorts of apples—green Granny Smiths, square-shouldered Red Delicious, little yellow crab-apples and so on—there are different sorts of wine grapes, and different sorts of grapes make different flavors of wine. The reason there are so many varieties is that different grape varieties do well in different places; different grapes grow well in hot southern Italy than in cold Germany. The nine major varietals we'll consider make most of the wine you'll find out in the world.

Field Guides

Each of these nine varietal chapters will give you some important background information on the grape in question, and will also address one or more of the major factors that make wine what it is. Each varietal chapter also contains a Field Guide to the sorts of that varietal of wine you will find in stores—the different price points, the way different styles taste, what you're paying for when you pay more, and so on.

I'll categorize wines the way you'll find them displayed in most liquor stores. The phrase "bottom-shelf wines" refers, literally, to wines on the bottom shelves. Retailers put them there because that's the tradition, and also because they'd really rather you didn't buy them, because they don't cost much. Liquor stores, like most stores, make their profit as a percentage of the total sale, so they might make $30 on a $70 bottle of wine, but only $1 or $2 on a $5 one. Top-shelf wines are found, yes, on the top shelf; they are wines you stand beneath and admire—and that you can't easily knock over and break. Those cost more.

These Field Guides serve several functions. First, they provide a way of looking at the overwhelming array of wines in the store. Second, they tell you what's important in the wine shop aisle and what's not. Third, they allow you to select wines for a tasting so that you can know what the wines in question taste like in the only way that matters; in your very own mouth.

Speaking of tasting: As I've said, you must. That's why after every Field Guide, each chapter features a step-by-step guide to tasting your chosen varietal, addressing everything from what to eat with what you're drinking to what to ask yourself while you're drinking. In addition, I summarize each Field Guide in a small "wine shopping list" designed for you either to photocopy or to take physically to the store to point at while you talk to your wine clerk. I put this in so you wouldn't have the hassle of needing to thumb through the book in the aisles.

Tasting Markers

In the tasting section, each varietal chapter also contains a list of something I call *tasting markers*. Most of how a wine tastes is actually how it smells. If you've ever had a bad head cold and had all food turn into flavorless paste, you know what I'm talking about. Smell is critical when it comes to wine. But Americans don't have a great vocabulary for smell, we never talk about smell, we never practice smell, and so when we read wine notes like "It was peppery with leather, raspberry, and cassis notes," that seems strange and confusing.

I have, however, learned a trick that makes smelling—and thus tasting—the differences between and among wines much easier. Take peppercorns and stick them in an empty wineglass, swirl them around, and voilà! That's what pepper smells like in wine.

You may feel skeptical about this and think it peculiar, but I swear to you, do it once and you will never look back. Sticking a slice of apple in one wineglass, a couple of wet rocks in another, and a bit of vanilla extract in a third will take your Chardonnay tasting from something that vaguely makes sense to something in which the differences between the wines, and the elements of those you like, are head-slappingly obvious.

Truly, these should be called "scent markers," but in wine we talk about "tasting notes" and a wine's "taste" when we really mean smell, so I'm going to stick with that.

In order to make your wine tasting as productive as possible I've provided the most important tasting markers to put in wine glasses to help you understand the wine, but you'll want to keep the long list handy to glance at while you're tasting. Merely seeing the words is often enough to help you identify that scent that's just out of reach.

Tasting Party

In each varietal chapter you'll also find suggestions for a party to have with your wine—from simple cheese and appetizers for some to full dinner parties for others. Delegate a few dishes to your friends and spread the cost of buying the wine around, and you'll soon have not just a newfound understanding of wine but a blooming social life. Alternatively, there are instructions on how to taste the wines on your own, or with just one other person.

As you plan and conduct your tasting, I'll be at your side, coaching you on the order in which to pour your wines and explaining the broad-stroke differences you should expect to find in the wines.

I'll recap what you will have learned from your tasting and, in case you have fallen in love with the wine you have just tasted, a basic framework on how to turn yourself into a stone-cold expert in the wine in question. How long that takes will depend on how frequently you drink. If you have a couple of glasses of wine every week you'll move along faster than if you have a couple a month.

Near the end of each chapter you'll find a "cheat sheet" in case you need it—perhaps you haven't done the tasting and have an intense, sudden need to have something intelligent to say about Chardonnay, for instance. Or perhaps you did the tasting last year and want a refresher course before heading to a big dinner with clients. I put in the cheat sheets because I'd have liked to have had them if I had purchased the book when I was getting started in wine. That's the same reason I close every varietal chapter with a list of dream gifts for Pinot Noir lovers, Tempranillo lovers, or what have you; you can photocopy the page and hand it to your sweetheart before the holidays, you can use it to buy special treats for yourself, you can use it to buy gifts that will truly impress your dad, your boss, Dustin Hoffman, or whomever. I put in these gift wish lists because I get dozens of emails from readers every year asking something like, "My wife loves Chardonnay, I know nothing about it. . . ." And also because just reading the lists will typically add something to your understanding: "Oh, high-end Zinfandel is prized for its ability to age, yet that's true, I never do see any. . . ."

I've laid out the varietals in a roughly ascending order from easy to difficult. Sauvignon Blanc and Zinfandel are great grapes to start with because they're easy to learn, and they'll get your confidence up fast. They're easy the same way that becoming a general practitioner is faster than becoming a surgeon: fewer facts to master at the outset. They're easier the way learning to walk on a living room carpet is easier than learning to walk on ice: more predictable. This says nothing about the wines' inherent value. You may well enjoy a walk with a family doctor on stable ground far more than you would a scramble with a surgeon on ice. Or you may not. If you want to start somewhere other than with Sauvignon Blanc or Zinfandel, go right ahead.

If it were me using this book, I wouldn't read it cover to cover; what I'd do is read the beginning, then skip to whichever wine varietal interests you. Read, shop, have your tasting. Read the chapter again. Taste some more. And when you feel like you want to move on to another varietal, pick up another chapter and repeat. If it takes you a decade to work through the whole book, that's no problem; prices may change by a dollar or two, but the basic information should hold up. You'll notice as you go through the book that a lot of these wine styles have been constant for hundreds of years, and while fads come and go you can be reasonably assured that since people have had a taste for Burgundy for a thousand years, they will continue to do so. Do you have a taste for Burgundy? You are on your way to finding out.

At the very end of the book you'll find two chapters addressing the big questions that your own taste can't answer, namely wine price and how to deal with restaurant sommeliers. The mystery and mayhem of wine price bedevils every new wine drinker: What is the difference between an $8 bottle of wine and one that costs $25 or $80? Is the $80 one ten times better than the $8 one? Why not? Is there any way to game the system? The more you learn about wine the more you will find wine pricing confounding—until the day you don't. Understanding wine price is sort of like understanding the category of people you hope to marry. At some point, what makes men or women do what they do is the most fascinating and exasperating topic on earth, and at some point you make your own sense of it, and your own peace with it. That chapter is meant to help you wherever you are on that special journey of a person, her wallet, and her taste.

The book's last chapter is a close look at wine in restaurants and the people in charge of it, sommeliers. Why do they hand you a cork? You know how to judge restaurants generally—Did your seven o'clock reservation get you a table at nine o'clock? Was the lasagna ice-cold?—what criteria should you use to judge wine service?

Finally, the book ends with a Wine Drinker's Bill of Rights. Hopefully by the time you get to this you'll have done some wine shopping, wine talking, and wine drinking and will feel more confident in your taste and in the world of wine generally. What to do with all that confidence? How about transforming the world as we know it? You'll see. Skip ahead and read the Bill of Rights if you want, but it will mean something else once you've had some experience discovering and speaking up for your own taste. How important are you, dear reader, in the international, historical, endless parade of the world's wines? A lot more important than you now know.

And that's it! You're ready to experience wine in the only way that matters: in your very own mouth. When you're done, you'll know everything you really need in order to understand wine, and you'll leaf through this book and be shocked that there was a time when you didn't know what peppery wines were. And you'll be all done with me.

Most wine critics want to make themselves invaluable to their readers: "If you agreed with my 93-point score, you'll want to come back next vintage to see what I've got to say then!" Me, I really don't care. My goal is to be the last critic you ever read, because you'll know what you think about Pinot Noir and Syrah and every other major sort of wine and you won't need me anymore.

This philosophy springs from my one truly radical belief, which is that wine doesn't particularly matter, but *you* do, dear reader, as a person, as an intelligence, as a life that helps and supports other lives. Wine only matters to the extent that it allows you to have various moments in your life that are more interesting, more pleasurable, more nuanced, more flavorful, and more fun. My dream with *Drink This* was to help you realize that interest, pleasure, nuance, and fun more reliably and predictably than you ever thought possible. Enjoy.

DRINK
THIS

THE NUTS AND BOLTS OF DRINKING, BUYING, AND TASTING WINE

How do you drink wine? As Lauren Bacall might put it, you just pucker up your lips and sip—right? After all, meaningful, authentic, even enviable wine experiences have been had by millions—and especially millions of peasants involved in harvesting grapes—who did no more than that. However, since our goal here is to learn, gain insight, and class up the joint, we're going to do a little more.

Two at a Time

The fastest way to learn about wine is to taste two similar wines at the same time. If you're a haphazard or casual drinker, it's really hard to remember what that Sauvignon Blanc you had six months ago was like. However, if you have two in front of you at the same time, it's easy: This one is lemony, this one is fruity. This one smells of pepper, and *this* one smells of pepper. Drinking two bottles at a time—two Sauvignon Blancs, two Zinfandels, whatever—will put you on the fast track.

What You Will Need to Get Started Tasting

Nitrogen or Argon in a Can

Of course, drinking two bottles at a time leads to the problem of having two bottles open at a time. The reason wine goes bad when it's open is oxygen. You'll probably remember from your high school chemistry class that oxygen causes all sorts of problems in the world. It's what makes rust, fuels fire, and generally changes stuff. One stuff it really changes a lot is wine, via a process called oxidation. Don't believe me? Leave a glass of wine on the counter overnight and taste it the next day. *Blech.* Oxidation.

A little oxidation can be good—that's more or less what you're doing when you decant wine, or let it "breathe"—but a lot is bad. You can slow or prevent oxidation in an opened bottle of wine in a couple of ways. You can try to suck all the oxygen out of the bottle, using something like the Vacu Vin system or another gizmo that pumps the air out, or you can try to put a little blanket of a gas that's heavier than air on top of the wine to keep the oxygen from getting to it.

Some respected wine professionals prefer the vacuum, but for my money the gas works better. You can buy cans of wine preserver that are mostly nitrogen from just about any wine store. They go by all kinds of brand names: Private Preserve, Cork Pops, and Winelife are the biggest. They cost about $10 and will get you through about a hundred uses. Most of the big, fancy wine bars use a very expensive version of this nitrogen preservation system; that's how they can have so many bottles open at one time.

After you pour your glasses of wine, you stick the little hose jutting out of the top of the can into your wine bottle and spray. Now you've got at least a couple of days to finish it—more if you stick the bottle in the fridge. So for 10 cents you get another week or so to finish your wine. (Champagne and other sparkling wines provide their own gas to prevent oxidation, so there's not much benefit to gassing them. Use a lever stopper, discussed below, to preserve those.)

Put a Cork (Back) in It

Once you spritz a little nitrogen into an opened bottle, you need to seal it. If it's got a screw top, that's easy enough. If it's a regular bottle, replace the cork. If you don't like wrestling with corks, invest in a couple of lever bottle stoppers. They cost between $1 and $7, depending on how high-design they are, and seal bottles with an airtight seal. I like the Zyliss ones because they cost about $3 and last forever. I've had some in my kitchen now for eight years and they're still going strong.

Speaking of Corks

Much ado is made about corkscrews, but any one that works for you is good enough. I like the traditional one with the little arms that lift up; they usually cost less than $10 and will follow you to your grave. I've had a couple of the ones with the Teflon-coated helix (the curly goes-into-the-cork part) that makes pulling corks effortless, but they cost a lot and they always break. They're convenient, though, if you're frequently opening a lot of wine bottles. I admire people who can use a waiter's corkscrew effortlessly, but I'm not one of them (though I keep one in the car for picnic-related emergencies).

All that being said, if you spend more than five minutes in this lifetime thinking or reading about corkscrews, you're wasting your time. Magazine editors periodically assign stories about them, but I think this is mostly because they go to the store and don't know which one to buy, so they think it's an issue that needs getting to the bottom of. It isn't.

Decanters

Speaking of stuff you don't need, add decanters to the list. Decanters are for people who have old wine—as in, *aged* wine—that has developed sediment on the bottom. When you decant it, most of the sediment stays behind in the bottle, and then most of the rest stays behind in the decanter.

Sediment is a good thing, by the way. It's the sign of unfiltered, high-quality wine. In the bottle it adds flavor, settling to the bottom as harmless fine silt. (It's more common in reds than whites.) However, it's not particularly fun to have in your mouth. It's like earthworms in the garden: good, but best left in place.

Mostly, wine decanting is about sediment, but the process also gives the wine time to "breathe," or to come in contact with oxygen, as described above. Wine can breathe just fine in a plain old pitcher, however. I'd guess 90 percent of the decanters in this country are owned by people who think they *should* own them. If you want to try decanting, just pour your wine into any handy pitcher, or even a vase. Try the wine. Has it improved? If not, congratulations! You just saved $30.

Wineglasses

The one bit of wine paraphernalia that I do believe in is nice wineglasses. Nearly all of a wine's nuance is in its fragrance, in the little molecules that waft into your nose where you detect them as roses, pineapple, saddle leather, or what not. If you use a juice glass for your wine, those little volatilized molecules coming out of the wine simply dissipate into thin air, leaving you nothing to smell and enjoy. Wine in a tumbler, a juice glass, a rocks glass, a lowball? No matter how cute the glass, you just can't smell the wine. And if you can't smell it, you can't taste it.

Now I know some of you are thinking, "Wait a minute, I've been to Europe and I was served wine in a jelly jar and it was just fine." Indeed, the nice-glass paradigm only holds for nice wines: If you're drinking two-euro-a-gallon wine, by all means, stick it in a jelly jar, that's the best way to make lousy wine go down easy. (Also, put ice in it, which helps prevent the scent compounds from volatilizing.)

However, if you actually want to enjoy the wine you drink, you need a glass with a stem, which keeps the wine in the glass from warming in your hand, and a bowl that is broader at the bottom and narrower at the top. That gap between the top of the glass and the surface of the wine is where the aromatic compounds get trapped so that you can smell them.

How much you spend on a good wineglass is up to you. Personally, I really like drinking wine out of nice Riedel stemware, and I think I like it half because it improves the wine and half because it makes me feel special and fancy. I get the basic ones that run $10 to $15 a stem; I don't think there's a great difference between those and the bigger, more expensive ones, which break more easily and therefore stress me out more. However, the point of a wineglass is the same whether it's an $8, $15, or $50 stem: They're there to keep the wine at the right temperature and to capture its fragrance. The big difference between the $10 ones and the $50 ones tends to be the quality of the glass itself, and whether it was machine-made or handmade. If it makes you happy to have a $50 handblown stem—have that thing! If it doesn't make you happy—skip that thing!

Maximilian Riedel: King of All Stemware

Is asking Maximilian Riedel, CEO of Riedel Crystal of America, about wineglasses like asking the fox for tips on henhouse management? Yeah. But you'll also learn a lot.

What's the reason you go to restaurants? Sometimes the food is better, but it's entertainment. You want to switch off your brain and enjoy yourself. If you find yourself in an environment that is comfortable, where wine is being decanted and poured for you, the wine opens up, the flavor improves, you feel special. Here comes your wine, here's a chance to talk to the sommelier—this is all part of the entertainment.

Truly the shape of the glass makes a difference in the beauty of the wine on the nose and in the palate. When Morton's Steakhouses introduced Riedel stemware, maybe only two months in they found their wine sales going up sixty percent. Why? Because it's more entertaining, you feel more special, the wine tastes better, all of a sudden you're surprised to find the bottle is empty, and you order more wine.

Great restaurants like Per Se, chefs like Thomas Keller and Daniel Boulud, the sommeliers, they're smart businesspeople. If they sell you a great bottle of wine you love, they know they have a good chance of selling you another—this time or another day.

I've gotten lovely Riedel glasses at Target and seen charming ones at Pottery Barn. If you told me there were good-enough glasses at Wal-Mart I wouldn't be surprised. The basic Riedel white wine stem is wonderful for whites, and I think it's nice to have both a Burgundy ball shape and a taller Bordeaux shape for reds. My final thought: Get some nice wineglasses. You won't regret it.

Smell is such a huge part of taste that you should swirl if you want to get real pleasure from wine. When you swirl the wine in the glass, what you're basically doing is creating a tiny little tornado, a bit of uplifting wind over the glass that moves the scent of the wine—that is, the compounds in it that can become airborne—up away from the wine and toward your nose.

If it makes you feel weird at first, do it at home where no one can see you. Or try keeping the base of the stem on the table and moving it in a slow circle, never picking it up.

Wine Racks

Sometimes in home-furnishing store catalogs I see adorable little wine racks carefully arranged in the sunny front window of a dream kitchen, and I settle back in my chair and muse: "What dopes." Sunlight and its partner, heat, are the absolute enemy of wine. If you want to destroy wine, a cute wine rack in a sunny front window is the fastest way to do that. The ideal place to keep wine is in a cool, dark cellar. Cool is important so you can avoid enemy number one, heat; dark is important because then you skip enemy number two, light. If you're living without a cellar, some good places to store wine include: under your bed, in a closet, in a cupboard, in a file cabinet, or under the sink. Wine bottled under a cork is best kept on its side so that the cork doesn't dry out. Corks do dry out: I talked to the sommelier at a super-fancy steak house once, the kind that lines the walls with stock-pot-size ultra-prestigious bottles of wine, and he told me that they used to lay down all the bottles overnight once a month to let the corks get moist—until the morning he came in to find $7,000 worth of Champagne soaked into the rug. All you need to know? Keep your bottles on their sides, in the dark!

Temperature, Especially Cellar Temperature

Serving wine at the right temperature is a big deal. It's generally said about Americans that we drink our whites too cold, because we have them at refrigerator temperature, and our reds too warm, because we have them at room temperature.

Red wines should be served at "cellar temperature," that is, about 55 degrees, halfway between refrigerator temperature and room temperature. If wine is too warm, the alcohol smell dominates, like warm vodka. If it's too cold, the volatile compounds that give wine its good scents stay in the wine and don't give you the full flavor. White wines generally should be served a little colder, in the 45–50 degree range, like a colder cellar. For all the wine tastings in this book it's utterly important that the wines be served at the appropriate cellar temperatures. If you have all your Rieslings sitting out in the hot sun and taste them at 80 degrees you'll learn nothing, and waste a lot of money too. Cellar temperature! Words to live by.

In addition to temperature there's the issue of seasonality. Some people like to drink their wine with the seasons, big bold reds in winter and light crisp whites in summer. Some don't. What's the correct thing to do? The answer is personal. If you want to eat a hearty stew in August, go for it! It's your life. Case closed.

Shopping for Wine

There's a reason every critic tells you to find a specialty wine shop: Big box wine stores like Costco or Sam's Club and discount shops like Trader Joe's are confusing and haphazard even for bona fide wine professionals. They're often stocked with odd lots, discounts, one-off labels made specifically for the store (see the "Money, Money, Money"

Is It Ever Okay to Put Ice in Your Wine?

It's far better to put ice in your wine than to drink it too hot, which can kill the fragrance. Don't want to take my word for it? I was talking to Bob Lindquist, one of the pioneering vintners who led the path of Syrah in this country through his work at his vineyard Qupé (*cue-pay*). I asked him whether it was true that winemakers often add water to wine, in tanks or barrels, as part of the winemaking process. "Absolutely," he told me. "It's much more the exception than the rule," and is often done when dehydrated grapes make a wine that's too concentrated.

I told him I sometimes want to add ice to my glass in a wine bar when they bring me something too warm, but I always feel like a rube when I do. "I end up doing that all the time, too," he told me. "It seems like if it's the summer and you've got a big wine you're always in a restaurant that's serving it too hot. I'm more hesitant to [add ice] to a more elegant wine, but sometimes your hand is forced. There's this great event we do every year in Paso Robles, we call it Rhône and Bowl—it's held in a bowling alley. A bunch of winemakers get together and everyone brings wines out of their cellar and shares them. One time it was maybe ninety degrees in the bowling alley and someone had brought this six-liter bottle of Elderton Command Shiraz, one of the most sought-after, Parkerized, huge Syrahs in the world, and we were all putting ice cubes in it. You had to! All the geeky winemakers were standing around with ice cubes clinking in our glasses, we all agreed it was a better wine with an ice cube in it."

chapter later on for more details), or really big name national wines.

Some of these wines may change over the course of a year, or vintage to vintage. One year some generic Hawk's-View-Ridge-Crest-Mt.-Hollow red wine might say Cabernet

Conversations with Bigwigs: Jon Bonne

Jon Bonne is the wine editor for the San Francisco Chronicle, *and as such drives the best, most comprehensive wine coverage of any American newspaper. (If you have never seen it, pilot your computer to sfgate.com immediately.) Bonne tastes perhaps a hundred wines a week—and he's been doing it for years. I asked him why critics never seem to review anything that's easy to find.*

We sit down four times a year or so and plan out what we're going to taste. We'll do Napa Merlots this day, Argentine Malbec this day, and so on. Then we send out an editorial calendar [to wineries and distributors]. We get a couple hundred or more bottles a week. The wines we get that way form the core of the tasting. It's not always that effective. If we're tasting Napa Cabernet, many of the really good wines will never come to us. A lot of Napa vintners are so influential that they're able to get personal visits from the biggest wine critics, and they would rather do that than send wine to us.

In addition to the invited wines, we have wineries that spam us and send wine to everyone on staff whose name they know, so we have wine coming at us all different ways. Those wines might have gotten horrible reviews, or no reviews at all. A lot of time those wines are technically flawed, really bad, or both, and it takes us a certain amount of time just to weed those out. I don't know why they send them—if they don't know they're undrinkable, or if they know it and are just kind of hoping they catch us when we all have a cold.

Any national critic faces a fundamental problem in that most of the really interesting wines are not made or imported in large enough quantities to be [widely available]. I augment our tastings by purchasing several bottles a week of things that are in the market that are potentially recommendable; purchasing wines is actually a much faster way of finding wines to recommend. I'd say that 20 percent of what I taste that gets sent to us is recommendable, but probably 50 to 60 percent of the wines I buy in stores are wines I could recommend. If you see a bottle sold at retail, especially in a smaller shop, you have the advantage of someone having gone through the wines and sacrificed their palate on your behalf, and then made the financial decision that the wine was good enough to sell. Over time I've come to look at retail outlets as allies; they're doing work I'd have to do.

Sauvignon on the bottle and be made with 90 percent Cabernet Sauvignon and 10 percent Merlot, and the next year it might be made with 75 percent Cabernet Sauvignon and 25 percent Syrah, depending on what's cheap and available.

Furthermore, because importers and distributors make less profit on individual bottles (though more on volume) at big box and discount stores, they don't send the most highly sought after wines there. For the wine tastings in this book you're going to need some of those highly sought after wines. You will *never* find the six major styles of Riesling or Chardonnay in a big box store, so if you're only shopping at big box stores you'll never learn what various wine styles are like, much less your own taste.

Independent wine shops usually have one guy sweating over every case: "Am I going to make money on this one, or lose money?" It tends to clarify their decision making. There are two easy ways to find a good wine shop. You can ask people who care, like the general manager at your favorite nice restaurant; or you can call a shop and ask questions culled from the following wine chapters, such as: "I need to find two single-estate Zinfandels from the same producer, like Ridge or Edmeades. Is that something you carry?"

Once you get started on the tastings in this book, you will actually need to ask this question and a few others that only someone knowledgeable can answer. If the person you're talking to can't answer, move on. If they can, congratulations! You have found a good wine shop.

Aging Wines

The aging of wines comes up in every wine article and reference book, and on many bottle labels. Here's what you need to know about aging wine. Wine collectors are the main driver of high-end (over $20) wine in the United States; in 2009 a group called Pointer Media Network estimated that a mere 5.2 million Americans buy 80 percent of the high-end wine imported into this country. These people are buying wine not just to drink, but to age. This matters to you, because what happens if you buy wine meant to age, but instead drink it right away? Your whole mouth will prickle up and you'll feel like you've been sucking on a leather jacket. (Some wines meant to age, and thus best to avoid for a new wine drinker: Bordeaux, Reserva Rioja, and Barolo. Basically, if wine is very expensive, it's probably meant to age.)

If you want to try aging wine yourself, it's fascinating. Just buy a case of a red with a lot of oak to it (Bordeaux, Rioja, Barolo, some American Cabernet Sauvignons) and stick it in your basement or in the back of a closet, keeping in mind that heat and direct sunlight are the enemies of wine. Try a bottle when you buy it, try another a couple of years later, and another every year after that until you run out. Usually you'll find that it starts out good but tannic, eventually gets weird and awful (this is called "closed up" in wine parlance; you'll now be kicking yourself for having bought a whole case), but then often becomes beautiful (at which point you will be kicking yourself for not having bought three cases).

However, the most important thing to know about wines meant to age is: Don't buy them if you don't want to age them! I can't emphasize this enough. Mysteriously, many people read that a wine can age for ten to fifty years as a buying recommendation; it's only a buying recommendation *if you want to age it.* If you're going to drink it this month, what that little note on the back of the bottle telling you to age the wine is actually trying to tell you is to *avoid* it.

The Basics of Tasting Wine

Tasting wine is less complicated than it appears—and also more complicated. It's less complicated because there are really only five things to look for, outlined below. It's more complicated because the more wine you taste, the more you'll be able to say, think, and experience concerning any of those categories. It's like the difference between knowing the rules of football and playing it at a professional level: You see a lot more, and have a lot more to think about, the more you've played it. Actually, wine tasting has a number of things in common with football, except your knees can never give out and youth is no benefit.

Aromatics

Aromatics are the scents of the wine, be they the famous cat pee (yes, this is considered a good thing) or minerals of Sauvignon Blanc or the strawberries and saddle leather of Sangiovese. Always remember that when we say a wine "smells of" cat pee or strawberries, there is never anything else in the glass except fermented grape juice, and maybe some water or molecules that drifted off a barrel, or dead yeast—no one dunked melons, or strawberries, or pepper, or anything else in there. It would be more accurate to say that a wine *reminds us* of cranberries than to say it *tastes* of cranberries, but we don't say that. Smell and taste are so closely knit we generally consider a wine with a smell that reminds us of cranberry to "taste" of cranberries.

Mouthfeel, Weight, and Texture

Does the wine feel slippery in your mouth, weighty like whole milk, or make your tongue prickle up like you're sucking on a rock or a black tea bag? A good part of wine criticism and connoisseurship is simply identifying how wine feels in your mouth, and deciding whether you like it. How a wine feels in your mouth is known by the highly technical term "mouthfeel." Sometimes texture will be part of this mouthfeel: The wine might feel thick, thin, slippery, or even chewy. Sometimes weight will figure in: The wine might feel heavy, or light. Look to the dairy case for comparable examples of weight in liquids, and think of how cream feels heavy in your mouth, while skim milk feels light.

Sometimes you can see a visible manifestation of weight and texture by swirling a wine around so that it "climbs" the walls of your glass. A wine with a lot of weight trails down slowly in thick rivulets called "legs." Some people think legs mean quality. They don't—they just mean legs.

Acidity

Think lemons. Does the wine have a sour component, the way lemonade does? That's acidity. Acidity is usually easier to detect in the presence of food; it makes food taste better, in the same way that a vinaigrette makes salad taste better. Traditionally, high-acid wines like Sangiovese are food-friendly wines. Acidity counteracts the sweetness of a wine, so a high-acid wine with lots of sugar won't seem sweet, it will seem balanced. Acidity without sugar is what people usually mean when they describe a wine as being like paint thinner.

Tannins

Tannin is a common phytochemical that plants make to defend against pests large and small, such as microbes and insects. It's in many plants we eat: pomegranates, strawberries, persimmons, chocolate, tea, and so on. It's particularly strong in oak trees and the skins of wine grapes. Put the two together by aging red wine in oak, and you have the most tannin a human commonly encounters. I've read that a single bottle of red wine has the tannin of a hundred chocolate bars.

Tannin helps preserve wine, and it tastes good. If you like tea, chocolate, or pomegranates, chances are one of the things you like about those foods is the tannins. To get a sense of what pure tannin feels like, boil a couple of bags of black tea in water, and once it cools, taste the super-strong tea: that tongue-prickling stuff is tannin. Tannin is more a texture than a taste; it makes your mouth feel tight and parched.

Professional wine tasters distinguish between two types of tannin—oak tannin and grape tannin—by long experience with the way it makes their mouth feel. Grape tannin is most easily experienced by finding a red wine that wasn't aged in oak; usually it feels like something lively and sort of prickly in your mouth. Another way to experience grape tannin is to find some red table grapes and peel off the skins and chew them.

Oak tannin is most easily experienced in a red wine aged in oak for a really long time but then drunk as soon as it hits the shelves in the store. Find a just-released Reserva Rioja: That's oak tannin! Your mouth should feel so dry and prickly you can barely talk. Oak tannin is part of what allows reds to age for decades. The general idea is that oak tannins become mellower over time, dropping into the background and settling out of the flavor of the wine, like a woman taking off an opera cloak to reveal a ball gown. When they do drop away their work will be done; they protected the fruit, flavor, and overall integrity of the wine, allowing it to become much more magnificent than it was upon release.

Structure

Your perception of how a particular wine's acid, tannin, and fruit interact is called the *structure*. Does everything seem in balance? Is there enough acid (in the case of a white) or enough acid and tannin (in the case of a red) to support the fruit? If so, that's a wine in balance. If there's too much acid and not enough fruit, the wine is astringent. If there's too much fruit and not enough acid to counterbalance it, the wine can be jammy or flabby. If there's not enough of anything, the wine is watery.

In general, one of the nicest things you can say about a wine is that it has good structure, or, by way of synonyms, has a good spine or good bones.

And that's it! If you like, you might keep a memo pad handy with these five categories noted, and write down your thoughts about all the wines you run across. You may quickly find that you're a person who cares a great deal about aromatics, or someone who is mad for tannin.

Now that's *really* it. It's time to start drinking!

2

ZINFANDEL

REBELLION IN A BOTTLE

Pronounced: *ZIN-fan-dell*

Dear Dara,

It's the intimidation that gets me: I go to buy jewelry, and the saleslady loads on a rich tale about how special these particular pearls are, and I feel important. I go to buy a package of batteries, and as long as I don't try to steal anything or punch anybody, the cashier and I are buddies in the war against sloth (the sloth, that is, if he didn't have a job and my remote control stopped working). But I try to buy a bottle of wine and suddenly I'm taking some kind of IQ quiz that seems designed to ferret out my social status. I've never summered on the Rhine, or the Rhône, the Côte Rôtie or the Côte d'Or, and I have no clue if I like southern Rhône wine over northern Rhône wine. I also don't know my way around a yacht, I don't have stables, and the White House chief of staff never consults me before making ambassadorial appointments. I'm a failure! A loser! Uncle! You win again, wine!

—Baffled, and Intimidated

You and everyone else. I actually had a funny conversation once with Paul Einbund, the sommelier at the cutting edge San Francisco restaurant Coi (pronounced *Kwa*). He was telling me about an actual larger-than-life bodyguard he knows. "Okay, this friend of mine is huge," Einbund told me. "Bodyguard huge. He's six foot four, four hundred pounds, a giant monster of a man, he used to be a bodyguard for Eddie Murphy, then Michael Jordan, then Dennis Rodman. I mean, you look at him and your knees buckle, you can't help it. It's his job to be completely and totally intimidating, and he's very good at his job. But I went with him to the Joel Robuchon restaurant in Las Vegas, and you know who was intimidated? He was. He just felt totally judged by the staff."

I put that out there to tell you you're not alone. In fact, a lot of successful people order wine solely on price, that is, the highest price they can afford, purely as an offensive tactic to ward off that sense of intimidation and judgment. Any sommelier in the country will tell you that it's easier to move big-name $200 bottles than value-priced gems simply because people try to spend their way out of looking clueless. Take a bow for not picking that path.

But here's a secret for you: Want confidence, a sense of your own taste, and utter mastery that you can deploy in shops and restaurants while impressing yourself and all those around you? Then complete this chapter on Zinfandel. Familiarize yourself with the big issues in Zinfandel and taste half a dozen bottles, and you will quickly know enough about Zinfandel to talk to anyone in the country about it. You'll also prove to yourself that competence in wine is within pretty easy reach.

What's to Love About Zinfandel?

It's gutsy and powerful. It offers good value at low price points, unlike other powerful wines such as Cabernet Sauvignon. In the theory of like-goes-with-like, big robust Zinfandel goes well with big, robust things that Americans like to eat, including barbecued ribs, meat lovers' pizzas, and cheeseburgers. Because it's so big and powerful, it functions well as a cocktail wine—that is, a wine that doesn't need to be served with food and so goes well with standing around chatting with your friends or kicking back watching a movie. And it's all-American. You don't need to learn a thing about foreign geography or European wine laws to understand it. Better yet, it's beloved by Silicon Valley tech and design people, and thus is better represented on the Internet and more clearly described on bottle labels than any other wine.

So, you want easy mastery of a powerful red? Zinfandel is the wine for you.

What's to Hate About Zinfandel?

Zinfandel has a couple of major problems. First, its grape clusters don't ripen evenly, meaning that some grapes start to raisin on the vine while others are just turning ripe. As you will learn in greater depth in Chapter 4 (Riesling), sugar in wine grapes translates to alcohol in wine. For now, just know that this means a good number of Zinfandels will always be big and high in alcohol—15 percent or even 17 percent alcohol levels are not unheard of. (A fortified wine like Port is 18 percent alcohol.) After splitting a bottle in a restaurant, a small woman may find herself too tipsy to drive home.

This bigness also means it doesn't pair well with delicate

foods. Put a Zinfandel next to sole in a butter sauce and you will experience something in your mouth akin to King Kong stepping on the Easter Bunny. Because of these twin effects of bigness and high alcohol, many people find Zinfandel simply too big to work as a table wine.

Zinfandel's final problem is that it drives French wine people nuts. Tell certain French wine folks that you like Zinfandel and they will pester you to the grave trying to get you to change your mind. It's too big, they say. Too powerful! No finesse! You like that stuff, really? You can't. It's not even French! If you are not the kind of person who can stand up to French wine nuts, Zinfandel is not the wine for you. (There is a good side to this: Since other Zinfandel people experience this as well, if you become a Zinfandel person and you meet another Zinfandel person, you will have an instant bond, like two White Sox fans finding each other at Yankee Stadium.)

Conversations with Bigwigs: Van Williamson

No one in America embodies the rock-and-roll icono-clast face of Zinfandel the way Van "The Vanimal" Williamson does. The Vanimal is the winemaker for Ed-meades, one of the country's leading Zinfandel pro-ducers, and his entry-level Mendocino County label is prized as one of the most reliable bargains in the busi-ness; it sells for under $18. What does the Vanimal think you should know about Zinfandel?

One of my favorite things about Zinfandel is really the people—the people who grow it, and the people who drink it. I think because Zinfandel is so difficult [to grow and make], all the computer scientists, doctors, and lawyers, they want a normal, predictable process, they all make Chardonnay and Cabernet Sauvignon. But with Zinfandel it's kind of backwards, you know what you want and go through whatever crazy thing you have to do to get it.

Zinfandel drinkers are a different breed; they're kind of halfway between beer drinkers and wine drinkers. At ZAP [the annual Zinfandel Advocates & Producers festival] in San Francisco, the first time a glass breaks there's a huge roar—and then *every* time a glass breaks there's a roar. Zinfandel drinkers are like that, they're not your sophisticated Cabernet Sauvignon drinkers fussing over the investment-grade wines in the cellar.

People who drink Zinfandel, a lot of them drink Zinfandel *a lot*—there's huge loyalty, ten times more than with any other varietal. California Cabernet drinkers always are trying to compare their wine to Bordeaux. If you're a Pinot Noir or Burgundy drinker it gets very expensive, and very intimidating, figuring out all that label [text]. But Zinfandel drinkers don't have to worry about anywhere else—it's all California, and if you want to try every good one, you can.

What's the Story with Zinfandel?

Here's a two-second history of California: Once upon a time it held about zero Europeans or people from the much smaller United States of America that was stuck on North America's east side. Then, in 1848, came the Gold Rush, and suddenly there were tens of thousands, and then hundreds of thousands, and soon enough millions of Europeans and other non-native people in California. During those heady days there were two ways to make money: You could find gold, or you could sell things to people who had piles of gold stacked up in their houses. The second route was actually extremely profitable. There are records of single peaches going for $2 apiece, at a time when most Americans were making $1 a day. As you can imagine, one of the things miners, and especially homesick Europeans, craved most was wine. If they'd pay $2 for a peach, imagine what they'd pay for a whole bottle of wine!

No one knows how the first Zinfandel grapes made it to northern California. Wine geneticists used to believe Zinfandel's parent was an Italian grape called Primitivo, but they have now officially identified Zinfandel's origins in an obscure Croatian grape called Crljenak Kaštelanski (*sirl-YEN-ack kastel-AN-ski*). However Zinfandel made it to northern California, the people growing it there soon fell in love with it, propagated it throughout the region, and made it California's own.

What's White Zinfandel?

The Zinfandel grape is black as night, so how exactly does it make a light pink wine like white Zinfandel? Think about a plum—you know how plums have black skin, but when you bite into one the flesh is sort of yellow or pink? Now, think about a dark red or purple table grape, if you peeled it—the same thing, right? Yellowish flesh, a lot like a green table grape, under a dark wrapper. To make red wine, you crush your red grapes and let the juice soak with the skins; eventually the pigments from the skins migrate into the juice, turning it a dark color. To make rosé, blush, or pink wine, you just squash the grapes and drain the pale juice away from the skins as fast as possible; the faster you do it, the lighter the wine. There are plenty of white or pink wines made from dark grapes—blanc de noirs Champagne, for instance, means "white of black" and refers to Champagne, a white wine, made from black grapes, in this instance Pinot Noir. White Zinfandel is made with the same grapes used to make regular red Zinfandel, except instead of letting the skins and juice soak together the juice is rapidly drained away. The reason it's often sweet is the same reason that red Zinfandel has high-alcohol strength: Sugar in the grape makes alcohol in the wine, unless, as we'll see in more detail when we taste Riesling, the wine-maker chooses to use a winemaking process and yeast that don't convert the sugar to alcohol. White Zinfandel makers prefer to leave more sugar behind than red Zinfandel makers do.

These first Zinfandel makers fell in love with it because it makes supremely nuanced black-red wines of intense power. The Seghesio family, who have been growing Zinfandel since the 1890s, pass on family lore that Zinfandel used to be called "the boss grape," meaning it was the most important of all the grapes they grew. Because of this power and its roots in Gold Rush cowboy culture, a certain balls-to-the-wall, rock-and-roll spirit echoes around Zinfandel to this day. Ravenswood, a winery that was one of the pioneering popularizers of the grape, had as its slogan "No Wimpy Wines," which some Zinfandel fans actually have had tattooed on their bodies. Other Zinfandel fans have tattoos of maps or vineyard sites. No kidding. Zinfandel T-shirts abound, with slogans like ZINFANDEL INFIDEL. Zinfandel winemakers seem to compete with one another coming up with sassy names like Sin Zin, 7 Deadly Zins, InZinerator, Vine Agra, and so on. The Zinfandel winery Gnarly Head, named for the very old, gnarled vines its fruit comes from, has a Gnarly Gnation of fans and a custom Gnarly Harley motorcycle. Armida sells a wine called Poizin, "the wine to die for," packaged in an itty-bitty Goth casket. Château Potelle puts out a Zinfandel they label VGS for Very Good . . . you get the idea. Zin people, they're a wild bunch.

However, if you're thinking all this Zinfandel stuff is sounding very unrefined and unclassy, think again. America's premiere fine dining chef, Thomas Keller, founder and chef of the best restaurants in America, The French Laundry, as well as New York City food mecca Per Se, once told me, "Zinfandels are some of my favorite wines. And young Zinfandels as well. I *enjoy* that they're forward in fruit, big and juicy; I don't think that means they're therefore the enemy of food. I particularly have always liked Paul Draper's Zinfandels for their finesse. I've also been drinking them for many years. When you've been drinking a particular wine over many years you develop a more personal relationship with it, as you would with any place or person you have known for a great while, and that adds to the enjoyment. I'd encourage any young cook to seek out those wines [he or she can hope] to develop a long relationship with; you'll naturally have a very different experience with a wine you've been drinking for twenty years. I certainly have that relationship with Draper's Zinfandels and Monte Bello [Cabernet Sauvignon]."

If Thomas Keller isn't enough of a food bigwig to persuade you that Zinfandel is worthy of your time, keep in mind that Alice Waters, doyenne of America's farm-to-table movement, loves it too. (If you're a locavore above all else, there's an argument to be made that Zinfandel is your wine.) One of the leading intellectuals of America's still-young wine culture is in fact Paul Draper, the master of single-vineyard Zinfandels.

What is it that these brainy people like about Zinfandel? They like the taste, of course, but they also like the uniquely American contribution that Zinfandel makes to the worldwide conversation about *terroir.*

Terroir, of course, is the idea that a wine expresses a million little things about where it has grown. You likely have some small experience with *terroir* if you've ever done any gardening. For instance, have you ever grown tomatoes? If so, you know that to do so you found a good tomato growing site, maybe in some southern corner of your property protected from north winds by the garage. And you know that you rejected other places on your property, say beneath a maple tree, as lousy tomato growing territory. More or less, this is what *terroir* is, except writ large: The property in question is the planet earth, and we're trying to grow wine grapes, not tomatoes. And often once that sunny site near the garage is found, so to speak, it mysteriously is revealed that one section makes spectacularly blackberry-scented wine, another makes cedar-scented wine, and a third makes swamp water. That's why winemakers divide their vineyards into smaller sections, and why they'll sometimes have odd configurations. Still, it turns out that the very best places to grow wine grapes on the planet earth are places like the Napa Valley, Sonoma Valley, Rhône Valley, Mosel River Valley (which gives us Germany's best Riesling), and Garonne River Valley (which defines the area of Bordeaux).

What's with all the valleys? Wine grapes have huge root systems that can stretch thirty feet underground. If the roots are given too much access to water, the grapevines will make lots and lots of leaves and big, watery fruit. This is good for a grapevine plant in terms of growing big and having lots of offspring, but bad for us because big watery grapes make bad watery wine. What people like is a wine grapevine that is barely surviving, because it makes what is known as concentrated fruit. The best place for a vine to barely survive is on a steep hillside, the kind you get with a river valley. When a grapevine is barely surviving on a steep hillside it produces concentrated fruit, and when you crush it, those grapes make concentrated wine, and that concentrated wine will be different, will have a different flavor, and have different scents, than any other wine on earth. That's *terroir.*

Some people despise the idea of *terroir,* people like Fred Franzia of the box-wine Franzia family and the creator of Two Buck Chuck, who once said, "Does anybody complicate Cheerios by saying the wheat has to be grown on the side of

---

Conversations with Bigwigs: Paul Draper

The winemaker at Ridge, a onetime Stanford philosophy major and one of the godfathers of American wine, Paul Draper inspired an entire generation of terroir-*driven and environmentally conscious American winemakers.* Terroir, *he told me, is not something you do, like bicycling. It's essentially a practice, like spirituality.*

The "why" of *terroir* is a whole series of things. It starts with the individual, with the winemaker. The vast majority of winemakers are not interested in *terroir.* They're making shoes, they're making a commodity, [though] some of them don't even know it. And while every vineyard has a *terroir* it can express, the question becomes, is it something rather poor, or average, rather good, excellent, or great?

Only a limited number of people are really looking to purchase a wine that comes from an interest in *terroir,* so we try never to use the word. We talk about site-specific, single-vineyard, or single-site rather than *terroir.* When you have the intention to make a site-specific wine, then, what does that include? All the things that *terroir* does: that is, climate, the daytime and nighttime temperatures, the sunlight, drainage, soil, the variety you're growing, and so on.

But it's also the individual in charge, his decision on how he's going to work on that land, whether he will be farming conventionally, or organically, or biodynamically, by irrigating or not—so, man is part of *terroir.* When we focus on the piece of ground we take ourselves out of it, which is misleading.

If you were to talk to our two vineyard guys they would say: We have a preference for this soil over that soil. In [Ridge's famed] Geyserville vineyard we consider classic Geyserville to come from a "lens" of soil that is made of old river rocks from when the Russian River came all the way up to the sides of the hills. All of the Geyserville parcels are in this lens, it's a half-mile wide and a couple miles long. However, one of our classic Geyserville vineyards had a section that's more alluvial, what the French would call a mud-flat, it's different, softer, easier, though quite distinctive and nice. We just make a little wine in-house with it, and the part of the vineyard that is on the Geyserville lens goes into the Geyserville wine.

a mountain and the *terroir* in North Dakota is better than Kansas and all this horses**t? You put something in your mouth and enjoy it. If you spend a hundred dollars to buy a bottle of wine, how the hell are you going to enjoy it? It's a joke. There's no wine worth that kind of money."

While some people despise the idea of *terroir*, other people just like to pay lip service to it without actually taking the trouble that making a wine with *terroir* necessitates. There is in fact nothing to prevent someone charging $100 a bottle from saying, "My wine is so great because *terroir terroir terroir*," while engaging in all the *terroir*-obliterating industrial wine making processes in the world. I've even seen wine descriptions issued by wineries that say things like, "Taking advantage of the best *terroir* in California, Horse Hockey Chardonnay combines premium fruit from six highly valued sites . . ." That's meaningless. *Terroir* has to be from one place, usually defined by the shape of the place (a hillside, a valley bottom) and the geology that underlies it. But there are no *terroir* fact-checkers. Coming

from the mouth of a winemaker, the word *terroir,* like "plat-
inum level," "five star," or "plummy," can be meaningful or
meaningless, depending.

Happily, when it comes to Zinfandel it's particularly easy
to cut through the signal-to-noise ratio. Why? Because Zinfandel isn't that popular, so the financial incentive to lie
isn't as high as it is for Cabernet Sauvignon or Chardonnay.
Also, Zinfandel is more knowable than other wines because
Zinfandel only grows in Northern California, home to a
high concentration of tech-savvy wine drinkers who have
made it the most website-documented of all the wine varietals. Today, Zinfandel has become the rare ground on
which rebels, brainiacs, and people with highly developed
palates unite.

And that's the story of Zinfandel, from the Gold Rush
through Thomas Keller. Now let's go a little deeper and look
at the Holy Trinity of Zinfandel, and what makes it tick.

The "Holy Trinity" of Zinfandel

The Grape

Zinfandel is a black, thin-skinned grape that is typically
"head-trained," meaning it grows freestanding, like a rose-
bush or an apple tree. Because it grows like this, Zinfandel
is capable of surviving years of abandonment. This is critical to understanding Zinfandel in America, because the
world's most prized vines are "old vines" or "ancient vines"
that are 80, 100, or even 130 years old. Typically these
fields were "discovered" by modern vintners after having
been planted sometime between the Gold Rush and Prohibition and abandoned some time after that.

No matter how old it is, Zinfandel grows into clusters
that mature unevenly; when they're picked, some grapes in
a cluster will be almost ripe, others ripe, and others over-

ripe, even starting to raisin. When ripe, Zinfandel's black-red grapes are peppery, spicy, and brambly, with the flavors and fragrances of black fruits (fruits that are black when ripe, like plums, blackberries, and black cherries), and sometimes notes of blueberry or red fruit (fruits that are red when ripe, like red cherries, raspberries, and strawberries).

Tannin and color are found in a wine grape's skin. Because Zinfandel is thin-skinned, some winemakers choose to add grapes to the final blend that have a lot of color and tannin, like Petite Sirah or Mourvedre, also called Mataró. Some winemakers add Carignan, which ripens later than Zinfandel and provides acidity to balance Zinfandel's sweetness. Alicante Bouschet adds color. Syrah or Grenache "soften" the wine, lending fruit if the Zinfandel of a particular vintage turns out more tart than sweet.

Terroir

We covered a lot about Zinfandel's *terroir* because it's an inextricable part of the wine's story, but there are a few things to add. Belying its Gold Rush origins, Zinfandel's greatest home is in the counties around San Francisco: Napa, Sonoma, Paso Robles, Santa Cruz, Amador, Mendocino, Lodi, El Dorado, and Lake. That said, Zinfandel *can* grow anywhere wine grapes are grown, and you may find versions from Australia, South Africa, and Europe.

Winemaking

Just as there are different places to grow Zinfandel, there are different ways to make wine from the grapes. Broadly speaking, there is a hard way to do things, and an easy way. The easy way involves harvesting Zinfandel by machine, then using special designer yeasts bought from a winemaking supply house that have been designed to ferment Zinfandel quickly and completely. The resulting wine can then be tweaked using techniques such as removing alcohol, which is done by using filters or other mechanical processes, or bubbling in oxygen, or adding natural enzymes, any of which soften the wine. This process of machine-to-storebought-yeast-to-laboratory-to-bottle results in the Zinfandel that many people love most of all: sweet, soft, and round. In wine-speak, this is a "quaffable," "easy-drinking," or "international-style" wine. The hard way of doing things involves picking by hand, using the wild yeasts found on the grape skins to ferment them, which can take months, might occur in fits and starts, and requires constant supervision lest it turn bad. The resulting wine is left alone. If it was very alcoholic the alcohol is left there; any softening is left to time and nature.

Stop Reading, Start Drinking!

Zinfandel exists on a sort of seesaw with spice on one side and fruit on the other. Some will be very spicy, others will be very fruity. The spiciness comes in all sorts of guises: cedar box, cigar box, cinnamon, nutmeg, and a brambly, sort of bay-leaf quality. The fruitiness runs the gamut from black fruit to raisins to bright red fruit. Some people really love the light, spicy Zinfandels; some adore the intensely fruity ones.

Broadly speaking, your big Eureka moments with Zinfandel are going to come when you contrast small, *terroir*-driven single-vineyard wines with one another, or against inexpensive, industrially made wines. You're not going to learn much of anything comparing two inexpensive wines; all that's going to tell you is which you like better, which is roughly akin to comparing brands of chocolate ice cream, when what we're really trying to figure out is whether you prefer chocolate ice cream or chocolate bars.

Zinfandel FIELD GUIDE

A good wine shop will have lots of Zinfandels; the majority will be clustered between $12 and $25. The bottom-shelf, under-$12 segment of the Zinfandel marketplace is really hard to predict. That's where you'll find foreign entries trying to break into the American marketplace, and also raisiny, almost cola-like, quaffable wines. In the most crowded section of the Zinfandel marketplace, the $12 to $25 section, you'll find wines from big American producers as well as a lot of smaller wineries. Over $20 you'll start noticing single-vineyard wines. There are only a handful of over-$50 Zinfandels in the whole world. The following field guide looks at most everything likely to be in your local liquor store, arranged by price, low to high.

Miscellaneous bottom-shelf European, $12 and under

When you go into your wine shop you will probably see low-priced Italian wine labeled Zinfandel. By all means try it, but only after you feel you know Zinfandel really well and are willing to kiss some frogs in order to find some low-price princes. Till then it will just confuse you. For my money, most European Zinfandels are blocky (that is, they feel unharmonious and unbalanced), but that could change if someone were to pour money into making them better.

Miscellaneous domestic, $8–$20

Any decent wine shop should have a dozen California Zinfandels on their bottom and almost-bottom shelves, and as bottom-shelf wines go these are some of the most reliable wines to be found in North America. The differences will be where they're from, whether the vines are "old," and various details of winemaking.

What's the difference between the various $8 wines and the $20 ones? With some of the cheaper ones you'll get more industrial-style winemaking, more grape blending, and a softer wine for less money, while other times price tells you nothing. Some of the most reliable affordable Zinfandels: Rosenblum's basic Roman-numeral-numbered wine (like Vintner's Cuvée XXX, XXXI, and so on), Rancho Zabaco (and Rancho Zabaco's less expensive label, Dancing Bull), Ravenswood's lower-priced wines, Cline (more in the style of a French Côtes du Rhône, that is to say, more herbal and less aggressive), Beaulieu Vineyards (BV), Montevina (which tends to be a brawnier wine), Seghesio, Gnarly Head, and Renwood.

You'll notice that a lot of the bottom-shelf wines have top-shelf brothers and sisters, from the same producer, with similar labels; you can learn a lot by tasting these side by side. Typically you'll find the bottom-shelf ones more quaffable—that is, they offer less to think about—and the top-shelf ones more complex. Keep in mind that more complex doesn't necessarily mean better; plenty of people prefer Harry Potter to Marcel Proust.

Site-specific Zinfandels, $20 and up

Broadly speaking, expensive Zinfandels can be divided into two camps: those that aim to showcase the individual characteristics of their sites and vines, and those that aim to do that *and* have a riper, more international, universal style. The more terroir-driven, less ripe, site-specific Zinfandel producers tend to make a wine that tastes more French than American. It usually seems drier (even though it might have exactly as much residual sugar as the more polished wines below) and has a wider array of scents, more subtlety, and less full-throttle oomph. All of the wineries listed here bottle several different vineyards separately.

The granddaddy of site-specific Zinfandel makers is Ridge, a winery led by iconic American winemaker Paul Draper (see sidebar), who not only bottles an array of site-specific wines made from grapes grown in many different vineyards but also puts exhaustive information on his back labels. You might learn, for instance, that a particular year of the Lytton Springs Ridge Zinfandel experienced vine sunburns, and that ultimately grapes from only 20 of the parcel's possible 34 sections, or blocks, were selected for blending and bottling.

Edmeades, Ravenswood, and Rosenblum also have extensive bottlings from different vineyards. Sonoma County's Dry Creek Valley has about fifty vineyards and makes some of the country's most distinctive Zinfandel because it's usually cool and even, allowing the fruit to ripen but not to become overripe. Look for single vineyard offerings from wineries like Mazzocco, Seghesio, or Dry Creek Vineyard. However, getting wines made by the same producer from two different vineyards will tell you more about *terroir* in thirty seconds than my typing for the rest of the day. Enjoy!

Other top site-specific, not superripe Zinfandel producers include Green and Red, Benessere, Bella, Robert Biale Vineyards, Carlisle, Dry Creek Vineyards, Franus, Peterson Winery, Ravenswood, Seghesio, Joseph Swan Vineyards, Renwood, and Bucklin Old Hill Zinfandel.

Field Blends

When the first immigrants put in their Zinfandel plantings they recognized that Zinfandel often did better as part of a grape blend—in the style of Burgundy, Bordeaux, and so on—than solo. (At the time, wines were labeled with names like California Claret or Hearty Burgundy, and the names of the varietals didn't matter to consumers.) Because of this they planted Zinfandel in the same field with other varieties such as Alicante Bouschet, Petite Sirah, Carignan, or Grenache. At harvest time they would ferment all the different grape varietals in a tank together, using a technique we now call "co-fermentation." Sometimes these wines will have labels that read "field blend." Some of the most highly desirable Zinfandels in the world are still co-fermented field blends, including Zinfandels from Ravenswood, Ridge, the Bedrock Wine Co., Bucklin Old Hill Ranch, Bella Vineyards, and Carlisle Winery & Vineyards.

Expensive, ripe, rich, and polished Zinfandels, over $40

There are a very, very few Zinfandels in the world priced over $40, and only a handful over $50. Very, very rarely you'll see one in a store priced over $80, but this usually happens because the wine has been well reviewed and the wine shop had to buy it on the gray market (that is, someone who bought it first from the winery or a distributor, and later resells it). Typically the most expensive Zinfandels are the best critically reviewed ones, and tend to try to showcase their site-specificity using a very fat, ripe style. Your inside track to getting one of these is to ask for a Turley Zinfandel; these are famous as the ripest, roundest, richest, most polished of all. Few stores actually have them, but asking for one will usually get you something in a similar style. Other good high-end Zinfandels in this style include Gallo-Sonoma, Dashe Cellars, Beaulieu Vineyards (BV), Behrens and Hitchcock, Fife, Hartford, Howell Mountain Vineyards, Martinelli, Mazzocco, Murphy-Goode, Peachy Canyon, Wilson Winery, and Storybook Mountain Vineyards.

Late harvest, Zinfandel ice wine, or Zinfandel "Port"

Zinfandel grapes ripen unevenly. Look at a cluster a few weeks before harvest and you'll see a combination of green and ripe berries. Typically, by the time the green stragglers turn black, some of the early ripeners are shriveling. This is a good thing, and accounts for Zinfandel's wide palette of aromas and flavors. If you leave the grape clusters in the field until all the grapes start to shrivel, you get a seriously sweet, very appealing late-harvest, "ice wine" (wine made from grapes frozen after harvest) or Port-style Zinfandel. These are typically rather expensive, starting at $15 a half-bottle, but are delicious and can also tell you quite a lot about the character of Zinfandel, namely, that it has a beautiful chocolate-raspberry character when left to become fully ripe.

Conversations with Bigwigs: Will Bucklin

One of the oldest Zinfandel vineyards is at Old Hill Ranch, so old that it was being called "superior to any in the state" in the Pacific Rural Press *in 1871. Today the vines, many of which are at least 130 years old, are dry-farmed, meaning they aren't irrigated. They're also certified organic. If the United States cared about farms, vineyards, and winemaking the way Europeans do, the place would be certified as a national treasure and preserved under glass for future generations. Instead, it's preserved in glass under the Bucklins' own label, Bucklin Old Hill Ranch Zinfandel, and also through some Ravenswood wines. One of winemaker Will Bucklin's first tasks after taking over as winemaker for his family was to spend two years creating an elaborate map of his vineyard to find out what was planted where.*

I started from a place of complete ignorance about field blends. I walked up and down the rows and wondered, "What were they thinking? What were they thinking?" because since that generation is pretty much gone, we don't know what the family conversations were and why they planted what they planted.

When you first look at our vineyard it looks pretty random, but it isn't. Our number one variety is Zinfandel, about 75 percent or so, and the second most common variety is Grenache. While it's not unusual to find Grenache in a field blend, it is unusual to find it in a Zinfandel field blend as the second most dominant variety. Why? I don't really know the answer, except that the basic tenet I've learned about field blending is the basic tenet of co-fermentation: Whoever planted it clearly intended the two to be made together. A field blend forces your hand to some extent.

In most of today's world, if you want to make a blend of Zinfandel you generally go and find the Zinfandel, you ferment that. You find the Grenache, you ferment that. But we're fermenting them together, and so a whole different reaction happens in the tank. And not just those two—there's Alicante Bouschet, the tenth most planted vine in the world that no one knows about. It enhances color; [we use it as a] color component. It's a good 10 percent of our blend, our third most popular variety. After that we've got another couple dozen—Petite Sirah, Mourvèdre, Carignan, Syrah, Tannat; there are thirty different varieties in the vineyard. It's incredibly complicated.

But that's the beauty of a field blend. My goal is to make the wine as close as possible to how the founders intended it. My rationale is that there are so many wines in the world to choose from, so many that are similar and express simply what the trend of the moment is—they're homogenous. Yet, we have this very unique and unusual story that can be told through the wine, a story of who was here, how things used to be, and how they tasted. I feel it's so important to tell that story.

Food and Zinfandel

Following the wine pairing theory of "like goes with like," big, bold Zinfandel goes with big, bold foods: A cheeseburger, a rack of ribs, pepperoni pizza, spicy Chinese food like ma po tofu or hot and sour soup, beef stew, *al pastor* burritos, and lots of the everyday foods that Americans love to love are perfect with Zinfandel. In this instance the high level of alcohol wipes clean your palate of both the rich food and the fat-soluble spice (this is the same logic as to why you drink beer and not water after you eat something with hot sauce), allowing you to enjoy the next bite as much as the first. Generally speaking, the same people who pooh-pooh Zinfandel as not being food-friendly are the same people who don't eat pit barbecue because "it's not good for you." Personally, I think it's a narrow person who defines food and leaves out chili dogs, and a narrow view of wine in which food-friendliness only admits the existence of white-tablecloth restaurants.

Tasting Zinfandel
Step by Step

1. A Brief Road Map to Our Upcoming Zinfandel Road Trip

The plan when tasting Zinfandel is to taste five iterations of the grape in order to get a sense of what it tastes like and whether you like it. In pursuit of that you'll contrast top shelf with bottom shelf; you'll contrast *terroir*-driven, or site-specific, single-vineyard wines with one another; you'll taste the most critically lauded version of the wine; and you'll taste a late-harvest incarnation to learn what the grape tastes like fully ripe.

Notes on Tasting Zinfandel Solo or in Pairs

Zinfandel is an ideal takeout-and-movie wine. You'll actually be doing only two tastings, one of a bottom-shelf Zinfandel versus a terroir-driven single-estate one, and a second of another terroir-driven single-estate, a plush Turley-style wine, and a late-harvest Zinfandel. What will you eat? Since pizza, barbecue, burgers, or spicy Chinese takeout are perfect with Zinfandel, this should work out quite well with any life that involves a couch and some downtime.

Notes on Tasting Zinfandel by Party

Barbecues are ideal situations for tasting Zinfandel, because it goes particularly well with grilled meats like ribs, with their sweet and spicy accents, or even hamburgers,

with the sweet spice of their ketchup. So, you'll be drinking
Zinfandel and eating barbecue with your pals while talking
about wine. Sound like fun? It will be.

2. Shopping for Zinfandel

The hardest part of learning about wine is shopping for it.
See the full Field Guide above for detail; these suggestions are culled from those lists. Don't worry about the
exact names mentioned here; try to match the category,
not the specific wine. For your tasting you want the following:

1. Inexpensive American Zinfandel, such as Rosenblum,
   Rancho Zabaco (or Dancing Bull), Ravenswood, Cline,
   Beaulieu Vineyards (BV), Montevina, Seghesio, Gnarly
   Head, or Renwood. $8 to $15.
2. & 3. Two different single-vineyard bottles from different
   vineyards but made by the same producer. You could buy
   Ridge's Lytton Springs and Geyserville, for example. Or
   Edmeades' Piffero Vineyard and Perli Vineyard, Rosen-
   blum's Rockpile Road and Lyons, Bella's Big River Ranch
   and Lilly Hill. Or pair from Green and Red, Benessere,
   Robert Biale Vineyards, Carlisle, Dry Creek Vineyards,
   Franus, Peterson Winery, Ravenswood, Seghesio, Joseph
   Swan Vineyards, Renwood, or Bucklin Old Hill Ranch.
   $20-something each.
4. A more expensive, polished Zinfandel, such as Turley
   Wine Cellars, Gallo-Sonoma, Dashe Cellars, Beaulieu
   Vineyards (BV), Behrens and Hitchcock, Fife, Hartford,
   Howell Mountain Vineyards, Martinelli, Murphy-Goode,
   Peachy Canyon, or Storybook Mountain Vineyards. Ask
   the guy at the wine store for the roundest, ripest, richest,
   fullest, lushest Zinfandel he's got. $40 and up.
5. A late-harvest, ice-wine, dessert-wine, or "Port" Zinfandel. These often come in half-bottles, and that is enough

for a dinner-party-size group; any late-harvest Zinfandel will do. $15 and up.

3. Planning and Thinking About Tasting

Gather your wineglasses, dump bucket (a vase or pitcher works well), and tasting markers. Make your life easier: Put fresh or frozen blackberries or a dollop of blackberry jam in one wineglass and whole black peppercorns in another. If you have a garden and can cut some dried rose canes or berry brambles, consider yourself blessed and put some of those in a glass. For spice, whole cinnamon sticks.

Tasting Markers

Keep the following list handy so you can glance at it while you're tasting—it will help you name fragrances that seem just out of reach.

Zinfandel is most likely to offer fragrances of		
Blackberries	Balsam wood	Cola
Black cherries	Plums	Chocolate or cocoa
Sour cherries (or pie cherries)	Currants	
	Smoke	Dried herbs (sage, bay leaves, thyme, etc.)
Brambles and briars	Earth	
	Vanilla	
Pepper	Minerals (wet rocks)	Dried leaves or grasses
Spice (dried cinnamon, allspice, etc.)	Raisins or prunes	

Less likely but still possible		
Tea	Fragrant flowers	Tobacco
Licorice	Leather	Hickory wood smoke
Blueberries	Incense	
		Tar

4. Cool Things Off

Get your wine to cellar temperature! (See page 10.) For Zinfandel, that's around 55 degrees.

5. Pull the Corks!

6. Taste Your First Wine

Pour each guest an inch or so of your inexpensive American
Zinfandel. Now swirl the wine. Sniff it. Taste it. Pass around
the glasses containing your tasting markers. Do these spark
anything? Pepper? This wine is supposed to give you a baseline of what Zinfandel tastes like. It should be some degree of
fruity, some degree of brambly. Is it? Wine like this, as it
tends to be blended from many vineyards, should give you an
average, not specific, taste for what Zinfandel is.

7. Taste Your First Single-Estate Zinfandel

Pour everybody an inch of your first single-vineyard Zinfandel. How is it different from the first? How is it similar?
Do they seem like the same grape? Swirl. Sniff. Eat some
food. Does it make the wine taste better? Does the wine
make the food taste better? Do you like it more or less than
the last one? Dump wine to make way for the next wine.

Timing Your Tasting

Tasting a wine can take as long as you wish, from thirty
seconds to a few minutes. Generally, it's best to keep
everyone together and focused on the wine. If people have
time to wander off and have side conversations you can
lose the wine-tasting and just end up with a party. I find it
works best to just rip through all the wines quickly, in ten or
thirty minutes, depending on how much people like to chat,
and then let people go back and develop more nuanced im-
pressions on their own time.

(Note to solo tasters: Here's where you take a break. Pick up the remaining three another night, as soon as convenient. Try to do it within a few weeks—if you wait too long you'll forget the first two.)

8. Taste Your Second Single-Estate Zinfandel

Pour a second single-estate, terroir-driven Zinfandel from the same producer. How is it different? How is it the same, compared to the first two? Are the wines made of the exact same thing? Check bottle labels for information about blending partners, areas the wines come from, and so on. Raspberries? Black cherries? Spice? Pepper? Discuss. Move on.

9. Taste Your Turley-Style Velvety Zinfandel

Pour the high-end, critically well-regarded Turley-style Zinfandel. Is it more like the first wine? More like the last? Swirl and sniff: Anything leap out at you? It should be rounder, fleshier, and plumper; it should seem less like a horse and saddle and more like an opulent velvet cloak. Does it?

10. Taste Your Late-Harvest Zinfandel

Finally, pour your late-harvest dessert-style Zinfandel. Now pair it with some dessert. Do you love it? Are you indifferent? Some people really, really love it.

And now: Congratulations! The structured part of your tasting is done.

Time to ask the big questions: Which was your favorite? Which was worth the money? Was the top-shelf, critical-darling, Turley-like one more like the late-harvest, the bottom-shelf, or the single-vineyard? Which do you want for your birthday? Which for pizza night on the couch?

THE TAKEAWAY

Most people who do a Zinfandel tasting for the first time are surprised at how different, and yet the same, Zinfandels are. It's like discovering the five-act structure at the heart of most films: It's both astonishing to realize how similar such diverse projects are, and astonishing to see how unique they are.

Most important, now that you've tasted the spectrum of Zinfandels you should have a firm sense of whether you like them. If you do—congratulations! Taste another dozen this year, adding to your foundation, and you will know more about Zinfandel than 99 percent of humanity.

Five-second cheat sheet for people who didn't read the chapter and are reading this on their iPhones in a bar while they wait for the band to start

Zinfandel is a bold, spicy, nearly black red wine that finds its finest expression in the various mountainous places within a day's drive of San Francisco. Because it's bold and spicy, it goes well with the bold and spicy foods that Americans love. Got a rack of smoked ribs, a big old rare cheeseburger, an *al pastor* burrito, or a mess of barbecued brisket? Stick some Zinfandel on the table and you will be one happy Zinfandel infidel.

The major styles of Zinfandel include (1) inexpensive American, which tends to be ripe and strong, and (2) single-vineyard, which are the ones you find in fine restaurants. Some big names include Ridge and Edmeades.

Another major style is (3) rich, polished, plummy and chocolaty. Expensive and critically lauded, these tend to be ripe and plush, and are epitomized by the Zinfandels of Turley Cellars. Finally, there is late-harvest Zinfandel, a deep, rich, almost Port-style wine that goes well with chocolate.

Knock-Their-Socks-Off
Gifts for Zinfandel Lovers

1. **Anything old.** Zinfandel lovers are always insisting that good Zinfandels can age for ten or fifteen years, or more, but rarely do they get to put this theory into practice. Pick up something aged from a California or Internet store like J. J. Buckley Fine Wines (jjbuckley.com), especially something old from standard-bearer Ridge, and *especially* something old from defining American bottlings such as Ridge's Lytton Springs or Geyserville, and you will shock and delight them. While these might be hard to find, they're not too expensive—usually they're under $75, and often under $50.

2. **Anything Turley.** Turley Cellars is Robert Parker's darling, and while the wine is mostly available on restaurant wine lists, some of it does dribble out to various Internet wine shops like nyvintners.com or jjbuckley.com; snag a bottle and you'll definitely impress any Zinfandel nut who reads wine ratings.

3. **Anything ultra-small-production.** Lots of the big names in Zinfandel, and some of the little ones, make certain wines in teeny-tiny lots of, say, 40, 70, or 300 cases, so little wine that none of it leaves California except through the tasting room of the winery or via the Internet. Let the Internet be your friend! Check the websites of Claudia Springs, Rosenblum Cellars, Bucklin Old Hill Cellars, Carlisle Winery, A. Rafanelli Winery,

Robert Biale Vineyards, Storybook Mountain Vineyards, Dry Creek Winery and others for these rare bottlings.

4. **Wine clubs.** How do you get those super-rare offerings without going through the secondary market or paying secondary markups? Buy your Zinfandel lover a year's subscription in a wine club like the one from Linne Calodo, Ravenswood (their Zinfomania club costs $39.95 for two rare bottles a month), Dry Creek Vineyard, or Haywood Estate Winery, and they'll think of you all year.

5. **Tickets and a hotel for ZAP.** If money is no object, take the Zin lover in your life to the annual festival of the Zinfandel Advocates and Producers—it's a carnival of Zin love and takes place over four days in San Francisco during the last weekend in January. If a trip to San Francisco isn't in your budget, check ZAP's website, www.zinfandel.org; they sometimes go on national tours and might be coming to your city soon.

3

SAUVIGNON BLANC

ZESTY!

Pronounced: *so-veen-yohn blahnk*. Also known as: Sancerre, Pouilly-Fumé, Fumé Blanc

Dear Dara,

I guess I'd like to start by asking: What's with all the names up there? How many French names does one wine need? Furthermore, I guess since I get to ask questions under the sweet cloak of anonymity, I'll confess that I don't really know why there are so many wines at all—why do we have Chardonnay, Sauvignon Blanc, and Riesling? Is it like we have sporty sedans and also eighteen-wheelers, because they do different things, or is it the way we have Mountain Memories Tide detergent and Mango Sarsaparilla Tide detergent—because they're just trying to take up space on the shelf so you don't see the competition?

—Baffled

Good questions all. But why not take it back even a step further? Why do we have wine at all? Your high school health teacher probably told you, again and again, that wine never solves any problems. But actually, while wine cannot solve problems like your wife moving in with your boss or your Camaro getting repo'd, wine does solve one specific problem quite neatly: If you have a lot of grapes during your October harvest, and no food at all, and specifically no grapes, the rest of the year, wine solves that problem. Wine turns highly perishable grapes into a shelf-stable product that will dispense both calories and nutrients—see all the health studies about wine and cardiovascular health or longevity—not just all year, but over decades. Wine turns a perilous never-ending hunt for sustenance in a world of feast and famine into a place where you can have civilization, and eventually civilization's highest form, fake Wikipedia entries.

Of course, grapes and wine aren't unique in mankind's arsenal for staying alive through the natural cycle of harvest and famine; we also figured out how to cultivate, dry, and mill rice, wheat, and other grains, feed some of that grain to egg-laying chickens, smoke or salt meat and fish, and make cheese, sauerkraut, fruit preserves, and so on. The beauty of wine, though, is that not only does it turn grapes into food for years, it makes all those other foods— the wheat, the eggs, the salted meat, and all the rest—taste better. More on that in a second, but for now I think it's valuable to have this in your personal arsenal against all wine snobs: *What is wine?* It's a way to be a French farmer and not die in January.

As to the reason there are so many different wines— Chardonnay, Riesling, and Sauvignon Blanc, for example— that's simply the same question as why peaches grow in Georgia and apples grow in Vermont. Over the thousands of years that various farmers lived in various pockets of Europe, they determined what grew best where. And just as some people strongly prefer peach pie to apple pie and some people like both, today we have Chardonnay and Sauvignon Blanc living side by side in wine aisles.

But back to how wine makes everything taste better: It really does. That's why it's such a big part of the European table. And no, I don't mean it makes food taste better like beer goggles for food; this improving trait is really just a simple trick of the human palate. A little bit of something sour just makes all the other flavors—sweet, meaty, bitter, salty— taste better. This is the same logic that governs us when we pour vinaigrette on salad, squirt ketchup or mustard on a burger, squeeze lemons onto a slab of fish, add tomato sauce to pizza or pasta, and so on. When wine critics and professionals talk about this good sourness in wine, we call it acid.

And there's no better wine to help you understand acid than Sauvignon Blanc. Why? Because Sauvignon Blanc is a high-acid wine, and the whole trick to making a good one is balancing the acid and the fruit. Think of acid and fruit as a seesaw: A good Sauvignon Blanc will seem balanced, the sweetness of fruit and the tartness of acid in correct proportion, like two kids of the exact same size on a teeter-totter, each suspended perfectly in the air. A bad Sauvignon Blanc will seem like a seesaw with a hippopotamus on one side and a hawk on the other. One without enough fruit will be screamingly acidic and thin, like lemon water. One without enough acid will seem flabby and centerless, like water with a squirt of strawberry syrup.

What's to Love About Sauvignon Blanc?

I love Sauvignon Blanc. I love how it tastes—it's zesty, it's fragrant, it's chic and cheerful. It's also the perfect place for any beginner to gain immediate competency. Why? Because it's often bottled on its own, without any blending partners, and it usually isn't manipulated with the winemaking tools we'll learn about in later chapters of this book, so it mostly just sits in its bottles waiting to tell you about where it comes from, much like Zinfandel. In fact, if I ruled the world, everyone new to wine would make Sauvignon Blanc one of their firsts, because it's the simplest of the noble white wines but is also complex enough to be interesting for a lifetime.

Sauvignon Blanc, like most of the world's "noble" grapes, first enticed the world from its home soil in France. In this case, west central France, a couple of hours south of Paris, in the Loire River valley.

There's not a lot you need to know about the Loire. It's beautiful, they raise a lot of dairy goats, there are trout in the river, and if you can afford to go there, you should. The most important towns in the Loire for Sauvignon Blanc are Sancerre and Pouilly-Fumé (*poo-yee-fyu-MAY,* not to be confused with the lookalike Pouilly-Fuissé, which is made with Chardonnay.) There are some other Loire towns that make less famous Sauvignon Blanc, towns called Menetou-Salon, Reuilly, and Quincy. When Sauvignon Blanc comes from 99 percent of the world it is called Sauvignon Blanc, but when it comes from one of these extremely important towns it is called Sancerre, or Pouilly-Fumé, or Menetou-Salon, and so on.

These village names are so important that the French wine laws essentially treat them as brand names and protect them as such. This system of French wine laws is called the *appellation d'origine contrôlée,* abbreviated to either AC or AOC, and it works like this: When they decide a particular area makes wines of distinction, they specify what grapes can grow in that region, what the yield of the grapes can be, and often specify allowed or necessary winemaking techniques. This is meant to work such that when you see Sancerre or Pouilly-Fumé on a label it means that the wine should have some baseline level of quality.

Also, Sancerre makers are protected from some grower in Turkey putting out his own wine with the same name. There are red Sancerres, made from Pinot Noir, but these are rarely brought into this country, and when they are people should make a big deal of clarifying that they're not the expected Sancerre. There is only one exception to the rule of the rest of the world calling Sauvignon Blanc Sauvignon Blanc: Fumé Blanc, a made-up marketing name that some people in California and elsewhere sometimes use when they want to annoy the tar out of me.

What's to Hate About Sauvignon Blanc?

In the 1970s, Robert Mondavi, a California winemaker hellbent on annoying people forty years down the line, decided his Sauvignon Blanc would sell better under the sexier name of Fumé Blanc, which he created by going halvesies with the names Pouilly-Fumé and Sauvignon Blanc. Ever since then anybody who thought they'd sell more bottles with the Fumé Blanc label has been free to use it, since it's meaningless.

I've read that at some point in time most winemakers using Fumé Blanc meant to convey that their Sauvignon was aged in oak barrels, as *fumé* means "smoked," and thus Fumé Blanc might kinda sorta translate as "oak-smoked Sauvignon Blanc," but it's not that way anymore. (Okay okay, there was a reason Californians chose to use oak: When made in Bordeaux, as a Bordeaux Blanc, Sauvignon Blanc is typically both blended with Sémillon and aged in oak. As California in the postwar period sought to be a second Bordeaux, with Cabernet Sauvignon and Chardonnay plantings everywhere, this oak-aged Sauvignon Blanc was thought to be classy and would appeal to American Francophiles. However, this was also a time when puff-pastry was seen as the height of cuisine, and book titles like *Real Men Don't Eat Quiche* were thought to be a hoot. Time marches on!) Now it's just needlessly confusing. I say ignore them. If no one buys them and winemakers find the Fumé Blanc name a marketing handicap, it will go away. But don't ignore the other Sauvignon Blancs! They're some of the world's most likeable and table-friendly of all wines.

What's the Story with Sauvignon Blanc?

The contemporary world's love affair with Sauvignon Blanc began in the nineteenth century, when railroads connected Paris with the nearby Loire Valley, and Paris's café and bistro culture really took off. Sancerre and Pouilly-Fumé were very popular in the cafés and bistros because they were inexpensive, like all whites meant to be drunk young, and went divinely with what people liked to eat; they're the perfect companion to oysters, chilled shellfish, salads, and cheese, especially goat cheese. These Loire Valley Sauvignon Blancs were zingy and herbal, marrying a bit of fruit on the nose with a bit of minerality in a captivating way.

Having found admiration in Paris, the Sauvignon Blanc vines of the Loire spread around the world. This worked out well for the world because Sauvignon Blanc is a vigorous, happy, easy-growing vine, possibly the easiest-growing vine of all time. From this easy-growing grape comes easy-to-make wine. And, following the normal laws of economics, when something is easy to grow and easy to make, it's also cheap. World-class versions of Sauvignon Blanc are cheaper than world-class versions of any other wine, and $15 Sauvignon Blancs are routinely of higher quality than $15 wines made from other varietals.

Why is Sauvignon Blanc easy to make? Mainly because winemakers don't mess much with the plain old grape juice they start with. They usually don't make Sauvignon Blanc in expensive oak barrels, they don't age it for years in cellars before releasing it. Most of the time they don't even blend it with other grapes. Of course, as with everything in wine, there are exceptions. But the vast majority of Sauvignon Blanc is just nothing but Sauvignon Blanc fermented in steel tanks and rushed into bottles, as close to its grapes-on-a-vine original fruit-self as wine ever is.

Conversations with Bigwigs: Kristin Belair

Now that you know the basics of Sauvignon Blanc, want to go a little deeper? Here's some upper level stuff. Honig, the Napa Valley winery, inspires great devotion among its fans. Some love it for its valiant commitment to good environmental stewardship, manifested in everything from the solar panels that fuel its winery to local sourcing of bottles to the way they help local wildlife. Some love it for its playful marketing postcards featuring its staff dressed up as pop-culture parodies.

Probably, though, most love Honig for its benchmark Sauvignon Blanc, a graceful, richly textured, seamless presentation of rich tropical and citrus fruit built elegantly on a foundation of firm acids. I called up winemaker Kristin Belair and asked how she does it. The answer was both more complicated and simpler than you'd think.

Winemaking is in some sense a lot like cooking. You do a lot of tasting, just as if you were making a sauce, except what you're making you're doing on a huge scale and it takes months, and sometimes years, to see how it comes out. And every year it's different, the weather, the rains, everything. Our Sauvignon Blanc in '05 had a grassy character; in '06 it was more tropical; in '07 it was intensely tropical.

What we're trying to do is grow something delicious. There's a basic recipe for making wine; you need to know what the recipe is and understand the rules of it so that if you make changes you know what you're doing. It's like if you have your basic chocolate chip cookie recipe, if you want to substitute some oatmeal for some of the flour you can do that, but you have to know the basic chemistry; you can't substitute baking powder for flour.

Sometimes people say, "Oh, if you're following the rules, you're not being creative." But I remember a quote from a jazz musician who said, "The framework of the music, the rules, that's what allows you to be creative." I feel like it's the same thing with winemaking or cooking: You have your basic recipe, your basic chemistry rules, but within that you can be really creative, especially if you have an idea of what you're trying to achieve.

A lot of people feel really intimidated by talking about flavors or scents. Americans are very visual—we don't think about naming things that we smell and taste. When you're a little kid you sit there: "It's a green tree. It's a red apple." But no one ever says, "What does a tree smell like? What does an apple taste like?"

Once you learn to identify smells and tastes, it changes you. Now I'm one of those weird people who go through the grocery store and smell the produce. I can't think why you would buy an apple that doesn't smell like an apple, but people do.

The "Holy Trinity" of Sauvignon Blanc

The Grape

A white grape used to make a still white wine, Sauvignon Blanc has two faces—one more mineral, one more juicy— that emerge depending on where it is grown. (We'll get to that in a second; see terroir, below.) However, no matter where it is grown it is likely to have aromas of green grass and herbs, melons, apples, citrus fruit, and stone fruit like peaches and apricots; where and how it is grown determines the strength of any of those qualities.

While most Sauvignon Blanc sold in the United States is straight-up Sauvignon Blanc, made with no blending partners, you should know that in its second-most-important French home, the area of Bordeaux, its traditional pal is another white grape called Sémillon. Sémillon is fat, thick, sweet, and juicy; if any grape could be said to be like butter, it would be Sémillon. You add it to Sauvignon Blanc for the same reason you put cream in coffee: to soften it. Sémillon is almost always used in White Bordeaux (Bordeaux Blanc). Taking their lead from Bordeaux, the Australians like to blend their Sauvignon Blanc with Sémillon too: Sometimes you'll see inexpensive blends of the two with both varietals noted on the front of the label, and these will tend to be richer than other Sauvignon Blancs. Of course, wine blending rules in the United States allow a California maker to put up to 25 percent Sémillon in a bottle labeled Sauvignon Blanc without telling anyone—if you ever run into a cheap Sauvignon Blanc that seems oddly fat and rich, that may be what's going on.

Terroir

Sauvignon Blanc can grow all over the world. Anywhere wine grapes are grown Sauvignon Blanc is made. Anywhere. However, its two most popular manifestations come from the Loire Valley and New Zealand. When grown in the stony, mineral-rich soil of the Loire, and especially Sancerre, it makes stony, flinty, mineral-edged wines. When grown in cool New Zealand with its long, long days, it becomes tart with a wildly tropical bouquet, bursting with mangoes, gooseberries, limes, and so on.

Winemaking

The most popular way of making Sauvignon Blanc is basically to do it, as one winemaker told me, "fast, cold, and dirty." The goal is to get the grapes from vine to bottle as much like their original grape-on-the-vine selves as possible. To accomplish this, the grapes are harvested, often in the middle of the night, when they're coldest, then tossed, stems and all, into tanks, pressed, and, depending on the winemaker's choice, either the fruit solids and juice are separated immediately, or they're not.

Rarely, but notably in the most expensive Sauvignon Blancs, some or all of the wine is fermented in new oak barrels, making it toasty and oaky. If you see the words "toast," "oak," "vanilla," or "butterscotch" on a Sauvignon Blanc label, that's your clue that you're dealing with an oaked wine. Most of the time, however, Sauvignon Blanc is made in steel, glass, or epoxy-lined cement tanks, or older neutral barrels, which can give the wine a fatter texture without adding much oak flavor.

Because of this minimalist approach to "élevage," that is, the craft that elevates the grape to wine, most Sauvignon Blanc winemaking is done as the plants grow, through pruning the leaves, called "canopy management." Growers control the amount of acid and the flavors in the final wine by how many leaves they allow the grape vine to grow, and how much of the grape clusters are exposed to sunlight.

Stop Reading, Start Drinking!

Your main task in this chapter is going to be learning the difference between Sauvignon Blanc styles and finding a favorite, if any. My one caveat: No matter how tempting it seems, don't draw any conclusions about Sauvignon Blanc until you've tasted the different *terroirs* and styles—they tremendously vary. If you gather five diverse Sauvignon Blancs and five diverse people new to wine, they will just be flabbergasted at the differences between the bottles.

Sauvignon Blanc FIELD GUIDE

A good wine shop will have at least half a dozen styles of Sauvignon Blanc, priced from $5 to $50; most will be $8–$25. The cheapest ones are going to be domestic California or Washington, Chile, or Australia, and they'll be, if you're lucky, brisk and grassy. The mid-price ones will be all over the map—in this mid-price you'll find lots of zingy, serviceable ones from everywhere from Australia to Washington to Chile to California, you'll also find tropical whizz-bang New Zealand perfume-bombs, and silky high-end Napa Valley offerings made with a bit of toast. There should be one or two over-$25 Sauvignon Blancs in a good wine shop. These will be prestigious French Sancerre and Pouilly-Fumé, and possibly single-estate highly desirable New Zealand or California offerings. The following detailed field guide is arranged by price, low-to-high.

Bottom-shelf fruity, ripe, inexpensive New World Sauvignon Blancs, $6–$12

The biggest problem growers have with Sauvignon Blanc is that the grapes get too happy and healthy. Given too much sunlight and too much water they'll go crazy, grow all over the place, and taste watery and, worse, like water asparagus has been boiled in. However, given perfect growing conditions—not too much water, and enough sunlight for ripening but not enough for the vines to go nuts—Sauvignon Blanc will become round and fruity, with aromas of melon, grapefruit, mango, and guava.

How can you tell which are the juicy, fruity, simple Sauvignon

Blancs? Just look for anything under $14 from California, Washington State, or New Zealand.

Some names? Château St. Michelle, Brancott, Columbia Crest, or Hanna, but basically, anything in the $6–$14 price point from a cooler New World area like New Zealand or the West Coast of the United States should be more fruit than lean because the grapes will become fully ripe.

Bottom-shelf austere, lean, inexpensive Sauvignon Blancs, $12 and under

Sauvignon Blanc grows absolutely everywhere, including Spain, Chile, Argentina, Peru, Austria, Uruguay, and anywhere else on the planet that can support a wine grape. As a rule of thumb, the colder a place is and the less cash they have, the less likely they are to spend money manipulating the wine or trimming the leaves away from the grapes, so the more austere, lean, crisp, and dry it will be.

Chile and Spain both make reliable versions of lean Sauvignon Blanc under $10. The Spanish version made by Peñascal is a great option; it's so zippy it's stilettolike. Also nice is Chile's Veramonte, which is exceedingly fresh and crisp. Some of the words on the label that might give you a hint you're looking at lean and austere: "fresh," "crisp," and "acidity." Some names: Peñascal, Veramonte, MontGras, Arido, Vina Caliterra, anything from Chile's Casablanca Valley, and about a billion others. Basically, anything under $15 from South America or Spain that says Sauvignon Blanc on the bottle should be crisper than not.

New Zealand Sauvignon Blancs, especially ones from Marlborough, $12–$25

"Exuberant" is generally how people describe Sauvignon Blanc from New Zealand, especially from the Marlborough region on the southernmost island. The scents just seem to leap from the glass like fireworks. Think of a diced mango dumped into a bowl of freshly mown grass and you'll get the general idea. Other aromas: lemon, apple, pear, lime, melon, pineapple, grapefruit, white pepper, honeysuckle, passion fruit, and, as any wine writer is happy to tell you, most famously, gooseberry and cat pee.

Seriously—cat pee. This is not a bad thing; in small doses cat pee is considered good. *Sauvignon* means wild, and people talk about the cat pee being that very wildness. No, I'm not kidding. People love it. Well, some do. You might.

In any event, the Kim Crawford is widely available and a classic Marlborough Sauvignon Blanc; it is racy and lively and has a beautiful perfume of melons and pineapples. The Cloudy Bay is another nice one that's easy to find. But just about any Sauvignon Blanc from Marlborough should get you what you're looking for: exuberant fragrance and a racy body.

Top-shelf glossy Napa, Sonoma, and Australia Sauvignon Blancs, $15 and up

Over-$15 California and Australia Sauvignon Blancs will be all over the map—some will be very fruity, some will be quite lean, some will be oaky and toasty. Why? Because money means freedom: The more money a winemaker has to play with, the more decisions he or she can make to do whatever they want. Some will choose to pay growers to be very exacting in the way they raise the grapes, doing specific sorts of trellising, canopy management, and whatnot; others will do that and then also spend money on new oak barrels, wild-yeast fermentation, keeping the wine in contact with the grape solids and decaying yeast (called resting the wine on its lees). Because of all this you don't necessarily know what you're going to get.

In any event, expensive New World winemaker-directed Sauvignon Blanc is definitely one of the major styles of the wine, so you should try it. One of my favorites is the Honig Sauvignon Blanc from Napa Valley; it's a silky, stylish, very well knit, elegant wine that brings to mind esoteric words like "finesse." The Grgich Hills

Estate is another exceptionally pretty, fragrant, and elegant Sauvignon Blanc that shows what the wine does in the hands of talented winemakers. Some other good ones: Rancho Zabaco Russian River Valley, St. Supéry, Kunde Estate, Flora Springs Soliloquy.

French Sauvignon Blancs, both inexpensive and costly, $20–$40

Anything from the French towns of Sancerre, Pouilly-Fumé, Menetou-Salon, Reuilly, or Quincy will be Sauvignon Blanc, and they will be totally different from any other Sauvignon Blanc you try. Why? The soil here is all limestone. Seriously, if you could see a picture of the "soil" at Sancerre it looks like the white gravel in an American shopping mall that surrounds the little shrubs in a median strip, and not soil at all. Because of this limestone, the wines here get a famous "gunflint" nose. Smelling a Sancerre or Pouilly-Fumé can be, quite literally, like smelling a wet piece of slate. Why is this good? Who knows—but it really, really is. It's wonderful. A Menetou-Salon or Quincy will be less expensive, because they're less mineral and thus less esteemed, but should still show you good structure and restrained but attractive fruit.

Sancerres and Pouilly-Fumés are almost indistinguishable and are not just the gold standard of Sauvignon Blanc but are among the most important wines in the world. Being a wine lover who hasn't tasted a Sancerre or Pouilly-Fumé is like being a film person who hasn't seen *The Maltese Falcon*—you have to do it, and it's totally worth it. The wine is smoky, flinty, herbal, fruity, profound. In case you're penny-pinching you should also know that Sancerre and Pouilly-Fumé are some of the best wine bargains in the world. You'll usually find them in stores for $20 to $35 and on restaurant wine lists for twice that. They go well with just about any appetizer you can think of, all fish and shellfish, cheese, salads, asparagus, smoked things, and Asian foods. If you want to have a richer life, one rule of thumb is simply to look for Sancerre and Pouilly-Fumé as your no-brainer first-course wines.

Oak-aged Sauvignon Blancs, $20 and up

I find very oaky Sauvignon Blancs to be peculiar and unappealing, but I'm in the minority on this opinion. Lots of people adore them, and they command the absolute highest prices in the world of Sauvignon Blanc, so they must be the absolute best. Right? Well, try one and be your own judge.

Some of the most esteemed oak-aged Sauvignon Blancs? Robert Mondavi's To Kalon Fumé Blanc, a benchmark Sauvignon Blanc in America, meaning it's a Sauvignon Blanc that all Sauvignon Blancs must be judged by; the late Didier Dagenau's top Pouilly-Fumés, Pur Sang and Silex; Seresin's Marama; Cloudy Bay's Te Koko from Marlborough, New Zealand (not to be confused with its regular $20-something Sauvignon Blanc; you'll know it's Te Koko because it will say so on the bottle and you'll be paying more than $50); Château Souverain's Alexander Valley; Fritz Russian River Valley; Gary Farrell Redwood Ranch Sonoma County; Ferrari-Carano Winery; Mason; and Merry Edwards.

If you can't figure out whether a particular bottle is oaked or not, here are some clues: Frequently Sauvignon Blancs made with oak are called "Fumé Blanc," and any mention of vanilla, oak, toast, caramel, butterscotch, spice, or smoke on the back label generally points to the use of oak.

The rest of the story

There will be a million other Sauvignon Blancs in your wine shop. Ignore those until you feel you have a good sense of what the basic profile of Sauvignon Blanc is, and then go hog wild. Some to look for:

Sauvignon Blanc–based White Bordeaux. White Bordeaux is what it sounds like: white wine made in the French region of Bordeaux. Typically it is made with some combination of Sauvignon Blanc, Sémillon, and maybe Sauvignon Gris (a rare, sweeter version of Sauvignon Blanc), Muscadelle, or Ugni Blanc. If you fall in love with Sauvignon Blanc, by all means start asking sommeliers and wine shop folks to point you toward more Sauvignon Blanc–heavy White Bordeaux. A top Sauvignon Blanc–leaning region is Pessac-Léognan.

If your sommelier can't help you find a Sauvignon Blanc–based White Bordeaux ask him if he can recommend one that's higher in acid. That should weed out the predominantly Sémillon-based ones. If he still has no idea what you're talking about make eye contact and draw your finger across your throat as if cutting off your head, then curse in French.

South African Sauvignon Blanc. Cool-climate South African Sauvignon Blancs have been something of a fad the last few years, with critics often proclaiming them the next big thing. Are they? They're doubtless some of the best wine coming out of Africa, but whether this is akin to being the best coffee in Ohio remains to be seen. I mean, something has to be the best coffee in Ohio, and while that's a good thing to be, does it matter to anyone not in Ohio?

Late-Harvest Sauvignon Blanc. Rarely winemakers create a late-harvest dessert wine, or an ice wine made from Sauvignon Blanc from grapes left to get as ripe as they possibly can. These can be delicious, honeyed and fragrant. Honig makes one of the best.

Food and Sauvignon Blanc

The general rule of thumb when pairing wine and food runs that you *pair like with like*. This means that light, bright Sauvignon Blanc goes well with all light foods—foods that are light in color, or light in terms of the weight they create in your mouth. So Sauvignon Blanc goes well with oysters, shellfish, most every kind of fish but especially lighter fish such as trout, salads, cheese, Vietnamese and Thai salads and grilled foods, chicken, and so on. It does not go with things that are very dark colored or very big and weighty in your mouth—beef stew, pizza, burgers, and similar heavy things.

Tasting Sauvignon Blanc
Step by Step

1. A Brief Road Map to Our Upcoming Sauvignon Blanc Road Trip

You'll need to taste five or six Sauvignon Blancs, both bottom-shelf cheapies and top-shelf pricey ones, to get a sense of the personality of Sauvignon Blanc. You'll be trying to nail down the basic taste of the Sauvignon Blanc grape (grassy, citrus fruit) as well as what effect winemaking can have in making this basic fruit taste polished or more complex, and you'll also taste its highest expressions, in the wines of New Zealand and the Loire. Your main goal is to emerge from this tasting with an unshakable personal sense of what Sauvignon Blanc tastes like to you; your secondary goal is to figure out whether you like it, and if so, which style you prefer. When you figure out the style you like best, you'll be able to talk to sommeliers and wine shop staff for the rest of your life: I like stony Sancerre, I like New Zealand Sauvignon Blanc, and so on. Can't picture yourself saying that? Trust me, it's only a matter of getting six representative examples in your mouth and this will go from goobledygook to self-evident in the space of a few hours.

Whether you're tasting alone or in pairs, or by throwing a party, your plan will be as follows: Your first task will be to contrast two inexpensive Sauvignon Blancs, one austere and racy, from a cold climate like Chile, and one fully ripe, perhaps from Washington State. This pairing will teach you about the Sauvignon Blanc grape itself, what it's like fully ripe versus what it's like *not quite*. Second, you'll explore terroir—how the grape expresses the site it is grown on. For this you'll try a wildly scented Marlborough, New Zealand, Sauvignon Blanc. Finally, you'll get a sense of the poles of highest expression of the grape, by seeing what no-expense-spared winemaking and careful grape-growing can do for Sauvignon Blanc. For this you'll pair an over-$15 California Sauvignon Blanc with a real Pouilly-Fumé or Sancerre. Finally, if you want, you'll try an oaked Sauvignon Blanc, like Cloudy Bay's Te Koko or Robert Mondavi's To Kalon Fumé Blanc, and—that's it! Wham, bam, thank you ma'am, you now know Sauvignon Blanc.

Notes on Tasting Sauvignon Blanc Solo or in Pairs

You'll be doing the same tasting as the party, except you'll have some time between wines one and two, three and four, and five and six. Try to taste all your wines with some food, either full dinners if you're a cook or simply with some fruit, cheese, and take-out chicken or a Thai salad if you're not. Finally, try to taste all six wines as close together in time as you can, over the course of a month, say; if you stretch them out over a year you may find yourself forgetting what that first pair tasted like.

Notes on Tasting Sauvignon Blanc by Party

A Sauvignon Blanc tasting party is one of the easiest, nicest little gatherings you can throw because it's the consummate cheese wine, which makes entertaining easy. The cheese most associated with Sauvignon Blanc is goat cheese, especially fresh goat cheese, chèvre, or one of the many goat-cheeses-in-a-shape like the various pyramids and bells you'll find at upscale cheese counters.

Fun fact: The most authentic cheese you could get would be Crottin de Chavignol, which comes from Sancerre; *crottin* refers to its shape and means "horse turd." I'd like to have been at that marketing meeting. *Hey, I can't think of what would sell this shit . . . Wait, that's it!*

Where was I? In addition to a goat's-milk cheese an ideal Sauvignon Blanc cheese board would include some not-too-aggressive cheeses, maybe a Gouda, a not-too-old Cheddar, or a Monterey Jack or Dry Jack. Apples, grapes, and pears would be ideal accompaniments.

If you want to have a dinner party, trout is a classic pairing, but some more perfect options would include a simple grilled or roast chicken or any dish made with smoked salmon, like a risotto or a pasta. Vegetarians might consider a pasta or risotto with a walnut pesto and roast vegetables. For dessert, stick to things that are creamy or fruity: cheesecake, mango sorbet, berries, vanilla ice cream, apple pie, and such. Just avoid things that are black, very dark brown, or purple: no coffee sorbet, chocolate, pecan pie, or the like.

2. Shopping

For your Sauvignon Blanc tastings you'll need several bottles, gathered from the field guide above. This shopping list is summarized for your convenience, and the names of the specific wineries are simply provided to help; don't worry about matching the exact wines mentioned, just try to match the categories.

1. New World cheap, fruity, and juicy Sauvignon Blanc, such as Hogue, Columbia Crest, Brancott, Château Ste. Michelle, or just about anything in the $6–$14 price point. See Field Guide above for more names.
2. Cheap, lean, and racy Sauvignon Blanc, such as Peñascal, Veramonte, or anything from Chile's Casablanca Val-

ley. Possible clues: The words "fresh," "crisp," or "acidity," on the label; a price of $6 to $15.

3. New Zealand Sauvignon Blanc, preferably from Marlborough, such as Kim Crawford, Cloudy Bay, Villa Maria. See above for more names, but any Marlborough Sauvignon Blanc will do. $15 to $25.

4. Big-name Napa or Sonoma Sauvignon Blanc: Something expensive, winemaker-directed, silky, stylish, and chic, like Honig, Grgich Hills, Cakebread, St. Supéry, Kunde Estate, Mason Estate, Flora Springs Soliloquy. See above for more names. $20 to $40.

5. Real French Sancerre, Pouilly-Fumé, Menetou-Salon, Reiully, or Quincy. Tell your wine guy you're looking for an unoaked Sancerre or Pouilly-Fumé with lots of mineral and gunflint character. If there's no wine guy (or gal), just buy whatever you see that says Sancerre or Pouilly-Fumé on it. If there's no Pouilly-Fumé but there is Menetou-Salon, Reiully, or Quincy, get one of those. $25 to $40.

6. Optional: One oak-aged Sauvignon Blanc, like Robert Mondavi's To Kalon Fumé Blanc, the late Didier Dagenau's top Pouilly-Fumés Pur Sang and Silex, Seresin's Marama, Cloudy Bay's Te Koko (not their regular Sauvignon Blanc), Château Souverain's Alexander Valley, Fritz Russian River Valley, Gary Farrell Redwood Ranch Sonoma County, Ferrari-Carano Winery, Mason, and Merry Edwards. $50 and up.

3. Planning and Thinking About Tasting.

Gather your wineglasses, dump bucket, and tasting markers. Make your life easier: Cut some fresh grass and put it in a wineglass. Place some wet rocks or gravel in another, cubes of honeydew in a third, pieces of apple in a fourth, and a chunk of a citrus fruit such as an orange or a lemon in a fifth.

Tasting Markers

Keep the following list handy so you can glance at it while you're tasting—it will help you name fragrances that seem just out of reach.

When tasting Sauvignon Blanc, the scents and flavors you are looking for, and most likely to encounter, are

Fresh grass

Dried grass or straw

Meadow grasses and flowers

Fresh herbs (parsley, lovage, chervil, and so on)

Dried herbs

Melon (honeydew, cantaloupe, muskmelon, etc.)

Minerals (wet rocks)

Flint (sometimes written as "gunflint")

Chalk

Apples

Pears

Figs

Honey

Asparagus

Lime

Gooseberry

Tropical fruit (mangoes, papayas, guavas, etc.)

Passion fruit

Cat pee

Honeysuckle

Any and all citrus fruit

Any and all citrus fruit rinds, either fresh, zest, candied, or dried

Stone fruit such as nectarines, peaches, and apricots

Less likely, but possible

Green tea

Earth

Smoke

Jasmine flowers

Pineapple

Salt or ocean water

Kiwi

Green beans

Jalapeño peppers

Green bell peppers

Vanilla

SweeTarts

Key lime pie, lemon meringue pie, orange meringue pie

What the Heck Are Gooseberries?

Gooseberries are one of the defining characteristics of Sauvignon Blanc, especially Sauvignon Blanc from New Zealand. But for a lot of Americans, saying that is about as meaningful as saying that something smells like Martian rocks. Gooseberries are little green, yellow, pink, or red berries that grow on shrubs in northern places like England, France, Germany, Switzerland, and Sweden. They're cousins to currants, and of course black currants are one of the key tastes of Cabernet Sauvignon, which is a descendant of Sauvignon Blanc, so that makes a certain amount of sense: the child is like black currants, the mom is like gooseberries. (Cabernet Sauvignon's other parent is Cabernet Franc.)

If you really want to know what gooseberries smell like, you can find them fresh in many farmer's markets. Gooseberry jam or pie filling can be found in many grocery stores or via the Internet.

Cat Pee. No Kidding.

Sometimes you'll read a tasting note that attributes the scent of cat pee to Sauvignon Blanc, especially that from New Zealand. Yes, really, cat pee. It's the slightly ammonia, slightly musky, slightly salty smell that anyone who's been unfortunate enough to know a busy male cat knows well.

Sometimes hand in hand with cat pee—or should I say, bathroom stall to bathroom stall—comes the signature Sauvignon Blanc aroma of sweat, or as some put it, armpit or summer subway. These scents are thought to come from a compound in grapes called pyrazines, which dissipate in the sunshine as fruit ripens. However, if the grape doesn't fully ripen, or if the grape clusters are too well hidden from the sun by the grape's bushy leaves, the pyrazines don't dissipate and you get cat pee.

Believe it or not, lots of people love it. Why? The same reason some people love really stinky cheese: They just love what they love. Don't believe it? Check out the New Zealand winery Cooper's Creek and their jokey, but real, actual, widely distributed wine Cat's Pee on a Gooseberry Bush. The main thing you need to know about cat pee emanating from your Sauvignon Blanc glass is it's natural, and for many people, desirable.

4. Cool Things Off

Get your Sauvignon Blancs to a good white-wine cellar temperature, 45 degrees. (See page 10 for why.)

5. Pull the corks!

Or untwist the screw tops. Some of the most expensive Sauvignon Blancs in the world are bottled under screw tops—they're a better way than cork to keep young whites fresh.

6. Taste Your First Wine

Start with the first wine on your shopping list, the fat, fruity, juicy New World Sauvignon Blanc. Pour an inch or so into each guest's wineglass. Swirl your wine. Sniff it. Taste it. Glance at the list of tasting markers—do these spark anything in you? If not, that's fine, sometimes it takes quite a few experiences for the tasting markers to seem obvious, but for most people they will, eventually.

Swirl and sniff your bottom-shelf fruity wine again. Because it comes from the warm New World, it should taste good and ripe. You may pick up the scent of apples and other fruity fruits. You don't? Then this is a good time to pass around the glasses containing your tasting markers and sniff and sip again.

Questions to consider: Do you smell fresh or dried grass? What about melons? Does the wine's label tell you the wine is going to smell like anything in particular? Does it? Are they lying? Does the wine seem too sweet, too tart, or in balance? Do you like it?

7. Taste Your Racy, Austere Bottom-Shelf Sauvignon Blanc

Next, pour number two on your shopping list, your austere, lean Sauvignon Blanc, which will showcase the racy style that Sauvignon Blanc takes on when it grows somewhere cold. Swirl. Sniff. Taste. You should detect a grassiness, and it should be crisp.

Questions to consider: How is it different from the first wine? Do you like one more than another? Taste your wine with food. Does it make the food taste better? The wine taste better? If you've got your first wine, now try that one with food. Sniff each wine—can you tell the difference between the two?

(Note to solo tasters: You will now take a break. Try the next two wines as soon as convenient; the closer in time everything is tasted, the easier it will be to keep track of.)

8. Taste Your Marlborough Sauvignon Blanc

Next up, number three: New Zealand Sauvignon Blanc, from the region of Marlborough. Pour. Sniff. Swirl. Taste. This one should be intense: wildly scented, full of tropical and citrus fragrances.

Questions: Holy cow, is that insanely fragrant? What does that? (Answer: Where it's grown.) Other questions: Do you smell limes? Tropical fruits—mango, maybe even passion fruit and pineapple? Do you like it more or less than the basic bottom-shelf, Sauvignon Blancs? If you do prefer it, do you think it's the fragrance you prefer, or is the wine itself more in balance?

9. Taste Your Silky Napa Valley Sauvignon Blanc

Your fourth bottle will show us the face of big-name, big-money California Sauvignon Blanc. It should be silky and lush. Questions to consider: Does this wine smell of melons? Grass? Does it remind you of any of the other Sauvignon Blancs, or does it seem like its own animal? Do you like the more raw, rough-edged, bottom-shelf wine, or this more polished one? Remember—there is no correct answer!

(Note to solo tasters: Another break. See you soon!)

10. Taste Your Real French Sancerre or Pouilly-Fumé

Finally, we'll be leaving the Sauvignon Blancs of the New World and finding out why anyone plants this stuff in the first place. For that we must go to the Old World: to France! The whole reason anyone ever planted Sauvignon Blanc is because they were trying to reproduce the wines of Sancerre and Pouilly-Fumé, that is, the top-shelf Sauvignon Blanc of France.

The significant difference between the big-deal French stuff and the rest of the world's Sauvignon Blanc is supposed to be an extreme minerality. With this wine you should literally smell flint, wet rocks, wet chalk, and minerals, minerals, minerals. Pour. Swirl. Sniff. Taste.

Questions to toss around: Minerals? Melons? Grass? Does this wine seem markedly different from the others? If so, which do you prefer? Do you detect a "finish," that is, a pleasant taste in your mouth after you've swallowed the wine? If so, would you describe it as a long finish or a short one? Does your French Sauvignon Blanc finish differently than the others? Try your French Sauvignon Blanc with food—does it improve the food? Does the food improve the wine? Out of all the Sauvignon Blancs you've tried, does this strike you as markedly better? Worth the price?

11. Taste Your Oak-Rounded Sauvignon Blanc

All the Sauvignon Blancs we've tasted thus far, with the possible exception of the Napa Valley one, would have been made without oak. Some of the most expensive Sauvignon Blancs on earth, however, are in fact aged in oak, which gives them a toasty caramel edge. (Part of this expense comes from the barrels themselves; new French oak barrels cost as much as a thousand dollars each, which can add a couple of dollars onto any bottle's price.)

Pour your oak-aged Sauvignon Blanc. Swirl. Sniff. Things to consider: Do you like the toastiness the oak lends? Some people love it, some hate it.

And that's it! If you're at a party, take the time to cross-compare wines: Do the bottom-shelf wines seem more appealing or less, now that you've tasted all the styles? Some people go through a whole tasting and are delighted to discover that their favorite wine is one of the cheapies. Others are dismayed to find they prefer the most expensive. Still others find they have fallen in love with the glossy Napa Valley style, but that a Washington wine makes a good budget alternative.

Congratulations! You now know more about Sauvignon Blanc than most people. When sommeliers approach you can tell them you like fruity, exuberant New Zealand Sauvignon Blanc, or stony French Sancerre.

THE TAKEAWAY

Isn't it astonishing how different one single wine grape is when grown on different soils? Most people who go through a Sauvignon Blanc tasting for the first time and contrast even just a Sancerre and a New Zealand Sauvignon Blanc can't believe that the same thing is in the two bottles. It feels like you're comparing apples to oranges, when in fact you're just comparing apples to apples. The reason they're all so different is simply because of where they're grown and how they're made. How crazy is that?

Five-second cheat sheet for people who didn't read the chapter and are reading this on their iPhones in a Vietnamese-French fusion restaurant while they wait for a table

Sauvignon Blanc (*so-veen-yohn blahnk*) is one of the world's most important white wines, and is especially valued for its ability to pair with almost any food. Tricky foods like contemporary fusion cooking, but also French bistro classics from salads to oysters to cheese, and also chicken, fish, Vietnamese and Thai food, sushi—basically, anything that isn't aggressively wintry, such as beef stew, goes with Sauvignon Blanc.

The two benchmark styles of Sauvignon Blanc you'll find in most restaurants are (1) French Sancerre and Pouilly-Fumé (*poo-yee-fyu-MAY*), and (2) New Zealand Sauvignon Blanc. The New Zealand style, as epitomized by the brand Cloudy Bay, has a wildly fragrant nose, all lime, mango, and fruit basket, but a clean and zippy pres-

ence in the mouth. The other extreme of Sauvignon Blanc
is the brisk, crisp, minerally French wines Sancerre and
Pouilly-Fumé. They are considered some of the world's
greatest wines, brisk, dry, austere, and with a bewitching
mineral nose. They are also usually relative bargains on
wine lists, under $70 or so, and are a must-try for every
wine lover.

Knock-Their-Socks-Off
Gifts for Sauvignon Blanc Lovers

1. Sauvignon Blanc lovers tend to be pragmatists, and have little
   in common with those zany money-is-meaningless Cabernet
   Sauvignon lovers. This makes life easy for the people who love
   them, because there's really only one very expensive Sauvignon Blanc in all the world: Château Haut-Brion Blanc.

   Château Haut-Brion Blanc is supposed to present the aromatic complexity of a Sauternes in a dry wine. I've read it
   smells like almond praline. Have $500 burning a hole in your
   pocket? Be the first on your block to know for sure.

2. Any older white Bordeaux from Pessac-Léognan, the region of
   France considered home to the very best Sauvignon Blanc–
   based Bordeaux wines in the world. Consult with a specialty
   wine shop like California's K&L Wine Merchants and see what
   they can find for you.

3. Duckhorn Sauvignon Blanc: If it was good enough for everyone
   at Barack Obama's inaugural luncheon, it should be good
   enough for anyone. It was paired with seafood stew.

4. Merry Edwards Russian River Valley Sauvignon Blanc: A
   perennial award winner, in 2009 *Wine Spectator* critic James
   Laube called this "the greatest Sauvignon Blanc I've ever had
   from anywhere." Merry Edwards uses the Musqué clone of
   Sauvignon Blanc, a pinker, sweeter, more aromatic grape. Is

that what makes this wine so raveworthy? See if you develop the same crush on it: At press time it cost only $29 and should be readily available.

5. Sauvignon Blanc ice wine, late-harvest, or dessert wine: While they may be as rare as camels in New York City, there are a handful of intrepid—or mad—producers in the world making Sauvignon Blanc–based dessert wines. The Dolce winery in Napa Valley makes a Sémillon and Sauvignon Blanc late-harvest wine that's unctuous and ambrosial. Napa Valley's Honig makes an all–Sauvignon Blanc late-harvest wine that's as fragrant as a hundred fruits arranged among a thousand flowers. Austria's Weingut Heiss makes a Sauvignon Blanc–based ice wine. Chile's La Playa makes a late-harvest Sauvignon Blanc the color of straw. Set a bottle under the Christmas tree and the Sauvignon Blanc lover in your life will be singing Santa's praises all year.

4

RIESLING
GRACE, PRUDENCE, AND NERVE

Pronounced: *REEZ-ling*. Also known as: Johannis-
berg Riesling—and nothing else! What joy.

Dear Dara,
I've got enough problems, I don't need to add sweet
wine to my burdens. Let's skip Riesling.
—Baffled

It makes me so sad when people tar Riesling with the
sweet brush. It's not sweet! I mean, some of it is, but it's
supposed to be. Also, did you know that German and Austrian Riesling has been the cutting-edge hipster's favorite
wine for the last few years? True. This is because high-
quality Riesling delivers the Holy Grail of all wine: cheap
and sublime.

What's to Love About Riesling?

Riesling's is the most naked of all winemaking. You don't
use oak, you don't blend in any other grapes to fix it, you

don't do anything except grow it well, and you better really grow it well or all your flaws are going to be out there for people to see. As Bo Barrett, one of the founders of the Napa Valley winery Château Montelena once told me, "With Chardonnay you've got oak, all sorts of things you can do to the wine. But Riesling is a highly technical wine, and you better have your stuff together. It's like walking down the street in a Speedo." This naked quality of Riesling scares off bad actors: You don't plant Riesling if you're lazy, and you don't make Riesling with an eye toward buying low and fixing the grape juice in the tank, because you can't. Think of it as holding auditions for swimsuit models. Who's going to show up?

In addition to this naked quality, Riesling is exquisitely nuanced. Some wines can unspool their secrets for hours in a glass. Once you get accustomed to searching out these flickering evolutions and nuances, you may find Riesling as entrancing or relaxing as watching a fire in a fireplace.

What's to Hate About Riesling?

German wine labeling. Every cliché you can think of that applies to the Germans' affection for officiousness applies. Worse, the incredibly precise, rule-bound, and number-obsessed German wine labeling system actually misleads with its precision. Their labeling of wines as sweet, sweeter, and super-sweet, for instance, doesn't tell you how sweet the wine *tastes*, it just tells you the measured sugar level at harvest. On the upside, these baffling and misleading rules flummox most Americans, keeping the stuff artificially cheap. Still, German wine labels can be so unhelpful that they may as well write some of them in mirror text. Or Egyptian hieroglyphics. Or *German*. Oh, wait . . .

What's the Story with Riesling?

Let me lay out a little European history. No, don't run away! If you didn't want to participate in the grand pageant of Western culture with its attendant history you'd just drink vodka and Diet Coke, right? It'll be painless and quick, I promise.

Riesling is one of the world's great wines, many would argue the greatest white wine of all. Its original home is central Europe, where it was grown exclusively until the nineteenth century. Now it makes lovely wines in Australia, New Zealand, California, and all over the New World.

However, back before the New World got going, sweetness was hard to come by. You had honey and ripe fruit, but that was about it. Sugar as we know it only became common in the 1700s, when the sugar colonies in the Caribbean began to perfect the technology of sugar cane refining. However, sugar as we know it today was insanely expensive, and a high-cost luxury item for most of the world until the nineteenth century. Germany didn't have Caribbean and American colonies and outposts the way Spain and England did, so sugar was even scarcer there than in other parts of Europe.

Now picture a poor farmer in northern Germany in 1400, sugarless. He's just far enough south that he can grow grapes, but far enough north that the cool climate makes it tough. Also, it's before global warming, so it's even colder in Germany than it is now.

Winemaking is the process of turning fruit sugar into alcohol. If you don't have any sugar in your grapes to start with, you have a problem. So of course the grapes were bred for maximum sweetness. This doesn't mean that the wine itself was sweet; typically bad things would happen to the grapes on their journey to sweet. Bad things like cold weather, incessant cloud cover, or ill-timed storms. So the grapes would only make it part way to sweet—that is, they'd only get sweet enough to turn into a *dry* wine.

If perchance the grapes did make it to sweet, this was considered the luckiest possible development. Because suddenly—sugar! In a land with almost none. So, just as the Spanish love oak and the Spanish wine laws largely have to do with how much oak a wine is exposed to, the Germans prize sugar and the German wine laws regulate sugar. And so I introduce to you the German wine laws. (Oh, surely you knew that if the bait was European history, the reward was going to be something as awful as this, right?)

Deutscher Tafelwein is how Germans indicate the lowest of the low, table wine made from grapes that never got ripe. These wines have no sweetness and rarely make it to America.

Landwein is the second lowest. This wine has to come from specified wine districts, but the grapes can be unripe. Winemakers are allowed to add sugar so there's something for the yeasts to turn to alcohol. This process is called "chaptalization," and it's common in most cold-weather wine areas. Champagne is sometimes chaptalized. These *Landweins* sometimes get exported, sometimes not. I put *Landwein* and *Deutscher Tafelwein* in here so that you can understand German wine laws as they were originally meant: to tell consumers the most important thing that German wine authorities could conceive of, that is, whether the grapes got ripe enough to get any prized, oh-so-valuable sweetness in them to turn into alcohol.

Now we'll move into the wine levels you will actually see:

QbA is the second-best level. It comes from specified wine districts and specified grape varieties, but chaptalization is still allowed.

QmP is the best, because the grapes got ripe! The winemaker is proving it by making the wine with only the grapes' natural sugar, no chaptalization allowed.

If you haven't picked up on this yet, let me put a neon underline beneath it for you: Sugar and ripeness are so important to German wine that the only thing that matters to make the "best quality" wine is that the grapes actually got ripe—that is, sweet enough to make wine with.

Incidentally, if you're wondering what QbA stands for, it's *Qualitätswein bestimmter Anbaugebiet* ("quality wine from a specified region"). Anytime an American can pronounce it correctly while eating a sausage, a magical troll appears and hands out a Volkswagen. QmP is *Qualitätswein mit Pradikat* ("quality wine with special attributes").

Within this top QmP category there are four more levels determined by—you guessed it!—sweetness levels:

Kabinett wines got their name because they were once so prized you'd be keeping them in your home safe, your "treasure cabinet." Today Kabinett wines are bottom-rank, or the least sweet of the best.

Spätlese (*SHPAYT-lay-sa*) is riper and sweeter. *Auslese* (*OWSS-lay-sa*) is riper and sweeter still. And finally *Trockenbeerenauslese* is the ripest, the sweetest, true dessert wine. (Don't even try to pronounce it, everyone just calls it TBA. Okay, if you must: *TROken-bayrun-OWS-lay-sa*.)

Remember, the sugar in grape juice gets turned into alcohol. If you wanted to, you could take the sweetest grape juice on earth and turn it into the driest possible wine. All you need are super-yeasts to convert all the sugar to alcohol. Ciroc vodka, for instance, is vodka made from grapes. It's not sweet, it's the very definition of dry—it's vodka. Of course, people in the world's Riesling territories know perfectly well how to turn grape sugar into dry alcohol. When the Germans turn all the sugar from a wine into alcohol they have a special name for it: *Trocken*. Halfway to dry they

Conversations with Bigwigs: Terry Theise

The Riesling resurgence among Gen X and Gen Y, especially among young sommeliers, can almost single-handedly be traced to the influence of one man: wine importer Terry Theise. Young sommeliers love Theise largely because he has exquisite taste and his name on the back label is a guarantee of something delicious in the bottle, because he is unafraid to say harsh things when warranted, and because he is able to put some of the ineffable, mysterious qualities of wine into words.

I've been surprised lately at how many of these twenty- and thirtysomethings are passionate about my wine. Because it used to be that the audience for my wine began in people reaching middle age who got tired of bogus wine, wine that shrieks for attention, wine with no variation to it. Which I think is fine, if that really is your taste, if you're a headbanger and need an enormous amount of input, just a wall of loudness with no dynamic variation, I think that's fine.

But for others, that's an assault. They appreciate quieter wines. What is a quieter wine? It's like a person about whom one might say: Still waters run deep. They're serene, comfortable, calm, and have a quality of being lit from within.

Now, that's still pretty abstract. Say you taste a wine. The flavor is elusive. When you take your first sip, you don't know what it is, you see it out of the corner of your eye. As you sit with it awhile, you think, "It's this, it's that." As you follow it, a quiet space opens around you. People who are drawn to that quietness often appreciate it in other venues as well. They are often gardeners, or someone who might enjoy washing dishes, the sensual zone-out of the water running over their hands. It seems strange for these people that there would be any other way to live, and vice versa. Rieslings are often these quiet wines.

call *Halbtrocken.* In English this is often translated as "off-dry," or "half-sweet."

Sweetness, then, is not something that is unchangeable and nature-given—it's just a winemaker's stylistic choice. And it's not like you're going to just blunder into a TBA the next time you're in a wine shop. The stuff usually costs upwards of $50 for a half-bottle, and the reason it does is because it's amazing, profound, and wonderful, and collectors trample one another to get it. If you haven't heard about it before, that's just because it's one of those things that are so sought after and rare they just change hands quietly, at high dollar amounts, like contemporary fine art.

A lot of people haven't heard of Château d'Yquem either, one of the most hotly sought bottles of wine on the planet. It's super-sweet dessert wine too; a bottle from Thomas Jefferson's cellar once sold for $56,000. It's one of those things that people in the trade don't even talk about with people outside the trade. It would be like an orchid collector trying to explain why some tiny ugly phalaenopsis is worth $10,000. People on the inside know, and people on the outside don't care.

Sweetness, however, is actually something that lots of wine people adore: Sauternes, TBA, and Port, all sweet wines, are some of the most collectible, desirable, big-ticket wines on earth. If you asked me, I'd say that the big problem that sweet wines have is not sugar, it's James Bond. His constant harping on a "dry" martini, and the attendant idea that "dry" meant good, superior, *the best,* and wasn't merely a descriptive word, like "blue" or "salty," took on a viral aspect in the culture—and here we are. People new to wine are often shrilly hysterical when it comes to the idea of dry—They want dry!—when what they actually mean is they want to be like James Bond.

If you want to know what dry is, consider vodka. Vodka is

dry. Vodka lands on your tongue and evaporates, creating a feeling of dryness. People don't like dry wine as much as they like to say they do. Blanc de blanc Champagne, the driest, isn't nearly as popular as Champagne made with Pinot Noir grapes. The driest Chardonnay is Chablis, but it's nowhere near as popular as fruit-bomb California Chardonnay. The driest sorts of Syrah, those from the northern Rhône, get nothing near the popular acclaim of much sweeter Syrahs like the Australian 100-point wines in the style of Penfolds Grange Shiraz.

There will be people who will tell you that sweetness in wine is simply a matter of residual sugar, a scientific measurement of the remaining unfermented sugars in a wine. These people are absolutely right, especially if a laboratory hydrometer is going to be the one enjoying the wine. However, I think that it's much, much more helpful to think of residual sugar, or as wine nerds sometimes put it, RS, in terms of IQ, the famous test of intelligence. Who's smarter, the person with the IQ of 145 or the IQ of 190? What if the person with the IQ of 145 is a first cellist in the orchestra and deftly united civic and business leaders to end homelessness in his city—and the guy with the 190 IQ is a self-sabotaging virgin scribbling in Klingon in his parents' basement? Who's more intelligent now? I hold that, like IQ, RS is only meaningful *in context*. That is, it is only meaningful when considered with the rest of the wine. On top of that, like IQ scores, RS numbers are pretty well hidden from the general public, and if you make your understanding of dryness incumbent on RS you're going to be exactly where you don't want to be, relying on critics, winemakers, and other gatekeepers to tell you what you're allowed to like instead of relying on yourself and figuring out your own taste.

If you want to be a real wine insider, internalize this: Dry does not mean "good"; dry means dry. And too much dryness can be a fault. Good wine has several dimensions: Acidity, alcohol, tannin, energy, nerve, structure, fruitiness, and sugar are all poles that have to balance one another out. If a wine is all acid with no fruit, we call it thin. If it's all tannin, we call it bitter. If it's all fruit, we call it flabby. If all a winemaker had to do to make a breathtaking wine was to turn all the sugar into alcohol, there are plenty of super-yeasts that can do that for them. That part's easy, it's just chemistry, not art.

How to Drink a Strong Man Under the Table

Some German Rieslings, like those from the Mosel-Saar-Ruwer area of Germany, are incredibly light in alcohol, maybe only 7 or 8 percent. This means that they're half as strong as a high-alcohol wine like an American Cabernet or Zinfandel, which can weigh in at 15 or even 17 percent alcohol. Polish off a whole bottle of Mosel-Saar-Ruwer Riesling and you've essentially drunk two glasses of regular wine. Use this to your advantage the next time you find yourself in a *Raiders of the Lost Ark*-style drinking contest with backcountry barbarians!

Plus, it's not as if dry and not dry are the only choices. Consider bananas. You probably have some personal, highly developed idea of what the best possible state of banana is, and what states of banana you will eat and not eat. Consider a banana's common stages of ripeness:

1. Strongly green;
2. Green starting to yellow;
3. Bright yellow with greenish ends;
4. Uniform bright yellow;

5. Yellow with a smattering of brown freckles;
6. More brown than yellow;
7. Brown.

I prefer my bananas in the 3–4 zone. I don't like the greenest bananas (which taste the driest), nor the sweetest, though in a pinch I'd prefer a 2 over a 6, but a 6 over a 1. And you? Where do you fall in the banana hierarchy?

Winemakers confront something like this, gauging a grape's ripeness according to three measurements. One is Brix, a scientific way of gauging how much sugar a grape contains. Another is "physiological ripeness," a human-eye and human-mouth evaluation as to whether the grape skin, seeds, and flesh have all become ripe. The third is instinct as to what point of ripeness will translate into the best wine.

As it goes with the bananas above, so it goes for wine grapes. A winemaker could choose to harvest their grapes at any stage of ripeness. At every stage they'll get different qualities. Pick your Chardonnay a little earlier, for instance, and you might catch it emphasizing lemon peel flavors; a little later, tropical ones.

So, what do we mean by a sweet wine? Undeniably it's one with residual sugar. I think the answer that will bring you lasting happiness is that a sweet wine is one of two things. It's either a wine in which the acid, fruit, or structure is out of whack such that the wine becomes lopsided; or it's a wine that strikes you as sweet. After all, one person's perfect banana is another man's too-green or too-ripe one.

Is there any more perfect wine with which to explore sweetness in wine than Riesling? No. It has all those sweetness levels, but is often made bone dry. I mean it, truly bone dry. And sometimes even when it does have significant residual sugar it is so well balanced with its other elements that it doesn't *seem* sweet at all. If you want to be an instant wine sophisticate, sort out what "sweet" really means to you. In the space of an hour you'll find yourself knowing more about dryness, sweetness, and wine than about three-fourths of the waiters in America.

So we're off. The plan is to try Riesling in its various manifestations, some rich, some bone dry, and see what the grape is capable of and what you like.

Blue Nun Was Not Riesling!

There's a popular misconception that runs that because Blue Nun is German, it must be Riesling. No, no, no. Blue Nun used to be made of Müller-Thurgau, a cloyingly sweet cross between Riesling and a very bordello-sounding grape called Madeleine Royale that became big in Germany because it could grow like a weed in basic farm soil. These days the company that owns Blue Nun is trying to rescue its image by using actual Riesling grapes in the mix, but if you ever had Blue Nun and remember it tasting like Skittles consommé, don't think that was Riesling. Alternatively, if the idea of a soup made of Skittles intrigues you, consider floating flaming marshmallow islands on top of it, because that would be awesome.

The "Holy Trinity" of Riesling

The Grape

A white grape primarily used to make a still white wine, Riesling has many incarnations. Grown in Alsace or Austria it can be dry and steely, with, depending on the soil, a mineral or even gasoline-smelling nose. In Germany, its benchmark home, it combines a racy structure with fragrant lime and apple notes. When it comes from places that are hot it can be fruity and flabby, like pie filling. Wherever it's grown it will display scents of flowers, peaches, apples, nectarines, melons, and possibly minerals and spice.

Very, very rarely you'll see an Australian or other New World wine where someone has chosen to blend Sémillon, Riesling, and Sauvignon Blanc or Chardonnay, but this goes in the category of things people *can* do, like using taxidermy to create a rabbit-bird, and not things they *usually* do.

Terroir

You'll never find Riesling growing in truly hot places like Sicily, but it will grow anywhere that's got cold grape-growing land: Chile, South Africa, New Zealand, and so on. However, its three most famous expressions are Germany, Austria, and the Alsace region of France.

German Terroir

Grown primarily around the meandering, ever-turning Mosel River, and its tributaries, the Saar and Ruwer rivers, German Riesling is a world unto itself, but ideally combines lacy acidity with complex, haunting, yet subtle fruit aromas.

Alsatian Terroir

The French style of Riesling is dry and nervy, dry and clean, dry and fierce. It's got more structure than the Eiffel Tower. This has to do with climate and soil, but the typical "petrol" aromas that the wine has make it seem even drier than it is.

Austrian Terroir

The line on Austrian Riesling is that it combines the aromatics of German Riesling with the steely, austere structure of Alsatian Riesling.

Winemaking

Riesling is basically made in the fields. It expresses loudly every little thing that happens to it: the mineral content of the soil, too much autumn rain, and so on. It isn't blended with any other grapes and it isn't aged in oak. Riesling is aged in neutral wood (that is, wood that could be twenty or thirty years old and imparts no flavor), steel, epoxy-lined cement tanks, or glass-lined ones. Some Rieslings are made with extended fermentations "on the lees," that is, in contact with dead yeast and some grape solids that remain in just-crushed Riesling juice. Some of Riesling's aromatics are dictated by the yeasts used in the fermentation. A winemaker might use only the wild yeasts that came in with the grapes from the field, or she might use store-bought yeasts that generate particular qualities, or she might even divide her crushed grape juice into different batches and use one yeast with one batch to create strong melon aromas, and another yeast with another batch to create more structure, and then blend them. The resulting wine will still be 100 percent Riesling, can still even be from the same vineyard, but will thus achieve more complexity.

Stop Reading, Start Drinking!

In this chapter you will learn about Riesling, what it tastes like, the different styles, the different terroirs, the different price points. You'll also learn what ripeness and sugar levels are to wine, and how acidity and sugar in proportion act to create wines that taste either balanced, or too sweet, or too acidic, which will help you in all your wine drinking forevermore.

Riesling FIELD GUIDE

A good wine shop should have at least two dozen Rieslings, including inexpensive American ones like Fetzer and Hogue, as well as Alsatian, German, and Austrian wines. Not sure if your favorite wine shop is good enough? I've got two strategies for you. One: The premier Riesling importer in the country is a guy named Terry Theise; whatever shop in your city carries his wines is *the* Riesling shop. Check out his employer's website, skurnikwines .com, for a list of the distributors that carry Theise's wines, then call the distributor and ask which shops carry his wines near you. Strategy two: Call up your likely shop and say, "I need two Rieslings for a wine tasting, an Auslese (OWS-lay-sa) German Riesling and an Austrian one. Do you have those?" If the answer is yes, you have found your good wine shop.

Inexpensive domestic Riesling, $6–$12

Bottom-shelf domestic Riesling has two faces these days. On the one hand there are very sweet wines like Fetzer and Kendall-Jackson, which sell more than a quarter of a million cases a year between the two of them. On the other hand there are budget producers like Hogue, Columbia Crest, Snoqualmie, Covey Run, and Château Ste. Michelle, all in Washington State, that make nicely balanced wines with great fruit aromas. All in all, bottom-shelf American Riesling is about ten times better than bottom-shelf American Chardonnay. Look for strong peach and floral flavors and aromas.

Real German Kabinett Riesling, $12 and up

By German law, Kabinett wines are the least sweet, or bottom-rank of the best, the driest of the best, and the most affordable of the best. The most critically well regarded come from vineyards near the Rhine, Nahe, and Mosel rivers, all of which are edged by steep mountains.

These mountains give German Riesling two complexly inter-woven halves, the fruity half and the mineral half. The fruity half comes from the mountains, because they catch the sunlight and allow grapes to ripen, but because it's still cold, this takes a long time, which winemakers call a long "hang time." A long hang time means more flavor. This is where the fruity aromas and flavors of German Riesling come from: the long ripening grapes.

The mineral half comes from the lousy mountain topsoil. Mountains have terrible topsoil for two reasons. For one thing, they were recently all rock. For another, any topsoil that might build up is liable to run down the sides in erosion or avalanches. Grapes growing in lousy topsoil are forced to send their roots deep into the earth—in this case, rock—seeking water and nutri-ents. Riesling grapes are thus able to pull out all sorts of mineral notes from their treacherous mountainside home.

Top names: J. J. Prüm (*proom*), Selbach-Oster, Dönnhoff, Schonborn, Schäfer-Fröhlich, Müller-Catoir, Egon Muller, Monch-hof, Joh. Jos. Christoffel Erben, Künstler, Karthäuserhof, Fritz Haag, Erben von Beulwitz, Hexamer, Markus Molitor, Gunderloch, Dr. Loosen (*low-zen*), J. & H. A. Strub (*stroob*), Bürklin-Wolf, Rein-hold Haart, Bassermann-Jordan, Reinhard Löwenstein, Müller-Catoir, Christmann, Dr. Weins-Prüm, Robert Weil, Willi Schaefer, Schmitges, Von Schubert, von Buhl.

Don't see any names you recognize? Fear not, about 60 per-cent of the world's Riesling comes from Germany, from about 3 zillion *weingüter* (châteaux), many with extremely low produc-tion. It's a far better strategy in German wine to try the ones you find rather than holding out for ones you've read about. In my ex-perience about one out of every two bottles you run into is ex-cellent. Kabinett Rieslings generally cost between $15 and $50, with most priced in the $20-something range.

Alsatian Riesling, $14–$40 and up

Alsace is a French border region that has been bloodily traded back and forth between France and Germany, but it's been French since 1945 and that looks to be sticking. However, keep this history in mind when considering that Alsace isn't as French as the rest of France. Case in point: They're the only French region where it's legal to grow Riesling. These wines are steely, austere, nervy, crisp, and graceful as a samurai sword slicing through peach-tinged clouds. Seriously, people who try a handful of Alsatian Rieslings often become lifelong fans—the wine is so elegant. You should try at least half a dozen in your Riesling explorations, it's that important a benchmark of the varietal.

The best Alsatian Rieslings read "Alsace Grand Cru" and carry the name of the particular vineyard on the label along with the grape type. There are about fifty grand cru vineyards. The Alsatians also make sweet, late-harvest dessert wines that are like TBAs called *Vendanges Tardives* (VTs) and *Sélections des Grains Nobles* (SGNs).

Top Alsatian producers: Zind-Humbrecht, Trimbach, Hugel, Paul Blanck, Weinbach, Mittnacht-Klack, Marcel Deiss, Marc Kreydenweiss, Schlumberger, Josmeyer, Ernest Burn, Albert Boxler, Domaine Ostertag, Schoffit, Leon Beyer, and Dopff au Moulin. Alsatian prices in North America start at around $14 and climb; while the sky's the limit, most are in the $20- to $40-something range.

Single-estate American Riesling, $15 and up

The first wine I really fell in love with was the Estate Dry Riesling from Trefethen. I'll never forget how thrilled and surprised I was by the fine grace of that wine. It's like drinking a bit of pale yellow light. Even though the conventional wisdom runs that American Riesling is always a distant second to the German, Austrian, and Alsatian versions, I'll always believe that the best American Rieslings are lovable on their own merits.

Some of the best: Trefethen, Claiborne & Churchill, Stony Hill, Renaissance, Navarro, Bonny Doon, Smith-Madrone (considered by some to be the benchmark American dry Riesling), Argyle, Château St. Jean, Esterlina, and Hagafen Cellars. A number of American vineyards make dessert wine from Riesling, including Trefethen and Frog's Leap, home of the world's only Frögen-beerenauslese. Most American single-estate Rieslings run in the $20-something range, sometimes a little more.

Austrian Riesling

It will displease most educators to hear this, but I bet if you plumbed the average American's brain for thoughts about Austria you would get one brain cell blinking: *Sound of Music,* Nazis, Australia?, pastries, Arnold Schwarzenegger, Vienna, Gustav Klimt's *The Kiss,* and . . . done. Increase your competitive advantage over your countrymen by adding the following fact: Austrian Riesling, almost always bone dry, is one of the world's most underpriced wines. The best are from Wachau. Most Austrian Rieslings will cost $18 to $40 and should be nervy and highly perfumed with scents of everything from orange rind to roasted beets to fresh oak leaves. Overall, however, they should suggest apricots and stony minerals.

Good names: Alzinger, Leth, Brandl, Loimer, Hirsch, Nigl (rhymes with *eagle*), F. X. Pichler, Rudi Pichler, Prager, Bründlmayer, Schloss Gobelsburg, Ludwig Hiedler, Feiler-Artinger, Mantlerhof, Erich Salomon/Undhof, Hirtzberger, Knoll, Kracher, Karl Lagler, Weninger, and Nikolaihof.

Real German Spätlese & Auslese Riesling, $18 and up

I'd venture that out of all the German wine categories Spätlese and Auslese make the least sense to Americans. You say they're sweeter than Kabinett, so they're sweet, right? Wrong. Wrong! Freaking Germans. Personally, I think a better approach to Spätlese and

Auslese, classifications that both the Germans and Austrians use to refer to grapes picked a little later, and thus a little sweeter, than Kabinett grapes, is to think of it the way the Germans meant us to: These wines are a little "better" than Kabinett wines. They are often made quite dry, even bone dry, and in that case the label will usually say Riesling Spätlese Trocken or Riesling Auslese Trocken. If you want to have some authority in discussing Riesling, you should try at least one.

Expect Spätlese or Auslese Riesling to have a fruitier nose, greater weight and density, and generally more of everything than a Kabinett. Typically these are the wines that German wine-makers are most proud of. Top producers are the same as the ones for top German Kabinett or top Austrian producers, above. Prices: $20-something and up, rarely more than $40-something.

The dessert Rieslings

Finally, the sweet stuff! This category includes German and Aus-trian *Trockenbeerenauslese* (TBA, pronounced *trocken-BEARen-OWSS-lay-sa*), *Beerenauslese* (*BEARen-OWSS-lay-sa*), *Eiswein* (*EYES-vine*), Alsatian *Vendanges Tardives* (VTs, pronounced *vahndanzh tar-DEEV*) and *Sélections des Grains Nobles* (SGNs, pronounced *say-lek-sion deh gran no-bluh*), and American and Canadian Riesling ice wine. Riesling under any of these names is dessert wine.

TBA wines are made by leaving the grapes in the fields as long as possible, so that they hang there, get infected with a good fungus known as "noble rot," *Botrytis cinerea,* which does all sorts of things such as concentrate sugars, consume acids, and change enzymes within the grape, leaving a dry, shriveled mess behind. Botrytized grapes look terrible, as though they were roasted in a volcano and sprayed with ash. But these moldy, shriveled, neglected-looking grapes make the most ex-pensive, expressive, and highly sought after German wine on the planet. TBA wines are hand-picked, grape by grape, by someone who seeks out the exact ones that are just perfectly moldy and shriveled. This contributes to the price of the bottles.

There's also a plain old BA, which for all practical purposes is the exact same thing. The difference between the two is in their sugar levels; TBA wines are sweeter. Both TBA and BA wines are only made in select vintages, and can age for decades.

Eiswein, which is simply German for "ice wine," is traditionally made from grapes left to actually freeze in the fields. These late harvests mean that the grapes are as ripe as they can be; any late-harvest wine is always sweeter than its regular-harvest counterpart. Not only are the grapes for ice wine harvested frozen, they are then pressed frozen, so that a lot of the plain old water in them is left behind as ice crystals and the juice that is extracted is super-concentrated.

Modern makers sometimes now freeze grapes for ice wine in freezers instead of the fields; this is called *cryoextraction* and makes the wine more affordable.

All these very late harvest Rieslings taste like a magical potion of figs, white raisins, peaches, and honey with fragrances that you could pick apart for days and finishes that go on forever and ever. If you find yourself head-over-heels for real TBA and VT and you've inconveniently been denied a trust fund, start frequenting the bars at five-star restaurants and ask for the dessert wine list as soon as you sit down. Riesling dessert wines make great apéritifs—that is, drinks before dinner—and there's nothing better with cheese. Typically, these dessert wines are sold in half-bottles that start in the $20-something range and climb.

The rest of the story: Australia and the World!

Australian Riesling, $6–$40. Some critics will tell you that Riesling from Australia is terrifically promising, especially in the country's southern region, cold Clare Valley and Eden Valley, and Margaret River and Frankland River, in the west. They'll tell you that lime-scented, tightly acidic Australian Riesling stands a chance of being Australia's great white, a wine that tastes as if it comes from somewhere, not from nowhere like Yellow Tail and all the critter-label wines.

Judge for yourself, I suppose, but there are an awful lot of flabby, sloppy, Kool-Aid Australian Rieslings out there too. I'd stay away until you are able to judge the wine against the benchmark Rieslings of Germany, Austria, and Alsace. When you do try Riesling from Down Under, keep in mind that the characteristic fragrance of Australian Riesling is usually lime.

Outliers, $3 and up. Occasionally bottles from South Africa or Chile or even German sparkling "Sekt" Riesling will pop up. Again, my advice is to wait until you know the ordinary Riesling styles well before you venture forth. Canada and the Finger Lakes district of New York State make some Riesling; if you live in Ontario or New York, count your blessings and add those to your repertoire.

Conversations with Bigwigs: Paul Greico

Paul Greico, co-owner of the Manhattan restaurants Hearth and Insieme, has been one of the most fascinating forces in New York City wine over the last ten years. Why? He doesn't suffer fools—or the popular press, conventional taste, the lowest common denominator, or critics—gladly, and he doesn't care who knows it. Who else could get away with declaring a "Summer of Riesling"? Some years, from the first day of summer till sometime in August, the only white wine on the menu at Greico's cutting-edge wine bar, Terroir, is Riesling.

My partner at first thought I was nuts. I'm not arrogant enough to say, if someone wants a Chardonnay, screw 'em, but I guess in a sense I did say that. If you love big over-the-top New World Chardonnays there's nothing in the

Riesling world that I can give you, but if you are at least open-minded about it I know I will find something you love, and you could have a great time with Riesling.

Sometimes I think the measure of greatness for a wine should be: Can I sit down and drink a whole bottle of it? With so many reds today you would never get beyond that first six-ounce glass, because with that massive extraction, those huge amounts of new oak, your palate is destroyed. But with Riesling your palate is going to demand a second sip, a second glass. You're going to come back for more, and as you do you suddenly realize: This wine is in perfect proportion, perfect balance.

It's the greatest white grape on the planet Earth.

Food and Riesling

Due to its tart acidity, Riesling is considered a great food wine. Riper domestic versions like Hogue are perfect for spicy dishes like Thai curries because the sweetness in the wine works with the alcohol to restore your palate. Considering the rule of like with like, light, clean German and Austrian versions go with lighter foods: chicken, pork, scallops, shellfish, and fish. If you want to get in-depth with pairing orthodoxy, you'll want fatter, earthier Rieslings for weightier foods like ham, and more austere Alsatian Rieslings for the lighter foods like trout. The only thing that Riesling doesn't really go with are very red or black things, red meat like steaks, liver, lamb or stewed oxtails, or chocolate, molé, and so on.

Tasting Riesling
Step by Step

1. A Brief Road Map to Our Upcoming Riesling Road Trip

Whether you're tasting alone or by party, you're going to need about six Rieslings to get a lay of the land. Your first task will be to compare the basic taste of the fruit, the peachiness and apple-like qualities, as expressed in a basic domestic Riesling, and also in a Kabinett-level German Riesling. Then you'll be trying the two driest styles of the wine, Alsatian and Austrian. Finally, you'll pair two versions of the wine at its ripest, most esteemed form, a Spätlese or Auslese German Riesling, and a late-harvest BA, TBA, or ice wine Riesling. These three pairings can be done during a party, which makes it fun, spreads out the costs of the wine among your pals, and will contribute more voices to the project. However, you can also do the tasting solo or with a friend; you'll simply space the tastings out a bit.

Notes on Tasting Riesling Solo or in Pairs

Riesling is a food wine and you might not totally get it if there's not food around. If you're not a cook, a grocery store rotisserie chicken or take-out Thai coconut curry will do nicely. Or pick and choose from the foods sketched out below. A note, too, on the final dessert wine: This is something that can seem like paradise at the end of a meal with friends and ridiculously intense when you're alone with it in bright room, so if you're tasting by yourself, consider saving that one for the next time you see it on a restaurant wine list. Otherwise, try it accompanied by cheese or a dessert such as pound cake.

Notes on Tasting Riesling by Party

Since Riesling is one of the rare wines that truly works as well with cheese as with dinner foods, you have two options for your Riesling party: You can do either a cheese and cold snack buffet or a spicy curry dinner.

Wine and Cheese Menu

An assortment of crackers, both dry (like water crackers) and rich (like Ritz or club crackers); bread, if you like, both plain and more substantial like a sourdough or rye. Cheese: especially German, Alsatian, and Swiss. Brie or, in the unlikely chance that you can find some, real French Muenster, a pinkish-brown, Brie-like cheese native to Alsace; Gruyère, both the young kind and, ideally, one of the several-year-old Parmigiano-like ones that are called "cave-aged Gruyère." Or Emmenthaler, Comté, or Raclette. If you like, you could add jams or chutneys that mirror Riesling's fruits, like peaches, apricots, apples, and nectarines, or slices of the fruits themselves. Baking peach jam on top of a wheel of brie would be perfect. Cold ham also is a terrific accompaniment to Riesling, as are pork rillettes, pork or trout paté, and foie gras.

Dinner Menu

If you want to add a hot entrée for a true dinner party, classic Riesling pairings include pork and chicken, or something spicy like a coconut milk curry. A good vegetarian option would be a butternut squash risotto.

Desserts

Because of their sugar content and palate-cleansing acidity, many Rieslings are very dessert-friendly. Cheesecake, lemon or mango sorbet with berries, pound cake, apple pie, lemon tart, or a fruit tart would all work well. The only things that really wouldn't go are very black desserts: chocolate cake, espresso sorbet, blueberry pie, and so on, because the intense flavors would overwhelm the wine.

2. Shopping

Whether you're alone or having a party, your first task is to buy your Rieslings.

You'll need six bottles, selected from the field guide above. The names provided are simply suggestions to help you in your shopping; whatever your local wine shop has should be fine. Just try to match the categories, not the names. You want to end up with:

1. An inexpensive domestic Riesling, like Hogue, Columbia Crest, or Snoqualmie; $6–$12.
2. A Kabinett German Riesling, such as J. J. Christoffel, Strub, or Josef Leitz; $12–$25.
3. An Alsatian Riesling, such as Trimbach, Hugel, Paul Blanck, or Mittnacht-Klack; $12–$40.
4. An Austrian Riesling, like Alzinger, Leth, Brandl, Loimer, or Hirsch; $20–$40.
5. A Spätlese or Auslese German Riesling, such as Selbach-Oster, Gunderloch, or Fritz Haag; $20–$50.
6. A late-harvest dessert German Riesling, either a BA, TBA, or ice wine, such as Dönnhoff, Eugen Müller, J. J. Prüm, or Schloss Schönborn; $20–$40.

3. Planning and Thinking About Tasting

Gather your wineglasses, dump bucket, and tasting markers. Make your life easier: Put some fresh peach slices, frozen peach purée, or even peach preserves in a wine glass. You will instantly understand the qualities that emanate from a glass of Riesling. For "minerals" some clean, wet gravel or wet chalk in a wineglass is perfect. Grapefruit or lime sections (especially if you run a knife, zester, or rasp over the peel to release the aromas), apple slices, and honey in wine glasses can also be tremendously helpful.

Tasting Markers

Keep the following list handy so you can glance at it while you're tasting—it will help you name fragrances that seem just out of reach.

Above all

Peach and white peach	Melon	Lime
Minerals: Wet stones, wet chalk, wet slate	Green table grapes	Tangerine
	Flowers (the general impression of flowers, roses, irises, violets, etc.)	Orange
Apples, both red and Granny Smith		Honey, especially in dessert wines
Nectarine	Grapefruit	Spice (cinnamon, nutmeg, allspice)
		White pepper

Possibly

Pineapple	Coconut	Matchstick heads (from a sulfur treatment used to keep the barrels clean)
Mango	Green herbs (especially parsley)	
Apricot		
Passion fruit	Licorice (anise, fennel)	Salt
Lemon peel		
Creamsicle	Petroleum, kerosene, diesel fuel	
Butterscotch		

4. Cool Things Off

Ideally your Riesling will be chilled to a good white wine cellar temperature of 45 degrees. (See page 10 for why.) Pull a well-chilled bottle out of the fridge an hour before serving and you'll be right there. However, if your only options are to keep it on ice or let it get warm, keep it on ice and let it warm up a little in the glass before evaluating it.

5. Pull the corks!

6. Taste Your First Wine

Your basic American bottom-shelf Riesling will tell you what Riesling is like when it gets fully ripe, as it does here. Pour an inch or so into each guest's wineglass and swirl. Pass around your tasting markers if you've got them.

Questions to consider: Peaches? Flowers? Apples? Does it seem sweet or balanced? Do you like it? Try the wine with a bite of food: Does it make the food taste better? Does the food make the wine taste better?

If you've got only one wineglass, dump your wine. If you've got two, now is time to put forward the second glass and put some of the Kabinett Riesling in it.

7. Taste Your Kabinett Riesling

We're on to the second wine, the Kabinett Riesling. Pour about an inch into a wineglass for each guest. Swirl. Sniff. You should experience similar fruit to the first one, as well as liveliness and briskness.

Questions: *Nerve* is one of the defining qualities of Riesling, a hard-to-define energy that seems to pulse through the wine, making it lively and hard to catch just as it's hard to catch a piece of string whipping around in the air. Does this wine have nerve? If so, do you like it?

Try the wine with food. How is it? Does the wine improve the food, or vice versa? Do you like it more or less than the domestic Riesling?

The typical things people say about German Kabinett Riesling are that it's delicate, lacy, and elegant. Do you feel that any of those apply to yours?

(Note to solo tasters, or those in tasting in pairs: You are now going to take a break. Pick up the tasting of the next two wines as soon as convenient.)

8. Taste Your Alsatian Riesling

Pour an inch of your Alsatian Riesling into a wineglass. Swirl. Sniff. Taste. It should be wildly different from the other Rieslings. Ideally it will be bone dry, steely, austere, and powerful, and will smell like wet stones. This is called a "mineral nose." If you've got a wineglass with some wet gravel in it, now is the time to find out whether the scent of your wine has anything in common with it.

Questions to consider: Does it have anything in common with the first two Rieslings you tried? Remember, these are all 100 percent Riesling, fermented in neutral containers, so all the differences are simply because of where the wine was grown, and to a lesser extent the yeast. Again, try the wine with food. Does the bracing acidity improve the food?

9. Taste Your Austrian Riesling

Pour an inch of your Austrian Riesling. Swirl. Sniff. Pass tasting markers if you've got them. It's most likely halfway between bone-dry Alsatian Riesling and fragrant, delicate German Riesling. Do you get that from yours? More questions: Flowers? Nectarines? Honey?

(Again, a note to solo tasters, or those in groups of two: Another break! Pick up the tasting of the next two wines as soon as convenient.)

10. Taste Your Auslese or Spätlese German Riesling

You are now moving on into expensive, unusual territory: Auslese or Spätlese German Riesling. Are you ready to be this much of an international sophisticate? You may have to start telling friends you hate the movies but love the cinema. Watch out!

Pour. Swirl. Sniff. Taste. Now, while Auslese and Spätlese by definition mean this wine was very ripe when it was picked, that doesn't necessarily mean the wine itself is going to be sweet, because the process of making wine actually turns the sugar in the grapes into alcohol, and pure alcohol is dry. Theoretically, a well-balanced wine should be able to have some actual sugar in it but still read as completely dry. You might perceive the wine as sweet because it smells flowery, however. Do you?

More questions: This wine should also be powerfully fragrant, with notes of tangerine, mango, lime, and other tropical fruits. Has it got those? Most of all, though, focus on whether the wine seems in balance or out of whack. Which is it?

11. Taste Your Riesling Late-Harvest Wine

Tell your friends how much you spent—there's no reason you should be the only person burdened here! Pour your late-harvest Riesling. Swirl. Sniff. Taste. What do you think? Is your wine a magical ambrosia of figs, white raisins, peaches, and honey with fragrances that you could pick apart for days? Does it finish—that is, create a lasting, interesting impression—for a long, long time? It's supposed to. Try it with food, preferably cheese or dessert. This should be one of the most fragrant wines you've ever had in your life— is it? It also should be truly sweet.

Questions to consider after tasting these half dozen Rieslings: Which was your favorite? Which was worth the money? Which do you want more of in your life? Is Riesling different than you thought it would be? If you used the tasting markers, were they helpful?

You now know more about Riesling than most waiters do, and, most important, whether you like it and what it's like. You can ask people for dry, stony Alsatian Rieslings or delicate Kabinett Rieslings and know what you're talking about. Try another dozen soon after your tasting, at restaurants, wine bars, or wherever, and you truly will be an expert.

THE TAKEAWAY

Now you know why this is the wine that has captured the hearts of all the cutting-edge hipsters, wine writers, and sommeliers. Can you believe the variety and nuance that Riesling provides? It's the most complex of all the aromatic whites, and when the haunting fragrances are married to an elegant structure, it's more than a beverage, it's like the flickering flames in a fireplace, elemental and captivating.

Five-second cheat sheet for people who didn't read the chapter and are reading this on their iPhones while they wait for a table in the trendiest possible restaurant and trying not to gawk at that also-ran indie movie star whose name you can't remember

Riesling (*REEZ-ling*) is a white wine that has been the food and wine hipsters' darling the last bunch of years. They love it because it marries an almost infinite yet very subtle bouquet of flowers, peaches, and stones to a lacy, racy structure. They also love it because average Americans don't get it—most think Riesling is always sweet, and they think this because in the 1970s Blue Nun dominated the world. (But Blue Nun in its heyday wasn't even Riesling! It was made of a grape called Müller-Thurgau.) Some Riesling today is indeed sweet, but most of the stuff you'll see on restaurant wine lists isn't. The driest Rieslings are typically from the French region of Alsace and are a perfect match to most Asian fusion and all of the lighter typically European foods, from scallops to veal to pork to chicken. Next driest: Austrian and German. These Rieslings are prized for their abundant bouquet and the way they allow you to sink into them as you chase their fleeting aromas. A good Riesling will have an electric quality in your mouth that makes the wine feel energetic and lively. Some great American Rieslings include Trefethen and Smith-Madrone; budget Washington Rieslings from producers such as Columbia Crest and Hogue are often the best wines to be found on inexpensive Thai or Japanese restaurant wine lists.

Knock-Their-Socks-Off
Gifts for Riesling Lovers

1. Something Old: One of the things critics love most about Riesling is its ability to age, and any true Riesling fan will have read with fascination various accounts of critic blowout tastings where Rieslings from the 1890s, 1940s, and so on are sampled. At the same time, most Rieslings are released within a

few years of the vintage, and since they're so delicious young, who can age them? Liquor stores like New York City's Crush Wine & Spirits (www.crushwine.com) specialize in German Rieslings that are twenty and thirty years old, something that any Riesling lover would love to try. Prices are, for something that old, remarkably reasonable, starting around $50; many cost less than $100. How to pick something old? Call.

2. Something from Egon Müller's Scharzhofberg vineyard: Considered one of Germany's greatest wine estates, Egon Müller's Scharzhofberg vineyard might have been first planted in Roman times. It is currently revered because it is on native Riesling roots, not the grafted rootstocks that most of the world has worked with since the root pest called phylloxera devastated European vineyards starting in the 1800s; some connoisseurs believe that wines grown on native roots taste superior to those grown on grafted ones. These ancient roots, and the hundred-year-old vines that arise from them, are thought to make some of the world's most delicate, magnificent, and nuanced Rieslings. The "gold capsule" wines are even rarer than the usual ones, and while they're hard to track down, there isn't a Riesling person alive who wouldn't be impressed to receive one.

3. Clos Ste. Hune: The greatest of all the Rieslings of Alsace, wine from a "clos," that is, an ancient, walled-in vineyard. Owned by the great Alsatian winery Trimbach, Clos Ste. Hune covers only about three acres in its entirety, which makes the fact that its wines sell for less than $200 pretty remarkable.

4. Dönnhoff: One of the great forces in German wine in America for the last generation, importer Terry Theise, writes in his catalog that Dönnhoff wines taste "simply, like the most perfect Riesling that can ever be." Prices are terrifically reasonable, in the $20-something to $60-something range. If you can't find them near you, the Minneapolis liquor store Surdyk's (www.surdyks.com) and the upstate New York store Arlington Wine & Liquor (www.arlingtonwine.net) always seem to have some on hand.

5. Weingut Bründlmayer: For Riesling fans in search of great
   stony minerality, look no further than Bründlmayer, widely
   agreed to be Austria's best winery. Organically farmed with no
   herbicides, the *alte reben,* or old vine, Rieslings raised on
   Bründlmayer's Heiligenstein vineyard in particular are considered the ultimate expression of Austrian dry minerality
   married to richness and exotic perfumes.

5

CHARDONNAY
CHIC AND CHANGEABLE

Pronounced: *shar-dun-nay*. Also known as: Champagne, Chablis, White Burgundy, Meursault, and Montrachet. Also, less frequently, anything plus the word Montrachet, Pouilly-Fuissé, Mâcon, St. Veran, Beaujolais Blanc, Côte de Beaune, Corton Charlemagne

Dear Dara,

No way is Champagne the same thing as Chardonnay. Champagne is like—whoopee! Happy New Year's! Or: fireplaces and velvet couches, come on over here, baby! Or: criminal kingpins in underwater lairs. And Chardonnay is like: intermission on the terrace at the theater, or a wedding-shower brunch. This is like learning that Marilyn Monroe was also an avid student of political economy. It doesn't compute.

—Baffled

Agreed. It doesn't make any sense. But it makes *some* sense.

Because you know what wine grapes are a little bit like? They're a little bit like flour—flour, of course, being the main component of spaghetti, croissants, sourdough bagels, and doughnuts, depending on what you do with it.

Like flour, Chardonnay can produce many end products. Depending on where it's grown and how it's processed, pressed Chardonnay juice can be made into: noble, robust, silky white Burgundy; chalky, utterly dry Chablis; fat, ripe, ice-cream-lush Napa Valley Chardonnay; sour, headache-making plonk from anonymous corporate farm fields; or the driest possible Champagne. (Traditionally most Champagne is made by blending Chardonnay, Pinot Noir, and Pinot Meunier, but all-Chardonnay Champagne does exist; it is called blanc de blancs.

How can this be? The same way that flour can be made into Frosted Flakes. Some materials in life just respond well to human manipulations. Chardonnay happens to be the most malleable of all wine grapes, which makes it an excellent place to note the winemaking in wine. Of course, it's popular to dismiss Chardonnay these days, and a lot of people think they don't like Chardonnay—but they are wrong. They might not like *most* Chardonnay, but if they like white wine, they like Chardonnay. They just haven't had the right one.

If Chardonnay has one problem it's that it's too well loved. It defines so much of what's great about French white wine that it's been planted the world over, and in some of the places it has ended up, like California and Australia, it has made such exquisite wine that everyone wanted to emulate it—and then, well, things went wrong. But still, don't judge the Beatles by listening to car commercials with soundtracks by Beatles cover bands.

What's to Love About Chardonnay?

Chardonnay grapes make some of the world's most beautiful whites. The reason for this is that Chardonnay is vital and hearty and responds dramatically to various winemaking tricks and techniques, most notably malolactic fermentation, oak, and "sitting on lees." We'll come back to these terms in a moment, but briefly, *malolactic fermentation* is a way of converting grape juice acids from tart to soft; storing wine in oak barrels adds toast and spice to wine's flavor; and "sitting on lees" is a way of adding complexity to wine by fermenting it for a long time with its dead yeast and some grape solids, the way simmering soup stock for a long time extracts a lot more flavors from the things in the soup than cooking it briefly would.

What's to Hate About Chardonnay?

Like any superhero, Chardonnay can be used for good or evil. As noble as some versions are, Chardonnay also makes much, and maybe even most, of the foulest plonk at your local wine store, mainly because of the misuse of those winemaking tricks. All of the methods winemakers use to make excellent Chardonnay cost money, and lots of it. If you're a cheap bastard wanting to sell wine under the highly marketable name of Chardonnay there are all sorts of shortcuts you can employ. For instance, instead of using oak barrels, you can just dip giant teabags of toasted oak sawdust or oak pellets held together by glue into your wine vat. (This is one of the reasons wine can cause headaches: All sorts of things besides the oak char get dissolved in the wine and end up as "congeners," stuff dissolved in alcohol, that get stuck in your brain and hurt you.) Or instead of picking your wine grapes by hand when they have the ideal level of acid, you can just mechanically harvest them when it's most convenient and dump in whatever food-grade acid you need—malic, tartaric, citric, you name it—to try to mimic good wine.

What's the Story with Chardonnay?

Chardonnay is so ever-present that starting to talk about it seems goofy, like trying to summarize people. People: They have two legs, nurse their young, started out in Africa, and eventually there was a 24-hour cable news cycle. But in order to understand Chardonnay, it helps to ask this question: Why is there so much Chardonnay on this planet?

The answer, as with so many things in wine, goes back to the French. While much French wine has a pedigree that stretches back to Roman times, the land that Chardonnay comes from has an even (literally) richer history, in that not only is it land that has been under vine since Roman times, but it's land in the heart of the most politically stable, richest part of France, a place today known as Burgundy but once upon a time known as the Duchy of Burgundy. What's that? A place that was essentially an independent nation and whose business involved such matters as ruling an empire that included places we now know as the Netherlands and Switzerland, trading cloth, drinking wine, supporting monks, and, more important for our purposes, allowing winemakers to tinker, farm, improve, experiment, try again next year, and try again the year after that, instead of simply dying young, which was the fashion in the rest of northern Europe. All this stability and time to tinker and improve led to the most comprehensively examined, understood, and valued wine-growing land in all the world: Burgundy. The white wine of Burgundy? Chardonnay. (The red is Pinot Noir.)

The specific area that the best White Burgundy, the best Chardonnay, comes from is a place called the Côte d'Or, a series of more or less continuous limestone and chalk steep slopes that stretch a mere thirty miles or so southwest of Dijon, in eastern France. The southern half of this small thirty-mile strip is an even smaller area called the Côte de Beaune, and that's where the world's best Chardonnay comes from. The first thing you need to know about the where and why of Chardonnay is that as the Fertile Crescent is to Western civilization, the Côte de Beaune is to Chardonnay. Every Chardonnay on earth descends from here, all the Chardonnay-making techniques descend from here, and the top-ranked Chardonnays from here cost double, or quintuple, what the top Chardonnays from the rest of the planet cost.

What makes them so hot? Their ability to express that special Burgundian limestone terroir, the fact that they age well, the fact that people have been collecting them since back when everyone knew what a duchy was. Now, here's the bad news: The major Chardonnay villages and important vineyards of the Côte de Beaune pretty much all sound the same to untrained ears. There's the village of Meursault, which can appear on labels in either plain clothes (Meursault Bourgogne) or fancy ones, dressed up with an individual vineyard's name (Meursault Les Tessons). There's the village of Aloxe-Corton, which makes scores of wines, as well as the highly esteemed individual vineyard Corton-Charlemagne. You get the idea. Oh, you don't? Well, consider the Montrachets: there's the village Puligny-Montrachet and the vineyards Le Montrachet, Chevalier-Montrachet, Bâtard-Montrachet, and Bienvenues-Bâtard-Montrachet, the village Chassagne-Montrachet and the vineyard Criots-Bâtard-Montrachet. These sound-alike names are actually something you have to deal with because all wines from Burgundy are called after their vineyard or village—they don't say Chardonnay on the front of the bottle, they say Puligny-Montrachet and Le Montrachet.

Why do they all have the same words in them? Because they're relying on that sound-alike quality to sell wine.

Once upon a time the villages that the Grand Cru vineyard Montrachet were in were called Chassagne and Puligny, but they decided to stick Montrachet (*mon-ra-shay*) onto their names to help their less famous citizens sell wine. Montrachet itself is a mere twenty acres, and is owned, as of this writing, by eighteen owners and twenty-six producers, all of whom can put their own label on their wine.

Currently Burgundy has 700 appellations, and maybe 30,000 growers. The reason there are so many different owners and producers on a single plot of land is that Burgundy was subject to Napoleonic inheritance laws, which stated that a property had to be divided among all the heirs, not passed down intact.

Where do you fit in to all this gobbledygook? Sometime in your life you should definitely try a real French White Burgundy, something with the name Meursault or Montrachet on the label, just to find out how you like it; if you don't, you'll basically just be drinking Chardonnay through a game of telephone. Do you have to drink it twice? No, that's totally up to you and your wallet. In addition to tasting Chardonnay from the place that inspired the world to plant it everywhere, you also need to know that European winemakers gave the world a trio of techniques that are key tools used to turn mere wine-grape juice into art, and knowing about, and tasting, these techniques is absolutely critical to understanding Chardonnay. Those techniques are *malolactic fermentation, oak,* and *aging on the lees.*

Malolactic fermentation: This classic Burgundian method is one of the most important stylistic choices a Chardonnay maker can make. It's a little complicated, so pay attention and I'll try to make this as quick and painless as possible.

You know there are a lot of teensy-weensy microorganisms living in the world, right? They're flora, they're fauna, there are gazillions of them. Some live in your tummy and help you digest food, some are wild and live on every surface and in every corner of the world, and humans have harnessed many of them to do our bidding so that we can preserve food. Some microorganisms turn milk into yogurt, others turn cabbage into sauerkraut or kim chi, and still others are used in winemaking.

Most important, yeasts turn the sugar of grape juice into alcohol, just as yeasts turn the sugar in mash into the alcohol in beer, or the sugar in potatoes into the alcohol in vodka. However, there's a less obvious thing yeasts can do in winemaking, and that is to eat fruit acids. You eat fruit acids yourself: malic acid, particularly, is something found in high levels in both wine grapes and green apples. It's tart and delicious.

You know who else finds it delicious? The wee beasties that are introduced to wine to help it undergo malolactic fermentation. Malolactic fermentation, abbreviated to ML, is one of those phrases that has its meaning tied up right in its name: It refers to a fermentation that converts malic acid, the sour-apple acid, to lactic acid, the creamy acid found in milk. When the yeasts get going they eat the malic acid and produce lactic acid plus carbon dioxide plus something called diacetyl, a compound that smells so much like butter that it's used in microwave popcorn in place of real butter. Sour, acidic Chardonnay grape juice plus the regular fermentation plus malolactic fermentation equals buttery, creamy Chardonnay wine.

Malolactic fermentation isn't used just in Chardonnay, but that's where it's most detectable. It's also used in just about all red wines. In the old days malolactic fermentation was something that the wine often did on its own. Nowadays most winemakers make it happen because of the slight chance that wild, uninvited, unpredictable wee beasties could come in and eat the fruit acids while producing off flavors. Guiding the wine through a malolactic fermentation ensures there's nothing for uninvited wee beasties to eat.

When it comes to Chardonnay, malolactic fermentation is a really big deal. The French call it *le malo*. Wine geeks talk about it in shorthand, using "ML" or "MLF" and "malo" as both verbs and adjectives, as in, "He's planning to ML half the wine and steel-tank the rest." Or, "That wine was so malo'd it was like a melted Dairy Queen Blizzard."

And that's about all you need to know about malolactic fermentation. It's exceedingly detectable in Chardonnay. The softness and butteriness it can produce drive some wild with desire and is off-putting to others. However, it's not an all-or-nothing proposition. A winemaker can choose to put some fraction of his total Chardonnay production through a malolactic fermentation and blend it back with the rest, resulting in wine that can be as subtly creamy as he or she wants. Once you actually taste two glasses of Chardonnay, one entirely put through malolactic fermentation and one entirely not, you will understand so much more about Chardonnay, it will be like the difference between reading about driving and actually taking a car out for the first time.

Oak: The second big decision a Chardonnay winemaker faces is the use of oak. Oak barrels, or *barriques* (pronounced *barreeks*), have been used for hundreds of years to age wine. The original reason was probably purely practical, as wood contains tannin, which helps preserve wine and can allow it to age for decades, thus helping in the battle against starvation. Toasted oak barrels, though—that is, ones literally scorched on the inside with a flaming torch—were found not only to add to the longevity of the wine, but also added pleasant tastes of vanilla, toast, and caramel.

Today, this flavor of oak, the same flavor that Bourbon,

Conversations with Bigwigs: Steve Reeder

One of the United States' most historic wineries, Simi has been operating continuously in Sonoma County since 1876, surviving Prohibition by selling land even while still making wine. When Prohibition was repealed Simi had a full cellar to meet pent-up demand. Today Steve Reeder is the winemaker for the historic property, and his French varietals, especially his Chardonnay and Cabernet Sauvignon, are widely considered to be some of California's most reliable bargains, as most sell in the teens and $20s. Reeder's secret to making consistently good, affordable wine: blending.

I love blending; to me that's the true winemaker's art. In our Landslide vineyard [for Simi's Cabernet Sauvignon blend] we have 172 planted acres; we divide that into blocks and we have twenty different blocks of Cabernet, three blocks of Cabernet Franc, three blocks of Merlot, three blocks of Petit Verdot, and so on. We ferment each of those twenty blocks separately—we even split out some of the oldest blocks and ferment those separately, so we'll have 21a and 21b, because even though they are from the same root stock and clone there's a tractor-row that splits the block, and we see some differences. The differences might be subtle, just a nuance, a degree higher Brix [sugar content in the grape], different pH, a different size berry, or some water-stress or other factor that has caused them to grow differently.

I go through and taste them all separately, looking at things like how much color is released when I grind a grape in my mouth and spit it out. When you pop the berry in your mouth is it still very firm or is it falling apart? What are you getting, in your mouth? Perhaps sweetness, perhaps pepper and blackberry? I'm also paying attention to structure of the grape: Is the seed crisp and brown or still chewy? I grind the skins against my molars and ask myself what the tannins are like, the grape tannins—are they ready? All the different factors, different soils, different root stocks, they all give you different characteristics, from depth of color to aromatic aspects.

Near harvest time I spend five or six hours a day walking the vineyards and shoving grapes in my mouth. We send interns out to do measurements too, checking the Brix and pH. Science is the stuff I can explain when I'm out in that field, and the art is the stuff I can't. You could watch me out there and ask: Why are you doing that, Steve? I don't know. I've been doing this for thirty-one years, and it's what feels right to me. You can sit there with your calculator and all that crap, but that's not what it's about. You're taking these things, they could be colors, they could be spices, you have this vision of how they want it to be, you blend them together—that's art. Americans by and large don't understand blending.

Anyway, back to the blocks. We ferment the blocks separately, and then age them separately. We want a lot of diversity at this step too; some will go into 100 percent new oak, but I'll get that oak from two or three different coopers [barrel makers], because different wood sources bring different flavors. Then we go through and taste everything. [For Simi's Alexander Valley Cabernet Sauvignon] I start looking for big black brooding fruit in our Cabernet lots, and once I identify those I look and see if there's a hole, anything that needs filling out. Maybe it needs some Petit Verdot for structure and a little earth tone. Maybe it needs Cabernet Franc for great violet and blueberry aromas.

To me, there are certain grape varieties that do fantastic alone—100 percent Chardonnay is a great thing. However, to get a depth of flavor I pull Chardonnay from three main regions. From the Alexander Valley I get pear and tropical fruit characteristics, from Carneros more of a lemon-lime-citrus-grapefruit character with racy acidity, and then those

are balanced by the Russian River Chardonnay, which gives
length, structure, and green apple. So you get a stronger,
more complex, more interesting wine than you would from
a single vineyard—but it's still 100 percent Chardonnay.

A lot of people like to say great wine is grown, and the
day I go and pick the bottle off the vine is the day I'll agree
with them.

Port, whisky, and red wine makers rely on, is something
that some white wine drinkers prefer over plain, unoaked
wine. Are you an oak person or an unoaked person? This
Chardonnay tasting will tell, but before you go into it, know
that there's no right answer. Whether you like oak or don't
like it is a similar question to whether you like chocolate or
don't. It's a matter of taste.

People who do like oak find as much subtlety and variation in it as chocolate lovers find in chocolate. To wit, most
oak is either French, American, or central European. Within
these broad categories are more subtle tastes; for instance,
there is Missouri oak and Minnesota oak, and five French
"forest appellations." One of these appellations might be nuttier, another more peppery. When winemakers talk about
oak, they describe it as the "spice" they use to enhance their
wine, and they give a lot of thought to it. Some are fierce
French or American oak partisans; others might split a single vineyard into different batches, aging one in a French
barrel and a second in an American barrel, fermenting the
third in neutral steel, and then combining them all before
bottling.

In addition to the choice of a specific oak winemaker also
specify the level of "toast" or "char" that the barrel undergoes.
The cooper—that is, the person who builds the barrel—literally burns the inside of the barrel with fire, either by using a
torch by rolling it through a bonfire, or by setting the barrel

around a stationary fire. A heavily toasted barrel interior will be quite black, a medium-toasted one will be sparrow-brown and look like toasted bread, and so on. In general, the idea is that a less toasted barrel makes wine that tastes "oaky," while a more toasted barrel makes something that tastes "toasty." While it's sitting in the barrel, wine penetrates a couple of millimeters into the wood, picking up its flavors. A winemaker may take a single vineyard's harvest into several batches and age one in a heavily toasted barrel and another in a lightly toasted barrel and combine them all before bottling, just as they might mix wines from French and American barrels.

Like a tea bag, however, the barrel eventually runs out of flavor. The first year of a barrel's use gets you the biggest bang for the buck. The second year it just adds a little bit of toastiness and oak to wine, and by the third or fourth year a barrel is considered "neutral"—that is, it's thought not to flavor the wine at all, and to be roughly equivalent to a cement tank or a steel one, although it allows a little micro-oxygenation and so fattens the wine a wee bit.

Knowing a little about oak can be tremendously helpful in decoding wine labels. When a wine's label tells you that it all went into new oak, it's trying to tell you it's really, really toasty and full of vanilla. And it's also trying to tell you that it's supposed to be aged for a few years. However, if it tells you it was in 20 percent new oak, it's trying to tell you that oak is there, but subtly.

Real oak barrels are costly. French ones, as of this writing, easily run $700 and can cost $1,000, American ones about $400 to $600. If you figure you get maybe 300 bottles out of a barrel, you can see that new oak could add as much as $3 to the price of a single bottle's cost when it leaves the winery. Once the distributor and final seller add their mark-ups, you might be paying $6 or $12 just for oak.

Oak, however, isn't merely a spice; oak barrels are also

the most valued way of letting the wine breathe, slowly and
with great control, and develop and integrate flavors. It's
not unusual for some White Burgundies, that is, some
French Chardonnays, to be aged in oak for two years before
release. The winemakers who do this believe it creates a
more integrated and whole wine than could be achieved
any other way. Finally, oak tannins are critical to aging a
wine; a red wine aged in oak can last a hundred years or
more, thanks to preservative properties imparted by the
oak. White wines in oak can age sixty years, or maybe more.
The plan with wines that are meant to age is that they're
meant to be overpoweringly oaky when they're bottled, on
the theory that you're not going to drink them for five, ten,
or twenty-five years; as they age, the oakiness recedes and
the fruit character of the grapes comes forward. For this to
work you need both strong fruit character *and* strong oak
character. As the renowned French importer Bobby Kacher
told me once: "It's fashionable for people to complain about
wines being over-oaked. I say they're under-wined."

Sitting on the lees: Another major stylistic choice
Chardonnay makers have borrowed from their forebears in
Burgundy is called "sitting on the lees," or, in the French,
sur lie. ("Lee" and *lie* are interchangeable; *Lie* here is pronounced *lee.*) The first thing a winemaker does after harvest is to press the grapes. The resulting juice, however, is
unfiltered. It's cloudy because it still has some grape solids
in it. You introduce your various wee beasties, the yeasts
that turn the sugar into alcohol, the ones that turn malic
acid into lactic acid, and after they have done their work,
these little guys die. They drop down to the bottom of the
tank or barrel. This combination of dead yeast and grape
solids is called the lees.

At this point the winemaker has a couple of choices. She
can stick a tube in the tank or barrel above the lees and

Conversations with Bigwigs: Melissa Stackhouse

La Crema produces one of the most reliable Chardon-nays in Napa Valley, buttery but not too buttery, toasty and oaky but not too toasty and oaky, creamy but not too creamy—you get the idea. I called up La Crema's winemaker Melissa Stackhouse to find out how such a stylish wine is made.

Chardonnay is very malleable, but once we get the fruit in we actually take a very Puritan approach to it. After it's pressed it goes to barrel-ferment one-third in new oak, one-third in one-year-old oak, and a third in older. This gives it a nice toastiness, but I never want the oak in Chardonnay to be an elbow poking out at you. I feel like for a while people didn't even really know what Chardonnay was because it was so oaky, so creamy.

We take our Sonoma Coast fruit that has all these bright apple and citrus flavors, and this really juicy mouthfeel, and just sort of take the elbows off. I want green apple and citrus as the first note, and then a little butterscotch, toast, caramel, and butteriness. You have to be flexible every year because the harvest, the vintage are never the same, so one year you might end up with 21 percent new oak, and another year 30 percent, and end up with wines that are somewhat similar because the oak is only being used to balance the qualities of the grapes you are dealt.

New oak certainly gets the most attention because it's the most aggressive component, but personally, I think one-year-old oak is the sexiest of them all. If you ever tasted the various barrels before they're blended, chances are you'd never want to bottle the new oak component by itself, it's very toasty and driven by that char component, it has a tendency to overpower the wine. However, as a blending component it gives you the sturdiness and spice.

A year-old barrel is very different from a new one. The

> wine that goes into a one-year barrel comes out a little less
> aggressive, but you still get all the lovely components of a
> new barrel, just damped down and more approachable. As
> for the barrels, their life goes like this: We use them new, at
> one, two, and three years old, and then they go off to be
> planters.

siphon off the clear juice. Or she can filter or "fine" the wine,
by either running it through a physical filter or dropping in
an agent like egg white that makes the solids drop to the
bottom of the tank, thus clarifying the liquid. A third alternative is to leave the wine on the lees, which allows it to
pick up all kinds of flavors and complexity. The yeast cells
break open, and compounds—proteins, amino acids, pheno-
lics, what have you—enter the wine, adding desirable characteristics, scents, and textures. Some winemakers even
stir the lees to encourage the things in them to get up into
the wine.

As a general rule of thumb, a wine label that tells you
that the contents spent a long time "on the lees" is trying to
tell you that it is richer, fatter, lusher, and more fragrant
(and thus less crisp) than wine that has not been on the
lees. It's also generally more expensive, as all that sitting
around in barrels and being stirred costs time and money.

The "Holy Trinity" of Chardonnay

The Grape

Chardonnay is a relatively thin-skinned, light lemon-
green-colored grape that ripens early; this means it can
grow just about anywhere, and, if grown somewhere hot, it
can get very fruity and ripe. Hot-climate wines such as
those from the hotter parts of Australia or Central Valley

California tend to be fruitier and sweeter and to have more of a mixed-fruit-basket scent. Cold-climate wines, such as those from France, tend to be more acidic, tarter, and less fragrant.

Chardonnay is usually bottled alone, but there are exceptions. For instance, it is one of the three traditional components of Champagne, and it can be found in special proprietary blends with special proprietary names like Sokol Blosser's Evolution. But excepting the exceptions, if it costs more than $10 a bottle and says Chardonnay on the front, there should be nothing but Chardonnay inside.

Terroir

Various characteristics like the scent of pears, chalk, or lime peel arise in a glass of Chardonnay because of the particular *terroir*—the combination of soil, water, and spot on earth—where the grapes are grown. A limestone soil, for instance, will create mineral notes in the wine. Fertile, well-irrigated farm soil in a hot place will make Chardonnay ripen so quickly it gets only the barest lemon flavors before it ripens and then threatens to rot. A cool, well-drained, yet still sunny site that allows the grapes to ripen over a long period of time will encourage development of more complex aromas. That said, while there are generalities to be made about terroir, much of it still remains mysterious, and most experienced winemakers can point to some patch of land that makes different wine than they think it should and tell you they have no idea why.

Winemaking

In addition to the techniques we've already covered, much of what ends up in your final glass of Chardonnay is made in the fields, by such practices as carefully trimming the vines and managing the grape clusters over the course of the growing season. A more expensive wine typically will be hand-harvested, with a human being examining each cluster of grapes and throwing away any rotten or unripe individual grapes while a cheaper, machine-harvested wine just incorporates the lesser fruit.

Stop Reading, Start Drinking!

In this chapter's tasting adventures, you'll learn about Chardonnay—what it tastes like in its basic grape form, but also in various versions that use more winemaking craft, such as using oak barrels. You'll learn whether you yourself find oak delicious, which will give you a rock-solid place from which to talk to sommeliers, waiters, and wine clerks for the rest of your life.

Chardonnay FIELD GUIDE

About a third of all the white wines in a good wine shop will be Chardonnay. There will be the ones that say Chardonnay on the label—those will be the ones from everywhere but France—and they'll range tremendously in price, from a couple of dollars for bottom-shelf wines like Two Buck Chuck or the Australian critter labels, all the way up to $100 for top-of-the-line Napa Valley or Carneros California Chardonnay. Then there will be the French ones, which will be called after the place they come from; the most generic will be labeled White Burgundy, or Bourgogne Blanc, and then there are all the villages and individual vineyards, from Chablis to Meursault to Montrachet.

Miscellaneous bottom shelf, $3 and up
If this book teaches you only one thing, let it be this: If you want good, inexpensive white wine, look for miscellaneous unoaked wines from Europe—Spanish Cava, most table wines from the French Loire, Vinho Verde from Portugal—but stay away from

bottom-shelf Chardonnay. Sure, there may be an exception that proves the rule out there somewhere, but unless you taste it yourself and feel certain it's good, don't bother with the cheapies. The only reason it's sitting there is because it wants your desire for Chardonnay and your desire to get a bargain to overcome your knowledge of how the world works. Don't let it.

American and Australian midprice, $10–$25

The best Chardonnays in this affordable category will tend to be ones that come from single vineyards, not large anonymous regions. Most American wines will have labels on their backs using words that give some sense of what's in the bottle. They'll say they've got "vanilla and toast," which tells you the wine is oaked, or they'll specify "clear green apple and mineral" to tell you it's not.

Unoaked Chardonnays that have never gone through malolactic fermentation, $12 and up

Sometimes called "unwooded" or "naked" wine, Chardonnays that have never seen oak used to be something of a rarity, but they're gaining in popularity. It's harder to find a Chardonnay that hasn't seen any new oak and also hasn't undergone a malolactic fermentation, but there are some. Hendry is one of my favorites. It's a Napa Valley wine that is pretty and lively and offers the subtlest floral scents—it's just bewitching. Other unmalo'd, unoaked wines: Sierra Vista Vineyards unoaked; Pepi Chardonnay; Morgan Winery's Metallico Un-Oaked; Kunde Estate Nu Sonoma Valley; Snoqualmie's Naked Chardonnay; and Iron Horse's Unoaked Chardonnay. There are also a bunch of Australian ones, usually called "naked" or "unoaked" Chardonnays.

Unoaked Chardonnays that have gone through malolactic fermentation, $12 and up

In these you get the softness of malolactic fermentation without the caramel of oak. Tasting them really tells you a lot about both Chardonnay and malolactic fermentation. My favorite: Toad Hollow Unoaked. It's bell-clear with pretty apple and melon fruit character. Also good are Kim Crawford's New Zealand Unoaked Chardonnay and Kim Crawford's Marlborough Unoaked Chardonnay.

Oaked Chardonnay with no malolactic fermentation, $12 and up

If you want to be a true Chardonnay expert seek out one of these California wines that are aged in oak but prevented from having a malolactic fermentation: Far Niente; Stony Hill; Forman Vineyard; Hanzell Vineyards; and Russian Hill Chardonnay.

Oaky, buttery, malo'd Australian or American, $15 and up

Buttery and oaky are considered déclassé as I am typing these words, so if you ask any winemaker if they have a buttery or oaky Chardonnay, they will adamantly deny it. They only have Chardonnays that use oak appropriately to showcase the fruit! Whatever. Oaky and buttery is a nice style that loads of people love, and chances are good that you will absolutely love it too. The oakiest, most old-school Chardonnay I know of is the Rombauer Napa Valley Chardonnay, a lush, buttery, toasty, butterscotchy, expensive-tasting wine. The La Crema Napa Valley Chardonnay is another great example of a fat, oaky, lush-tasting Chardonnay; every time I've brought it to a tasting, about one out of six people will declare it the best wine they've ever had in their life and vow to drink nothing but. In the wine shop expect the most expensive and best-regarded Chardonnays to come from Napa Valley, Carneros, and the Russian River.

Generic French White Burgundy, $12 and up

There are thousands of tiny vineyards in Burgundy. Some are extraordinarily esteemed and make dizzyingly expensive wines. Others, often just down the road, are totally unheard of and make quite reasonably priced wines, say, $12 to $20 a bottle. All

White Burgundy is almost always and only Chardonnay. (There's a little of something called Aligoté, too, but it isn't often exported. If it is, the bottle will typically read "Bourgogne Aligoté," not "Bourgogne Blanc.") Still, while a particular vineyard's *terroir* and a particular year's vintage can make a big difference in that year's Chardonnay, you should be able to learn quite a lot about what Chardonnay tastes like in its native soil by just grabbing anything you can afford labeled Bourgogne Blanc. Most White Burgundies use both malolactic fermentation and oak, though the wines tend to be subtler than wines from the New World.

Unoaked, Expensive French Chablis, $20 and up

A lot of people find the name Chablis baffling; isn't that one of those things like Champale or Cold Duck that you're not supposed to drink? They think this because the name Chablis was hijacked and slapped on a lot of sweet jug wine in the 1970s. Chablis is actually the driest, and one of the loveliest, Chardonnays you can ever hope to taste. The good news about the name confusion is that it keeps the wine priced at about half what it's worth. Typically you'll pay $20 to $50 for a Premier Cru Chablis, the "second greatest possible" wines as classified by the French a long, long time ago.

Chablis comes from the northernmost reaches of Burgundy, where the soil is so full of limestone and ancient seashells that it's literally white. The wine itself tends to be steely and mineral-scented—a crystal stiletto. There are scads of Chablis producers, and just about all are good. Some names: Verget; Domaine Christian Moreau Père & Fils; A & F Boudin; Vaillon; and Domaine Vocoret.

Oaky, expensive French white Burgundy, Meursault, and Montrachet, $30 and up

A lot of critics think that White Burgundies—which are always Chardonnays from Burgundy—are the best white wines in the world because of their complexity, elegance, layered fragrances, and good structure. There are almost 600 Premier Cru vineyards in Burgundy, and another 33 Grand Cru ones, so don't expect to recognize all or even many of the names you see in a wine shop. Basically, any time you see the word Montrachet (*mon-ra-shay*), such as on Chevalier-Montrachet, Bâtard-Montrachet, etc., or the word Meursault, that's the good stuff. If you can't get anyone in the wine shop to help you, start looking at price tags. Does the Meursault or Montrachet you're looking at cost a lot of money? Eureka! That's what you're looking for. Expect to pay $30 to $90 for anything with the word Meursault or Montrachet on it.

Blanc de blancs Champagne, $35 and up

It's perverse of me to keep insisting on blanc de blancs Champagne as Chardonnay, but I'm going to keep doing it. The steeliest, driest Chardonnay possible is found in blanc de blancs Champagne, and if you want a vivid demonstration of what winemaking is, simply put any blanc de blancs Champagne on a table next to a buttery California Chardonnay.

Food and Chardonnay

Whether very oaky, very fruity New World "butter bomb" Chardonnays go with food at all is one of the big controversies in wine today. Leaving aside that minefield, which, as you can imagine, cleaves into predictable camps, Chardonnay has been prized over the centuries precisely because it goes so well with food. Following the wine pairing rule of like-goes-with-like, light-colored Chardonnay goes with all light-colored things: seafood, chicken, turkey, pheasant, pork, veal. The only meaningful exception to the Chardonnay-with-seafood rule is that oily fish, such as mackerel, sardines, or bluefish, don't go well with Chardonnay; they go better with reds.

Because there are so many different styles of Chardonnay, there are an infinite number of specific pairings you could do. You could pair the lightest-weight Chardonnays, like stony Chablis, with lighter-weight light-colored foods (Chablis with oysters or simple scallops) and the heavier-weight Chardonnays, like Montrachet, with heavier-weight light-colored foods (pheasant in cream sauce), but that's probably beyond the scope of this book. Basically, all you really need to know is that anything in the mild-and-medium world of food goes with Chardonnay, anything strong doesn't. And if you want to decide very oaky whites go with nothing, that's a choice you can make.

Tasting Chardonnay
Step by Step

1. A Brief Road Map to Our Upcoming Chardonnay Road Trip

The plan here, whether you're tasting alone or by party, is to taste five different styles of Chardonnay and thus get a sense of what the grape tastes like on its own, what it tastes like when dressed up in nice winemaking, and whether you like it in either form. First you'll taste a naked Chardonnay—that is, one with no oak and no malolactic fermentation—and you'll contrast that with a wine made with no oak but *with* malolactic fermentation. (Kind of like the difference between toast and buttered toast.) Then you'll sample a buttery classic Napa Valley Chardonnay, one made with both oak and malolactic fermentation. Finally, you'll taste a stony French Chablis and a well-built French White Burgundy. If you've got a big group you'll add a blanc de blanc Champagne. Having thus tasted all the major styles

of Chardonnay, you will know once and for all whether you
like it! This is something that often takes people who
haven't done this tasting twenty years to figure out.

Notes on Tasting Chardonnay Solo or in Pairs

You'll be trying three wines for your first tasting and two
for your second. Make sure you have a can of wine preserver (see pages 4–5) in the house or you risk wasting
some seriously nice wine! Not counting the super-oaky
styles, Chardonnay is actually a pretty good food wine; if
you're a cook, anything in the party outline below will work
well, and if you're not, take-out rotisserie chicken, a grilled
chicken or ham sandwich, or a BLT with mayo will work
just fine.

Notes on Tasting Chardonnay by Party

While oaky Chardonnays don't pair well with food, French
ones, particularly Chablis, are perfect food wines, so your
learning-about-Chardonnay party could be either a cocktail
party or a full-fledged dinner party. If you choose the hors
d'oeuvres route, know that because Chardonnay varies so
wildly, pairing with cheese can be tricky. A smoked Cheddar
will go well with the most lavishly oaked Chardonnay, while
the chalkiest, unoaked ones, like a Chablis, will go with fresh
goat cheese. (Logically, you'd think the goat cheese popularly
called Montrachet would go with a Montrachet wine, but not
really, as the cheese is just an imposter borrowing the famous wine's name.) Some of the really rich triple-cream brie-
like cheeses can be nice with unoaked Chablis. In addition to
cheese, anything salmon works well—hot smoked salmon,
cold smoked salmon (lox), salmon spread, or poached salmon.
Fruit is essential: Green grapes, pears, and apples all go
nicely with Chardonnay and help you cement the association
between the apple scents of Chardonnay and real apples.

If you want to have a dinner party, roast chicken, roast

pork, or grilled or roast fish are all great choices. The only caveat is that you want to stay away from dark sauces.

For dessert, anything on the plainer or creamier side of the spectrum will be perfect. Pound cake and ice cream, cookies, panna cotta, or cheesecake all work well.

2. Shopping

Whether you're tasting alone or having a party, your first task is to buy your Chardonnays. This is going to require the most looking at bottles and restoring them to the shelf of any tasting in this book, so give yourself plenty of time, and be sure to keep hydrated and stretch. You'll need six bottles:

1. An unoaked, unmalo'd American or Australian Chardonnay, perhaps one from Hendry or Iron Horse. Australian ones are usually labeled "naked" Chardonnays. $15 to $25.

2. An unoaked but malolactically fermented Chardonnay, such as one from Toad Hollow, Kim Crawford's New Zealand Unoaked Chardonnay, or Kim Crawford's Marlborough Unoaked Chardonnay. See longer field guide above for more names. $15 to $25.

3. A Napa Valley, Sonoma Valley, or Carneros Chardonnay that has been aged in oak and undergone malolactic fermentation, such as one from Rombauer or La Crema. If in doubt, look for words like "buttery" and "vanilla." $20 to $45.

4. A bottle of French Chablis, which is typically unoaked; any Premier Cru Chablis will do. Some names: Verget; Domaine Christian Moreau Père & Fils; A. & F. Boudin; Vaillon; and Domaine Vocoret. $20 to $50.

5. An oaked Premier Cru French White Burgundy; anything with the word Montrachet, such as Chevalier-Montrachet or Bâtard-Montrachet, or the word Meursault will do. $60 and up.

6. Optional: If you have a big group and want to taste more than five wines, add any French blanc de blanc Champagne to the mix. $40 and up.

3. Planning and Thinking About Tasting

Gather your wineglasses, dump bucket, and tasting markers. Make your life easier: Put half a lemon in one wine glass, fresh apple slices or apple juice in a second, a bit of vanilla extract or a whole vanilla bean in a third wineglass, and a piece of white bread, toasted and torn to fit, into a fourth. You will instantly understand the qualities that emanate from a glass of Chardonnay.

Tasting Markers

Keep the following list handy so you can glance at it while you're tasting—it will help you name fragrances that seem just out of reach.

Above all		
Lemon	Nuts (a general quality of nuttiness, most likely hazelnuts and almonds)	Butter
Apple		Vanilla bean
Green apple		Caramel
Pear		Pound cake
Apricot		Toasted bread
Melon	Honeysuckle	Cinnamon
Fig	Peach	

Less likely, but possible		
Earth	Minerals	Mint

4. Cool Thing Off

Ideally Chardonnay should be at around 50 or 55 degrees. Chill a bottle in the fridge an hour before serving and you'll be right there. However, if your only options are to keep it on ice or let it get warm, keep it on ice and let it warm up a little in the glass before evaluating it.

5. Pull the Corks!

Or untwist the screw tops; typically you'll find "naked wines" and some Chablis under screw top because they're meant to be drunk young, and more expensive French and Napa Valley wines under a cork, as they're capable of aging.

6. Taste Your First Wine

Start with your basic unoaked, naked Chardonnay that did not undergo malolactic fermentation. Pour an inch or so in each guest's glass. Swirl the wine. Sniff. Taste. This wine is a good starting point because it's just the juice. It should taste like lemons, apples, and pears, possibly like flowers, and it should feel zingy and light in the mouth. Questions to consider: Anyone smell apples in this wine? Lemons? Pears?

Ideally, it will be mouthwatering and will make you crave a bite to eat. Try it with some food: Does it improve the food? Does food improve the wine? Do you like this naked Chardonnay?

Now it's time to move on to the unoaked Chardonnay that *did* undergo malolactic fermentation.

7. Taste Your Second Wine

Pour an inch of your malolactically fermented but not oaked Chardonnay into each guest's glass. Malolactic fermentation is something done to turn tart fruit acids into buttery milk acids. This wine should be different from the first wine in that it should be creamier, softer, and fuller in the mouth, less like lemonade and more like milk. Is it? Other questions to consider: Again: Apples? Pears? Lemons? But now also: Butter? Pound cake? Do you like it more, or less, than the last one? Take a few moments, and try it with food. When you're ready for the next one, dump and move on.

8. Taste Your Napa Valley or Carneros Chardonnay

Pour the third wine. Swirl. Sniff. Taste. First we tasted Chardonnay juice alone, and then Chardonnay juice with malolactic fermentation, we now have the whole kit and kaboodle—juice plus MLF plus oak. How do you like it? This is the real deal, Napa Valley or Carneros Chardonnay. Pass around the toasted bread in the wineglass, and the vanilla bean, if you've got them. Do you detect vanilla or toast in your fancy wine? Consider the old questions: Apples? Pears? Lemons? Butter?—but add in some new ones: Caramel? Toast? Butterscotch?

Most important, do you like this wine more or less than the first few?

(Note to solo tasters, or those in tasting in pairs: You are now going to take a break. Pick up the tasting of the next two wines as soon as convenient.)

9. Taste Your Chablis

If you've never had Chablis, prepare to have your mind blown. Chablis is 100 percent Chardonnay from the French area of Chablis, but it's cold there, so the grapes don't get very ripe, and the "soil," as it were, is mostly rocks. This results in wine that is like a stiletto: stony, austere, like a steel blade plunged through a lemon's skeleton. And here it is, right in front of you! Pour an inch of wine for each guest. Swirl. Sniff. Taste. What do you think? Anyone detect the classic mineral, chalk, and stone aspects? It should smell, literally, like wet rocks or stones. The other questions to ask are all the ones that apply to the other Chardonnays: Apples? Pears? Lemons? You shouldn't get toast or oak, because most Chablis doesn't see oak barrels. Do you like it? This is the wine that Chardonnay haters always greet in disbelief: Surely nothing this lean could be Chardonnay? But it is. Try it with food. That's Chablis!

10. Taste Your White Burgundy

Now is the time to bust out the big guns: your Premier Cru French Montrachet or Meursault. Pour. Swirl. Sniff. Taste. How is it? It should have both oak and malolactic fermentation, as well as qualities of Chardonnays you have tasted, like the fruit scents of apples, lemons, and pears, as well as the malolactic scent of butter and the oak scents of vanilla, toast, and perhaps caramel. Part of what you're paying for in real White Burgundy is all that, plus more: a grandeur, a scent of earth perhaps, or mineral.

Questions to consider: Is it worth the money? Invite your guests to backtrack through the five wines, seeking a favorite.

11. Tasting Your Optional Blanc de Blancs Champagne

If you're lucky enough to be tasting a blanc de blancs Champagne, pop the cork! Pour a bit for each guest. Swirl. Sniff. You should get scents of biscuit, bread, toast. The bubbles in Champagne come from another dose of yeast, so Champagne often smells a little more like bread than any other type of Chardonnay, from which it is made. Blanc de blancs Champagne starts life as still Chardonnay wine, and during that period the winemaker can make all the choices we have thus explored, using oak or not in whatever way she prefers. What do you notice in the Champagne that you've noticed in the still wines you've tasted? What seems different. Do you love it? Do you understand it? Do you understand it more than if you hadn't explored Chardonnay? Knowledge is power!

Congratulations! You are now ready to go forth and drink Chardonnay from an informed position. This puts you ahead of a good 90 percent of people nattering on the Internet. For the rest of your life you'll be able to tell wine-shop people what you want in a Chardonnay: Apples? Acid? Toast? When you bump into Martha Stewart and she tells you her favorite wine is white Burgundy, you'll be able to respond intelligently. Drink another two dozen Chardonnays and you'll be a stone expert.

THE TAKEAWAY

Now you know all the faces of Chardonnay—its happy, fruity side, its stony, austere side, its oaky depths, its buttery wealth. Hard to believe one grape does all that, isn't it? That's why Chardonnay is the most popular white wine on earth. You also now know how profoundly winemaking choices affect the final taste in your glass, and, hopefully, which winemaking choices lead to tastes you enjoy. Finally, you also have rejoinder to all the people who think it's fashionable to say they want "ABC"—anything but Chardonnay. Oh, those simpletons. Don't they know that Chardonnay is many things, many gorgeous things?

Five-second cheat sheet for people who didn't read the chapter and are reading this on their iPhones in a bistro while they wait for a table

Chardonnay (*shar-dun-ay*) is the world's most prominent white wine grape, used to make the driest Champagne, dry, food-friendly wines like Chablis, and also oaky, buttery, silky "fruit-bomb" cocktail wines. Chardonnay responds dramatically to *terroir* and winemaking. Grown in hot places, like parts of Australia or California, it can get very sweet, even tropical. Grown in cold places, like the Champagne region of northern France, it is steely and acidic. Oak barrels can make Chardonnay profoundly oaky and toasty; malolactic fermentation can make it buttery and creamy. Chablis (*sha-blee*) comes from a cold place and is usually not made with oak, which results in a dry, steely wine; some Australian and Napa Valley Chardonnays are just the opposite, they're so rich and caramel-tinged they're the wine equivalent of a butterscotch milkshake. Because of this wide variation, it is more important with Chardonnay than with any other wine that you know what you're ordering. Whenever possible, ask for a taste of the Chardonnay you're considering before you order a bottle.

Knock-Their-Socks-Off
Gifts for Chardonnay Lovers

1. Château Montelena Chardonnay: In 1976, a wine competition was held in London that forever changed the world. It changed the world because it pitted a bunch of California wines against wines from the most important wineries in France—and the California wines won. This competition was called the Judgment of Paris, and the white wine winner came from Château Montelena. While the winemaker at the time was Mike Grgich (see below) you can touch the hem of history by tasting a bottle of Chardonnay from the Chardonnay-growing-grounds that

changed everything. Best of all, Château Montelena Chardonnay usually costs only $40-something.

2. Grgich Hills Napa Valley Chardonnay: Mike Grgich is aging—he was born in 1923. As of this writing, he still oversees production at his winery, but these may be the last years for those who want to try Chardonnays that are true to the vision of the man who shocked the world.

3. A Grand Cru Montrachet or Meursault: The gold standard of white Burgundy. Look online at Internet liquor stores such as haskells.com, wallywine.com, astorwines.com, or samswine.com.

4. An Aged Grand Cru Chablis: Again, one of the world's gold standards for Chardonnay. Aged ones should be both honeyed and mineral-scented; ten years is a decent age.

5. Talbott Vineyards Chardonnay: This Monterey County winery is a critical darling, once even scoring a perfect 100 from *Wine Spectator*. Check its website for limited-edition super-special wines: www.talbottvineyards.com.

6

CABERNET SAUVIGNON
DRINKING WITH ALPHA MALES

Pronounced: *cab-er-NAY so-ven-YON*. Also known
as: red Bordeaux, Meritage, Claret, Pauillac, Margaux, St. Estèphe, St. Julien, Pessac-Léognan, Haut
Médoc, and Médoc

Dear Dara;

*I almost don't want to ask you about Cabernet
Sauvignon, because that's the ultimate wine of jerks,
right? I mean, I work with this guy who seems to stake
a good deal of his ultra-wannabe-rich personality on
the fact that he only drinks Cabernet Sauvignon, which
he calls "Cab."*

*Also, he doesn't move his jaw when he talks, and
every time he makes coffee he spills water on the break
room floor and doesn't wipe it up. Who is he, Jesus? No.
He's a gift to trip-and-fall lawsuits. Anyway, I hate
him.*

*I get the sense from umpteen company retreats that
the reason he drinks only "Cab" is because if I knew
anything about the world I'd drink only "Cab" too,
which both attracts and repels me. What's the deal?*

—Baffled

It's true, Cabernet Sauvignon attracts the most aggressive members of the species. To prove their alpha maleness, many Cabernet devotees spend their lives pursuing extremely expensive "cult" wines, which are generally distinguished by their high scores from critics and their lack of availability to most everyone else. Once these Cabernet collectors get their cult wines they like to notch their bedposts, discuss the wine's "attack"—that is, first impression—and compare the size of its finish (how long you perceive a wine after you've swallowed it). Mostly though, they like to talk about price.

But don't blame Cabernet Sauvignon! It's not its fault that it is so well loved. Cabernet Sauvignon is one of the most important red wine grapes in the world, if not *the* most important. You need to know it, but there's also a good chance you'll fall in love with it—it can be incomparably compelling. They don't call it the king of reds for nothing.

However, before we get going here there's one important thing you need to know. Like a real-life king, Cabernet Sauvignon owes much of its power to its supporters. Unlike the other wine grape varieties we've tried so far, Cabernet Sauvignon is rarely bottled all alone. On its home turf, in Bordeaux, France, Cabernet Sauvignon is usually part of a team of red grapes that includes, above all, Merlot, but also Cabernet Franc, Malbec, Petit Verdot, and, infrequently, St. Macaire, Gros Verdot, and Carmenère. This team is not a team of equals. I like to think of it as a small acting troupe with a king (Cabernet Sauvignon), a queen (Merlot), and a lot of bit players: In some acts the king is showcased and the queen helps, in other acts the queen stars and the king adds a little support, and usually the bit players rush around the stage's edges and do minor but critical things to make the show work. Every once in a rare while the king or queen stands alone, every once in a while a bit player takes a larger role—I'll stop belaboring this analogy now, you get the idea.

Even when it's planted elsewhere, in the United States, say, or in Australia, Cabernet Sauvignon tends to be grown and bottled with its royal troupe.

Many of you are probably now thinking: No, no, no! I see Cabernet Sauvignon on wine lists alone all the time, and I've drank it plenty of times and no one ever mentioned kings, queens, or supporting bit players. True. But this is due more to a tradition of wine labeling than to facts on the ground; in California a bottle can read "Cabernet Sauvignon" or "Merlot" or what have you on the front, and as long as the wine inside is 75 percent of the named grape they don't have to tell you any more. Is 25 percent a big deal? Yes. Imagine a glass of 75 percent apple juice, and you add 25 percent purple grape juice. Or 95 percent coffee to which you add 5 percent cream. Or 99 percent water to which you add 1 percent lime juice. Even a little something extra can often make a difference. This king, queen, and supporting player tradition has been normal in wine ever since time immemorial, and only becomes a problem when you're trying to get a handle on what you like. How can you know if you like Cabernet Sauvignon if every time you taste it it's busy being burnished by a cast of supporting players? The way I see it we have two options: Either we can try, or we can give up. And I say we will try.

We will try by stacking the deck and choosing the wines where Cabernet Sauvignon stands more alone than usual, but we're going to do this keeping in mind that sometimes when we think we're just staring at the king, he's actually being propped up by a very good support staff.

What's to Love About Cabernet Sauvignon?

Cabernet Sauvignon is not just a noble grape, as wine writers call the most significant wine grapes, but a *regal* grape, and it makes many of the world's most collectible, most pursued, and most influential wines, such as red French Bordeaux, some Italian so-called Super Tuscans, and the big-gun wines from California, Washington, and Australia. Why are these Cabernet Sauvignons so collectible? Big, bold, and knee-weakening strength, plus grace, plus magnificence, plus beauty. Some wines seduce; Cabernet Sauvignon awes.

What's to Hate About Cabernet Sauvignon?

The money, the money, the money. Because it's the most collected wine in the world, and because it can age and appreciate greatly in value, high-quality Cabernet Sauvignon commands higher average prices than any other wine on earth. Note I said "high-quality." Made poorly, Cabernet Sauvignon can be awful: blocky, reeking of green peppers, watery, overly acidic, screechingly tannic. However, because so much of it is so expensive, and because people really, really want it, some sucker is always going to be poised to snap up that $11 bottle, hoping against hope. If you're very lucky your bottom-shelf Cabernet Sauvignon will merely be overripe, jammy, and innocuous. When it comes to bottom-shelf red wines, Cabernet Sauvignon is the riskiest choice you can make, hands down.

What's the Story with Cabernet Sauvignon?

Unfortunately for those of us who are put off by crowds of men standing around talking about how much it cost and how long it is, Cabernet Sauvignon is not a wine you can, or would want to, ignore. It's one of the big ones, if not the biggest one—the wine of kings, beef, George Washington, JFK, and Eleanor of Aquitaine.

Oh, yeah, Eleanor of Aquitaine. Remember? Quite a life she had. She was the most eligible bachelorette in Europe in the 1100s, thanks to her great beauty and spirit—and the enormous quantity of France she inherited. She eventually had a few marriages, led a few crusades, gave birth to a few kings, including Richard the Lionhearted, became queen of England, and just might have invented the jury system as we know it. It was a pretty good life, especially for the Middle Ages, when the big trends in royalty seem to have been dysentery, marrying your cousin, and dying young.

However, let's not dwell on the romance of dying young from dysentery after marrying your cousin, let's ponder this: Why did a French heiress become queen of England? If you want to understand the importance of Cabernet Sauvignon in the universe, you first have to reacquaint yourself with a little European history. Like: France wasn't always France, and Great Britain wasn't always Great Britain. And the rest of us didn't exist at all.

Once upon a time the world was very small, and all of it was in the middle of Europe. This world consisted of lepers, wolves, wars fought with bronze weapons, the Mediterranean Sea, the Atlantic coast . . . and that about wraps it up. Transportation was, to say the least, difficult. If you wanted the quickest road between point A and point B, your best plan was to have a lot of heirs and hope they built one.

Yet this one river, the Gironde, in what is now France, worked pretty well for transport. It led from the Atlantic Ocean, not too terribly far from the English Channel, all the way into the heart of France, to about Toulouse, where a brief portage overland led to the Aude River. Float down the Aude and you'd end up out in the Mediterranean. This Gironde to Aude route wasn't the Panama Canal, but if you wanted a shortcut from the Atlantic to the mid-Mediterranean, it was as good as things got.

People who were lucky enough to live on the shores of the

Gironde began trading with whoever floated by. They found that what people really liked to get in trade was a bottle of the local wine. As a result, by around A.D. 300, Bordeaux winemaking was going great guns.

Let me reemphasize, in case anyone drifted off there: Winemaking has been going on in Bordeaux since A.D. 300. The year 300. That's when Christianity was just getting going, and way before anyone was speaking any language we would recognize today. It was before there were, as we know them, nations, states, laws, or brand management. However, an argument could be made that all those things were born in the cradle of Bordeaux, one of the first really stable parts of modern Europe.

It's not hard to find a château, a French winemaking estate, where the same land is thought to have been under vine since Roman times. You might even say that Château Haut-Brion, whose Bordeaux is especially prized today, is the world's earliest known product brand name. I've read that in the late 1600s you would pay seven shillings for a bottle of Haut-Brion in London, while mere Spanish wine ran two shillings a bottle. So rest assured that even in the seventeenth century there's a good chance that the guy in the horse-drawn carriage next to you was bragging about how much he paid and how superior was his red Bordeaux.

What wine these fourth-century, ninth-century, and thirteenth-century French farmers—or, really, pre-French farmers, because there was yet no France—were making isn't entirely clear. What we do know is that through trial and error, tinkering and playing, planting, replanting, propagating, and more trial and error, the local farmers came up with that royal suite of grapes we now call the Bordeaux varietals. Generally speaking, on one side of the Gironde farmers found that Cabernet Sauvignon did best, though usually softened with Merlot, and on the other side of the

Gironde Merlot did better, though usually structured and lengthened with Cabernet Sauvignon. There are a lot of exceptions; it's not hard to find a property on one side of the river or the other that bucks expectations and uses more Merlot than you'd think—or more Cabernet Sauvignon. However, I find the one point you have to internalize about Bordeaux to stop being overwhelmed by it is this: The United States is less than three hundred years old, and we have an inexhaustible wealth of important cultural nuance and detail. Bordeaux has had people making wine there for more than fifteen hundred years, so imagine how much cultural nuance and detail they've packed on in that time. It's fine to start your wine life being overwhelmed by Bordeaux; if you weren't, it would mean you're not really grasping the enormity of the situation.

To understand the significance of Cabernet Sauvignon in Western culture it's important to understand that not only do several Bordeaux châteaux predate Columbus's cruise, but Bordeaux was actually part of England, by marriage, for some three hundred years, because Eleanor of Aquitaine married Henry II. And the Hundred Years War was fought because England really, really, *really* did not want to relinquish control of Bordeaux and its wines.

By the bye—you think any current wars are quagmires? Imagine how people with an average life expectancy that precluded a midlife crisis felt about a war that ran, on and off, from 1336 to 1565. Yes, that is a two-hundred-plus-year war. But the British are modest. Also, Château Latour refers to a tower that marked one of that war's big battles.

I digress. When Bordeaux was part of England, distinct tax advantages were granted to Bordeaux châteaux, and Bordeaux wines became the default red wines of the English aristocracy, who referred to them as Claret. Rhymes with "carrot."

You know who else found the nomenclature of French Bordeaux annoying? Napoleon III. So annoying that he demanded that the château owners of Bordeaux cut out the game of telephone that is Bordeaux connoisseurship and just tell him exactly who had the best wines.

At first the château owners balked, but Napoleon ruled, and so eventually they were forced to announce a list ranking themselves Most Important, Second Most Important, and so on. These are the "classed growths," or *crus classés,* which came out of the Classification of 1855. We still use this 1855 ranking today; it's phenomenally important to high-dollar, upper level collectors.

How much do you need to know about the Classification of 1855? Not much when you're getting started in wine. All you really need to know is that there are only a handful of these top-ranked-in-1855 First Growths, or Premiers Crus, and you can't afford them. A single bottle of the latest vintage of Château Lafite-Rothschild costs around $800 from a

---

Quick and Dirty Merlot Guide

One of the great sadnesses of my life as a writer is that at some point in every project you have to be satisfied with what it is, and not what it isn't. With this book a line had to be drawn, lest the book cost $200 and weigh sixty pounds. Merlot, unfortunately, was one dramatic place where that line was drawn—which isn't fair to Merlot! Poor Merlot. One of the most important grapes in the history of the world, there's actually more Merlot planted in Bordeaux than Cabernet Sauvignon, but right now Merlot is terribly out of fashion. This is punishment for its popularity in the 1990s, which earned it a scathing critique in the movie *Sideways,* which made Merlot appear to be the worst thing a wine in America can be: uncool. Sad. But such is American wine life right now. Just this morning I saw a series of gift tags for wine from a company called PoppTags.com which read: "The wine store guy said this was good." And: "The wine could be terrible but the label is so pretty!" And: "Nothing says 'Thank You' like a wine I know nothing about." Ouch. With consumers like this who needs enemies? But don't make Merlot your enemy—it's good stuff.

Here's your quick and dirty Merlot guide: If Merlot was a couch it would be a deep, velvety, very comfortable one. The wine is typically plummy, round, generous, fleshy, and lively; ideally it offers scents of plums, black cherries, black tea, and, if you're lucky, violets or even oranges. The best in the world comes from the French Bordeaux district called Pomerol, it's also very big in that part of Bordeaux called St. Émilion. In the 1990s Merlot was very fashionable in the United States and too much of it was planted in hot, fertile places where the wine grew too abundantly. In its worst guises, Merlot is like that big velvety couch but with all the supports blown out: You sink in, and it's flabby, has no structure, and threatens to suffocate you with dull lushness. That said, dull and lush is not the worst thing a wine could be, and when you're stuck at the theater and jockeying for wine during intermission Merlot is likely to be superior to the other cheap and mysterious wines you're offered. It's especially better than bottom-shelf Cabernet Sauvignon. At a higher price point you could make a good argument that any $25 Napa Valley Merlot is as good as a $50 Cabernet Sauvignon—because Merlot is so unfashionable right now it's underpriced. The Napa Valley growers still producing it are doing so because they love it, and they do so mainly for the core of sophisticated American wine drinkers who drink following their own taste, not the trend du jour. Be one of those people!

To hold your own Merlot tasting like the longer tastings here, assemble five wines.

1. A bottom-shelf Washington State Merlot, like one from Hogue or Columbia Crest—the long days and accompanying long hang-times allow Merlot from up north to develop more complex black-fruit flavors.
2. A slightly more expensive and complex Merlot, from either California or Washington; Sonoma County's Sebastiani is terrific and reliable, I also have loved Chateau St. Jean, and Blackbird, as well as Leonetti, from Washington.
3. A Napa Valley over-$25 Merlot, like one from Flora Springs, Duckhorn, or Behrens and Hitchcock.
4. A Pomerol or St. Emilion; this'll cost you, but don't worry too much about the producer—just ask your local wine shop for "A good Pomerol" (*poe-may-roll*). If your wine shop has any, that will do.
5. If you live in the New York City area, consider adding a Long Island Merlot; they've often been touted as the next great thing.

Put them all on the table and have dinner. Beef, chicken, duck, lamb, mushrooms, pork, meatier fish like swordfish, tuna, or salmon—Merlot is a dinner-table workhorse. (The only thing to avoid is foods that are very aggressive in some dimension—very spicy ones, or very sweet, or very lemony, as extreme foods can overwhelm Merlot.) What do you think?

Whatever you do, though, don't invite the most closed-minded people you know to this Merlot tasting. Merlot these days has what could be called Jean-Paul Sartre syndrome: Its big problem is other people.

reputable merchant, and if you find a cheaper bottle on the Internet, you're in counterfeit territory.

What is good to know when you're getting started in wine is that the Classification of 1855 made it much, much easier for anybody who suddenly became very rich to know exactly where to spend their money. It was, effectively, the first 100-point system of scoring wines. Today the most esteemed Bordeaux wines continue to be that handful of First Growths and the best from the second growth, called Super Seconds.

Unless you have more money than God, I think this is all you really need to know about Premier Cru Bordeaux, because since the 1855 Classification, French Bordeaux prices have stayed right where Bordeaux château owners like them to be: with God in his heaven. However, in the same way that it's good to know about the Magna Carta if you want to understand the American system of government, it's good to think about First Growth Bordeaux, with God in his heaven, if you want to understand contemporary wine.

So, back to the history. Eleanor of Aquitaine danced off this mortal coil. Wine flowed. Time marched. Some of the things that time marched in: the British Empire, Americans (Thomas Jefferson was a big Bordeaux guy), Japanese guys with cell phones the size of bricks, Texas oil barons, Manhattan cardiologists—trace the history of wealth since 1855 and you can trace exactly who was buying Bordeaux, building wine cellars for their Bordeaux collection, and bragging to their friends.

So, to recap: There's one wine that, essentially, predates Europe. There's one wine that all but invariably increases in value as it ages. (They call First Growth Bordeaux "investment-grade" wine.) There is one constant that has marked the status of Western men among one another and their grandfathers since Roman times—and it ain't a goddamn car. As the Bible is to Western literature, Cabernet Sauvignon is to global winemaking. It's the one grape that New World winemakers, and especially those in California and Australia, really do backflips trying to ace. The so-called Judgment of Paris, the 1976 wine competition that shocked the world by giving top prizes to California wines instead of Bordeaux first growths, and subsequently was

---

Tricky Dick

President Richard Nixon used to be a big fan of Château Margaux, an exceedingly expensive First Growth Bordeaux. In his book *Real Life at the White House,* John Whitcomb writes, "He was not inclined to share it with congressmen. For run-of-the-mill guests he ordered a $6 bottle of wine and had his Château Margaux served to him in a plain carafe or a bottle wrapped in a towel."

Others have written that at state dinners Nixon had the wine served blind, in decanters. Nixon's decanter was filled with Château Margaux, while the decanters on the rest of the table were filled with plonk. However, other records show that karma eventually caught up with him.

---

featured on the cover of *Time* magazine and turned California from a hinterland to a cult-wine world-beater in the space of a few years, mattered because it involved red Bordeaux. If it had been a Sauvignon Blanc or Syrah competition a few people would have cared, but not that many. The fact that the competition involved the most important red wine in the world is what made it historic news.

The "Holy Trinity" of Cabernet Sauvignon

The Grape

Tannins, the things that preserve wine and allow it to age, come from grape skins and grape seeds, or pips. Because blue-purple Cabernet Sauvignon is a small, thick-skinned grape with a lot of seeds in proportion to its size, it seems designed by heaven to age. In addition to its tannic qualities, Cabernet Sauvignon fruit has the scent of black currants and other black fruits such as blackberries, black cherries, and plums, as well as mint and green pepper.

The primary classic Bordeaux blending partners for

Cabernet Sauvignon are Merlot, Cabernet Franc, Petit Verdot, and Malbec. Here's what they do:

Merlot

Cabernet is the skeleton and Merlot is the flesh. Put them together and you get a whole person. Conveniently, Merlot grapes bud and ripen earlier than Cabernet Sauvignon, so farmers growing them together don't have to harvest every vine at the same time.

Cabernet Franc

Cabernet Franc is one parent of Cabernet Sauvignon (the other is Sauvignon Blanc). Used as a blending partner, Cabernet Franc gives a wine a greater sense of fruit and some perfume—blueberry, tobacco, and, famously, the scent of violets. So if you ever detect a strong scent of violets in a Bordeaux, feel free to draw your fingers through your beard and murmur, "The Cabernet Franc adds a lovely sensuality."

Petit Verdot

Winemakers rarely make a wine that contains more than 1 to 3 percent Petit Verdot. They use it for color (in the Médoc region of France in particular, Cabernet Sauvignon doesn't get very dark), for tannin, and for spice.

Malbec

Malbec is another grape used for color and spice, especially pepper. Typically a Bordeaux or California Bordeaux-style blend will use very little Malbec, just a percent or two. It is bottled on its own in the French district of Cahors and in Argentina and can be excellent.

Syrah

Syrah, the subject of Chapter 7, is not a traditional blending partner for Cabernet Sauvignon anywhere but

Australia. They've got Syrah, which they call Shiraz, coming out of their ears, and what else are they going to do with it? Feed it to the chickens? Not bloody likely, mate. Drunk chickens. That's no way to raise chickens!

Seriously, though, Cabernet Sauvignon is often quite tannic on its own, and once oak tannins, from oak barrels, seep in to the wine they can make a wine buzz-saw tannic. Put Syrah/Shiraz in it as the Australians do and you get more color, but also a softer, more glycerin finish and a fruit-forward, more easily approachable and quaffable wine. Because of this, some American box wines blend Syrah with their Cabernet Sauvignon. If you feel like you've got a handle on Cabernet Sauvignon and Bordeaux and suddenly get a wine that totally confuses you, it's probably got Syrah in it.

Terroir

Cabernet Sauvignon is one of the most widely planted grapes on earth. Wherever wine grows, Cabernet Sauvignon grows. That said, its two most significant sites are in Bordeaux and California's Napa and to a lesser extent Sonoma valleys.

Bordeaux Terroir

Bordeaux is essentially at sea level, at a place where three rivers run into the cold Atlantic Ocean. The action of those rivers, and the action of ancient glaciers coming down from the nearby Pyrenees Mountains, deposited millions of years' worth of gravel here. This gravel holds heat from the sun so that the vines stay warm, but the gravel's inability to hold moisture or nutrients prevents the vines from truly thriving. Thriving, happy vines make big, watery fruit; suffering, barely surviving vines make intense, highly valuable fruit. Some of the most valued Bordeaux properties, such as Château Haut-Brion, have gravel fifty feet deep.

The Napa Valley

The Napa Valley is very new, geologically speaking, formed when faults caused the mountains on either side to pull apart, allowing lava to bubble in. Later, rivers filled the valley floor with sediment and rocks, some in what's called an alluvial fan, the deposit that occurs when a fast-moving, steep stream slows and widens. Both volcanic soil and the rocky soil of the alluvial fan are prized for their *inability* to hold water and nutrients; remember, struggling vines generate small, concentrated fruit. The mountainsides of Napa Valley are also prized for their inability to coddle plant life; ditto for Sonoma Valley mountains and all the other California mountainsides.

Conversation with the Biggest Wig of All: Robert Parker

You cannot talk about wine in America for ten minutes without someone bringing up the Wine Advocate's *founder Robert Parker, the most influential, the most controversial wine critic in the history of the world. His 100-point scoring system—the first 50 points are free, anything under 80 can't sell, anything over 90 flies off the shelves, anything over 94 makes a career and a fortune—is beloved by many for clearly advising what's in all those unknown bottles. But it's also despised by many for reducing the work of lifetimes to a score that is neither here nor there—say, an 88; imagine how irked you would be if someone you never actually met looked at your life achievements from his office in Baltimore and said: B+. His critics insist he likes overblown wines that are too big in every dimension—too fruity, too oaky, too alcoholic—and that he likes them because they stand out in a blind tasting, which is a very different experience from enjoying wine with dinner.*

However, there's no arguing with his fans: Parker makes the winemakers whose wine he likes millions of dollars, because a high score from him opens doors and wallets around the world. And so, his critics contend, he has remade wine in his image, as wineries globally hire "flying winemakers," consultants who know the tricks to making a wine more to his taste, a process they've dubbed "Parkerization."

What does Robert M. Parker, Jr., the great man himself, think of all this? "Parkerization," he told me, is a load of hooey:

The idea that I can change wines is like saying I have enough power to bring the dead from their graves. I've read all the rhetoric—"he likes big oaky blockbuster wines"—and that is so patently false that its falsehood can be established by picking up any of my fourteen books or any issue of *Wine Advocate.* It's something that's very easy for people to say, and nearly impossible to disprove. You will never find someone who says that who is able to provide an example of a wine or winemaker who changed their product for me.

Of course, my critics will say: No one will go on the record because they don't want to alienate you. How can I possibly respond to that? There are producers who were making horrible wine who, because of my criticism, started making better wine, and then their wine quality improved dramatically. Are those wines meant to please me? No, but they did. Should they have kept making bad wine?

I got into the business because I was influenced by Ralph Nader and the journalists who were working during the Watergate years, and back then the entire wine writing industry existed on the largesse of the wine industry. Everything was *good good good* because everything was paid for. I went in paying my own way, not accepting freebies in any way, writing for consumers, not to flatter the industry.

If wine has changed it has to do with an expanding

worldwide market and the increased level of education and sophistication of wine lovers around the world, not with me. And the idea that I want all wines to be the same is just absurd. Wine can be so compelling because it is so different, not only each glass of a great wine can be different as it evolves, but all the wines in a region, in a vintage, in the world. Why would anyone want them to be the same? If you want a standardized taste you should drink Budweiser or Jack Daniel's.

There are wonderful wines from every important wine producing region on earth. In some regions those great wines are big wines, in other regions those great wines are the more delicate wines. I think what makes a good wine is universally obvious. By and large there is strong agreement among all people who taste a wine as to what is good. There was great wine, and bad wine, long before I was born, and there will be great wine and bad wine long after I've faded from the scene.

I certainly hear the criticism of me. And I think frankly it's that a lot of wine writers are jealous, and that their attitude toward consumers is condescending. This jealousy comes up because they feel they have no influence and no voice, and they feel that way because no one listens to them.

Winemaking

Cabernet Sauvignon makers have many, many choices to make: How much yield should they get from their grapes? Hand harvest, or machine? Wild yeast, or commercial? How long to ferment? Almost all Cabernet Sauvignon is aged in oak barrels, or otherwise given the flavors of toast, vanilla, and caramel that harmonize beautifully with Cabernet's black fruit. (See Chapter 5 on Chardonnay for the full story on oak.) The difference in your final bottle will spring from the grapes, the *terroir,* and these winemaking choices.

Stop Reading, Start Drinking!

You're about to learn about Cabernet Sauvignon—what the personality of the grape is like generally, what the wine tastes like in both expensive and inexpensive New World iterations, expensive and inexpensive Old World Bordeaux styles, and some other style of your choosing. Most important, you'll learn whether Cabernet Sauvignon, the king of reds, is your cup of tea, which is something that, if you want to be a wine drinker, you really have to sort out.

Cabernet Sauvignon FIELD GUIDE

Most wine shops will have at least a few dozen Cabernet Sauvignons. In some shops a quarter of the reds will be Cabernet Sauvignon—it's just that popular. You'll pay from around $8 to $100 for most of them. The least expensive will be either Washington State wines, California Central Coast wines, or Australian wines blended liberally with Shiraz; for my money, the Washington State ones are the most reliable. Generally speaking, the French Cabernet Sauvignons will be dryer and the North American ones will be richer. There is no absolute correlation between price and quality: Half the time a $50 wine will be better than its $80 neighbor. See Chapter 11 for more on this vexing situation.

Inexpensive Central Valley California Cabernet Sauvignon, under $15

In the hundred thousand acres that stretch south of San Francisco called the Central Valley, grapes have it easy. Lots of sun, plenty of water, and lovely rich soil. Conventional wisdom about wine is that when the grape vines have it too easy, they make dull wine. So these wines have a reputation for being the fruitiest of all Cabernet Sauvignons: ripe, lush, cherry-berry fruity, and happy as cupcakes. Or the most noxious of all Cabernet Sauvignons: big dark bottles of watery green-pepper juice. Which will you get? You pay your money, you take your chances.

Washington State Cabernet Sauvignon, $6–$15

Washington State's vineyards aren't on the rainy Pacific coast, but inland, toward Idaho, where Cabernet Sauvignon grapes live a life that's dry and cool, and one in which the shorter northern growing season is compensated for by longer summer days. This tends to result in small fruit that ripens slowly but completely and that makes wine with big flavors of chocolate, black fruit, cherries, black olives, mocha, and cassis. The nicest examples of Washington State Cabernet Sauvignon combine that fruit with good structure, and will seem really lively in the glass. Less exciting examples can seem flabby and won't have much aroma, like flat Coke. Good affordable names: Hogue, Columbia Crest, and Snoqualmie. Good high-end names: Leonetti and Quilceda Creek.

South American Cabernet Sauvignon, $6–$20

People love South American Cabernet Sauvignon because they're considered such great values. Of course Chile and Argentina are quite large, so generalizing about them is tough, but here I go: Mostly these wines are made in a Bordeaux style, and tend to have meaty, bacony, spicy, and cedar-scented aspects, with notes of tobacco and wood smoke on top of black fruit. People who like French reds also tend to like South American reds.

Miscellaneous other European Cabernet Sauvignons, $8 and up

Because Cabernet Sauvignon has name recognition and can more or less grow anywhere wine grapes grow, you will often these days find Cabernet Sauvignons from Italy, Spain, Croatia,

New Zealand, Lebanon, Uruguay, and such. Should you try them? No. At least not until you can lean back in your chair, close your eyes, and summon to your mind exactly what Cabernet Sauvignon from major areas like France and California tastes like. Once you feel that you do know what Cabernet is, by all means, let all the little bright lights shine.

Australian Cabernet Sauvignon, $3–$100

Because Australia's climate ranges from rain forests to deserts to mountains, there is no one style. That said, here in the States we tend to get two sorts of Australian wine: the very costly and the very not. The cheap ones will be critter-label cheapies festooned with cute animals; inside the bottles is a blend of Cabernet and Syrah/Shiraz. The critter-label Cabernets will tend to feel very round and fat in the mouth, thanks to the Syrah. Meanwhile, the expensive Cabernets can be anything depending on where they're from; the best regions are Coonawarra and Margaret River. Generally, expect more red fruits, herbal notes including sage and mint, lower tannin, and higher acid from high-end Australian Cabernet Sauvignon.

Inexpensive French Médoc wines, known as Cru Bourgeois Bordeaux, under $30

As mentioned above, the birthplace of Cabernet Sauvignon is the Gironde River; the left bank of the Gironde is called the Médoc. This is important because the Médoc is the baseline for all Cabernet Sauvignon worldwide. Inexpensive Médoc Bordeaux tends to be brilliantly structured and spicy, but can lack fruit. There are so many names they'd be impossible to list, but if you want to find one, ask. When the wine guy at the store asks if he can help you find something, say "You can help me find Médoc Cru Bourgeois Bordeaux" or "Cabernet Sauvignon from the Médoc" or "cheap Bordeaux."

**American Meritage, Claret, and, bafflingly, "Red Wine,"
$10–$100**

As touched on above, when Cabernet Sauvignon is grown on its native soil of Bordeaux it is rarely bottled alone, but instead is combined with its traditional blending partners. Many winemakers feel that this is the one true and right way to make Cabernet Sauvignon, and that a Cabernet Sauvignon without, say, Petit Verdot and Merlot is like a chicken soup without black pepper and carrots—you could make it, but why?

What Americans can do if they want to make the same combination as Bordeaux is join the Meritage Association (at a cost) and call their wine a Meritage, which is a made-up word combining "merit" and "heritage" (rhymes with "heritage"). If they don't want to join the Meritage Association they can call their wine Claret, or they can give it a proprietary name, that is, a name they trademark and own, say, Tapestry, Seduction, or Complexity; typically the labels on these bottles will say "red wine" somewhere.

These non-Bordeaux Bordeaux blends will—hopefully, cross your fingers—be like premium Bordeaux: lots of structure, full-bodied, an abundance of aromas knit together into a tight, not-too-exuberant melody, with nice fruit. Meritage wines tend to be expensive, winemaker-driven, look-at-me wines, and as such are almost uniformly really good.

Napa Valley Cabernet Sauvignon, $15 to infinity!

Why do people go bazonkers over Napa Valley Cabernet? Generally, a high-end wine should have all of the qualities we've discussed above—appealing fruit, good structure, spice, oak, aromas, weight in the mouth—and knit them together into a whole that is larger than the sum of the parts. A lot larger. You should feel a resonant profundity, a passionate thrill, a thrum in tune with the universe. What, you shelled out $135 and felt no resonant profundity? It tasted sort of like flat Diet Coke? Sucker. It happens.

That's why Napa Valley Cabernet has its detractors. Flora Springs and Honig are my go-to affordable Napa Valley Cabernets; for around $35, I find they offer the joy of Napa without the fierce ante-in.

Expensive French Bordeaux, $30 to infinity!

So we know the most esteemed Cabernet Sauvignon in the world comes from the "left bank" of the Gironde in Bordeaux, from the regions of Pauillac, St. Estèphe, St. Julien, Margaux, Haut-Médoc, Médoc. Keeping in mind that most red Bordeaux are blended wines made up of king Cabernet Sauvignon, queen Merlot, and their court of helpers, traditionally the wines of Paulliac are going to have the highest proportion of Cabernet Sauvignon, sometimes even 100 percent.

You should be able to find a Pauillac (*poy-ack*)wine from a single Château for between $40 and $120. (Practically speaking, today the various levels of classification—Fifth Growth, Second Growth—are meaningless, except for the staggering prices of First Growth, which are always interesting.) Some of the more affordable great Pauillac names: Château Lynch-Bages, Château Duhart-Milon, and Château Pibran.

Generally you should be able to walk into any wine store with a good French selection and say, "I'm looking for an affordable Pauillac."

This is such an insidery thing to look for that you will gain instant credibility. Your wine clerk will almost invariably reply, "Aren't we all." And you're off.

Here's what you should get when you taste real, single-Château Bordeaux: staggering grandeur. All the structure in the world embroidered elegantly with beautiful fragrance and lush fruit. Majesty.

Conversations with Bigwigs: Celia Masyczek

Napa Valley cult Cabernet is one of the great forces animating wine today. It drives critics into frenzies, either awarding blockbuster scores or sniping at the wines; it drives collectors into buying sprees, and it drives the rest of the world's noncult winemakers into fits as they try to emulate the cult wines. These cult wines are generally available only by Internet mailing list, mailing lists that often have years-long waits to get on them. The reigning queen of the latest greatest cult Cabernets is Celia Masyczek (pronounced ma-chess-key), a winemaker for lots of different small Napa Valley brands, including her own wine, Corra, and Scarecrow, the hottest ticket in town. (The wine is called Scarecrow because the vines were planted by J. J. Cohn, the producer of The Wizard of Oz.*)*

Someone called me the diva of Napa Valley Cabernet once. I was horrified. *No no no*—I'm not a diva, never use that word. I'm a consultant and contract winemaker. I just happen to be one with a love for Cabernet. What can I say? I love the variety. It is delicious to drink. It goes so well with so many different types of food, and I actually find it refreshing with a plate of food that has a lot of different flavors to it. The nuances and complexity of Cabernet can be profound, and I'm really just trying to build something under my own name that I feel is just a perfect balance of that fresh juicy character of Cabernet with some sweet bay leaf and anise character, but not overly on the green side, but a little green because that's a true varietal expression

You have to be careful when you use the word *green*—you're never trying to make something that smells like asparagus water. Then on the other hand there are people who are against anything except berry and jammy flavors and take their Cabernet to a ripeness level where that's all you get. My personal preference is not to take it to that level because I think it's more complete, more appropriate, and better with food when it's not at that level. Black olive, black tea leaf, I think those are a more traditional style of Cabernet—some call it French, but it's also California fifteen or twenty years ago.

The phrase "cult wines," I think that's been overused to the point that it's starting to lose its meaning. It has gone from meaning something that was exceptional to something that is unattainable. Cult wines are, historically, a recent phenomenon. What happened was, there used to be fewer—a lot fewer—wineries and wine brands in Napa Valley. In general Napa Valley was about growing fruit that went to a large winery; you would be selling to Beringer, Mondavi, Sterling, or one of the large wineries, and this was true whether you were taking exquisite care of your fruit or were pretty careless, the quality really didn't matter. Maybe they made your wine into a reserve or a regular Napa Valley offering, but the ceiling was pretty low for a grower. With the advent of the Internet and increased awareness in the wine media, increased awareness among growers about the benefits of replanting vineyards on better root stocks, trellising, and that sort of thing, not to mention a lot of capital in California as Silicon Valley was booming, a lot of people suddenly realized they could go out on their own with just a couple hundred cases and make it. The individual personalities of those pieces of ground were able to be recognized as something different than a 100,000-case blend.

What's different about a 400-case wine? It's inefficient in a way. At the same time, you can never make wine at 40,000 cases they way you can at 400. I can tape off individual vines and say: Don't pick these today, wait a week. I can taste every barrel and say: This goes in, this does not. Another way of saying "cult wines" might be "attention to detail wines."

Food and Cabernet Sauvignon

Beef, beef, beef. Also lamb, bison, elk, caribou, venison, and duck. What kind of beef? All kinds: Pot roast, osso bucco, prime rib, beef tartare—the works. But above all, steaks on the grill. There's something about the char and a rare interior that just morphs a good Cabernet Sauvignon into a hedonistic experience. Cabernet Sauvignon's black fruit and toast make it perfect with rare red meat. Fruity, simple Australian and Central Coast California Cabernet Sauvignons can go with burgers, Thai curry takeout, and similar bold and sweet dishes. Dry, austere Cabernet Sauvignon from Graves also goes with game birds like pheasant or grouse.

Don't serve strong, tannic, big and bold Cabernet Sauvignon with anything particularly delicate. Have it with sushi and you might as well be eating wet crackers for all the fish you'll taste.

Tasting Cabernet Sauvignon
Step by Step

1. A Brief Road Map to Our Upcoming Cabernet Sauvignon Road Trip

Whether you're tasting alone or by party, you're going to need five Cabernet Sauvignons to get a sense of what the wine really tastes like and whether you like it. Your first task will be to discover the basic personality of the grape—the black currants and other black fruit. To do this you'll taste a mass-market bottom-shelf American Cabernet Sauvignon. You'll contrast that with a basic Cabernet Sauvignon grown in France, a Médoc Cru Bourgeois Bordeaux, which will give you a clear taste of Cabernet's bracing structure and fierce tannins. With those two poles of fruit and structure in your mind, you'll taste another Cabernet from somewhere of your choice—Australia, perhaps, or Washington State. This will show you how *terroir*—growing conditions, soil, and wine-maker choices like wild or cultivated yeasts—affects the taste of wine. With that basic idea of Cabernet, you'll move on to the big guns: a Napa Valley Cabernet and a fancy Bor-deaux. With these you'll taste the basic elements of Cabernet, plus a whole lot of oomph, nuance, complexity, and depth.

Notes on Tasting Cabernet Solo or in Pairs

If you're tasting your Cabernet Sauvignons solo, plan to do your tasting with some food. French Cabernet is a food wine, and you won't totally get it if there's no appropriate food around. A steak on the grill is perfect, but if you're not a cook, take-out roast beef, a hamburger, or a pile of beef brisket from a barbecue place will do.

Notes on Tasting Cabernet by Party

Fire up the grill and invite your friends over for steaks or good burgers. You're looking at one of the nicest barbecues you can throw. If it's winter and your grill is under a snow-drift, you could splurge on a standing rib roast, beef ten-derloin, or another big beef cut. Cabernet also goes with lamb and other red meats, as well as game birds and duck, particularly with a red-wine reduction.

If you're a vegetarian, think of earthy foods: grilled mushrooms, beets, or eggplant and pasta, risotto, or polenta combined with Parmigiano Reggiano or cave-aged Gouda.

If you prefer to have a wine-and-cheese tasting instead of a full-blown dinner party, go primarily for the nuttier, firm cheeses: Parmigiano Reggiano, cave-aged Gouda, Gruyère, a smoked cheese, and aged Dry Jack or a good Cheddar. Many people believe Cabernet goes well with Gorgonzola, the bigger-than-life blue cheese, but I've never thought so; if the idea appeals to you, try it.

Add some of the following to your cheese board: figs, cherries, walnuts, and oil-cured black olives; these will draw out some of the wine's flavors. If you can add some meat to the cheese selection it will help you understand the wine more. Look for *bresaola* (Italian dried beef, sort of like ham in the tradition of prosciutto, but made of beef), a paté with mushrooms, or lamb or duck sausage.

For dessert, chocolate, figs, cherries, coffee-flavored sweets, and plums are the classics here. Coffee or chocolate sorbet or a nice chocolate bar will do, or go for a full fig tart or cherry pie if you like.

2. Shopping

Whether you're alone or having a party, your first task is to buy your Cabernet Sauvignons. You'll need five bottles, selected from the field guide above. The names provided are simply suggestions to help you in your shopping; whatever your local wine shop has should be fine. Just try to match the categories, not the names. You want to end up with:

1. A mass-market, bottom-shelf Cabernet Sauvignon, ideally one whose label proclaims it entirely Cabernet Sauvignon. Beringer's Third Century is a good choice, as are Bogle, Hess Select, Hahn, and Guenoc. $9 to $14.
2. A basic French Médoc Cru Bourgeois Cabernet Sauvignon. You'll need to visit a decent wine shop, where the clerk will probably start trying to sell you something else on the logic that for only another ten bucks you can get a much better wine. Resist. You're looking for something with fewer bells and whistles, not more, because you're trying to find what the grape tastes like unadorned. (To

get them off your back you can also buy your classified-growth Bordeaux from them; see the final item in this shopping list.) $25 to $50.

3. One outlier: a Washington State, South American, or single-estate Australian Cabernet Sauvignon. You're looking for another expression of the grape; anything will do. The main thing you *don't* want is something blended with a non-Bordeaux varietal, like Syrah/Shiraz. Some names: from Washington, Hogue Genesis, Snoqualmie, Columbia Crest; from Chile, Casa Lapostolle or Veramonte; from Australia, d'Arenberg. $15 and up.

4. One nice Napa or Sonoma Cabernet Sauvignon—and there are zillions. I like the Honig and Flora Springs for value, Duckhorn, Spring Mountain, and Whitehall Lane if I want to spend more. Basically, anything for which you're paying more than $35 should do very nicely.

5. One nice Cabernet-heavy French Bordeaux from a recognized château. This will be your most difficult shopping experience, requiring the help of a wine store clerk. The best value-to-price ratio here is going to be the Super Seconds, classified growths that aren't as expensive as real First Growths. Good names: Château Lynch-Bages, Château Léoville-Barton. Also, some of the top châteaux make "second labels." These usually cost $70 to $100 and are very good. Look for Bahans-Haut-Brion, Pensées de Lafleur, or Les Forts de Latour. $70 and well up.

3. Planning and Thinking About Tasting

Set out your glasses, your dump bucket, and your tasting markers. Make your life easier: Put some black currant jam, or cassis liqueur, in a wineglass. You will instantly understand the central fruit quality that emanates from a glass of Cabernet Sauvignon. Put some torn pieces of dark toast in another glass, and a couple of oil-cured black olives in another. If you happen to have fresh mint around, put that out, too.

Tasting Markers

Keep the following list handy so you can glance at it while you're tasting—it will help you name fragrances that seem just out of reach.

Most likely

Black currant (fresh, as jam, or as crème de cassis)

Blackberry (fresh, as jam, candied, stewed, or with any other descriptor)

Black cherry (fresh, as jam, stewed, as cherry liqueur, etc.)

Cherry (ditto)

Plum (ditto)

Fig (ditto)

Black olive

Graphite, pencil lead, or pencil shavings

Raspberry (ditto)

Chocolate

Toast

Bay leaf

Anise

Eucalyptus

Mint

Chocolate

Green bell pepper

Possibly

Tea leaves

Asparagus water

Leather

Cedar

Black pepper

Cinnamon

Vanilla

Toast

Smoke

Caramel

4. Cool Things Off

Get your wine to cellar temperature (see page 10). Ideal temperature for Cabernet Sauvignon will be around 55 to 60 degrees.

5. Pull the Corks!

6. Taste Your First Wine

Your basic American bottom-shelf domestic Cabernet Sauvignon should tell you what Cabernet is like when it gets fully ripe, as it does here. Pour an inch or so into each guest's wineglass and swirl. Taste. Pass around your tasting markers if you've got them.

Questions to consider: Black currants? Blackberries? Herbs? Black olives? Do any of the other scents from the long list jump out at you? Be especially on the lookout for figs, eucalyptus, mint, and cherries. Does the wine seem sweet, or balanced? Do you like it?

Now either dump your wine, or, if you've got a second glass, pour everyone an inch of the French Cru Bourgeois Bordeaux.

7. Taste Your Second Wine

Pour about an inch of the basic French Cru Bourgeois Bordeaux into a wineglass for each guest. Swirl. Sniff. Taste. You may feel your tongue prickle up and feel your whole mouth get tight inside. That's tannin. Cabernet Sauvignon is one of the most tannic grapes there is, and when it grows in a cool place like France, it gets more tannic than when it grows in a hot place like California. How do you like it?

Now taste for structure, the element of wine that makes it seem brisk and well-knit, like it's off on a march. Do you get that at all? You might get aromas of black currants, toast, pine forest, mushrooms, rose petals, spice, oak, burnt coffee, or cedar; your tasting markers and list will help you identify individual scents.

Compare it to your first wine: Which is fruitier? Which has more structure? This wine will be thinner, more plainly acidic, and more bracing than any other Cabernet Sauvignon you'll try. You'll either love it or you won't. More likely it will be your least favorite when you start drinking Cabernet Sauvignon, but a favorite later.

Try the wine with food: Does the tart acidity help food taste better? Do you like it more or less than the domestic Cabernet Sauvignon?

8. Taste Your Outlier

The point of this wine is to get another taste of Cabernet Sauvignon, so tell everybody what you got: Australian? South American? Washington State? Pour an inch of your outlier Cabernet for everyone. Swirl. Sniff. Taste. How is it different from the first two? More fruity? Less? More tannic? Less? Is it better knit? Pass the tasting markers if you've got them; does that help you notice anything? Consult your long list of tasting markers: Anything in this wine jump out at you? Most important: How do you like it?

(Note to solo tasters, or those in tasting in pairs: You are now going to take a break. Pick up the tasting of the next two wines as soon as convenient.)

9. Tasting the Big Guns: Napa Valley

Next, the wine everyone's waiting for: the pricey Napa Valley Cabernet. Tell everyone what you got! Admire the nice bottle: It's so heavy so that it can age for years and years in your cellar. Does it have a really deep depression at the bottom? That's called a *punt;* it's to collect the sediment that would separate out of the wine as it aged over many years.

Pour. Swirl. Sniff. Taste. This one should be very concentrated and fruity, plush and big in your mouth, and dancing with lovely aromas.

Questions to consider: What does this have in common with the first two wines? Does it have the fruit of the domestic cheapie plus the structure of the French one? It should. It should also have more than that: Oomph, wow, some drama. Does it? Check your long list of tasting markers: Do you get any fruits? Herbs?

10. Tasting the Big Guns: Real Bordeaux

Here we are, finally, at the wine that started the world's love affair with Cabernet Sauvignon: expensive stuff from

France's Bordeaux region. Pour. Swirl. Sniff. Taste. It should
have structure to burn, an immense depth, and fruits, spices,
and other notes woven into a seamless whole. In other words,
all the good points of everything you've tried so far, plus fireworks and melodies. Does it?

Take time to consider the big questions: Which wines
most improved, or were themselves most improved by, food,
and which were best on their own? Which was your favorite? Which would you buy again?

And that's it! You now should have an unshakable sense of
what Cabernet Sauvignon is, and what you think about it.
Try another dozen Cabernet Sauvignons in the coming
months and you'll have a lifelong ability to talk about
Cabernet Sauvignon with waiters, sommeliers, and clerks
in shops. Do you like New World or Old World Cabernet?
Fruit or structure? Tell 'em what you think!

THE TAKEAWAY

Now you know why this wine has captured the
attention of wealthy and powerful men for hundreds of years. Can you believe the depth, the
power, the magnificence? It's an awe-inspiring beverage in the way that Coke, beer, or little country wines
can only dream of. The way the fragrances coil around
that taut strength, the way it seems powerful and
bold, the way the power is backed with subtlety and
grace. Yowza! That's drinking.

*Five-second cheat sheet for people who didn't
read the chapter and are reading this on their
iPhones while they wait for a table at the million-
dollar steakhouse*

Cabernet Sauvignon (*cab-er-NAY so-ven-YON*) is a red wine that has been the drink of kings and millionaires ever since the days of knights and jousts. The powerful love it because it, too, is powerful. It combines an iron fist of structure with a velvet glove of cassis, blackberry, herb, and cedar box notes. Cabernet Sauvignon is the ultimate steak, prime rib, or beef tenderloin pair, though it also goes gangbusters with all red meat, game, and duck. That said, cheap Cabernets are dicey; if you're reading this in a burger place or grocery store, a better bottom-shelf pick would be the Syrah. Everyone in Napa Valley trips over one another trying to make a better Cabernet, so Napa Valley Cabernets are pretty much always a safe bet. Some of the most affordable American ones include those from Flora Springs, Honig, and Château Montelena. When it comes from France, its birthplace, Cabernet Sauvignon is called Bordeaux. Some affordable reliable French names include Château Lynch-Bages, Château Léoville-Barton, or affordable "second labels" like Bahans-Haut-Brion, Pensées de Lafleur, or Les Forts de Latour. Broadly speaking, Napa Valley wines are fruitier and more powerful, Bordeaux wines more structured with more finesse.

Knock-Their-Socks-Off Gifts for Cabernet Lovers

Can you afford to knock the socks off a Cabernet lover? Many Cabernet hounds are hard to please, like diamond collectors. That said, here are some ideas:

1. Here are the planet Earth's top five Premiers Crus, the First Growth Bordeaux wines—if you can afford one, everyone will be well impressed: Château Latour, Château Margaux, Château

Haut-Brion, Château Lafite-Rothschild, and Château Mouton-Rothschild.

2. Ridge Monte Bello Cabernet: Don't know whether your recipient is more of a French wine lover or an American wine lover? Hedge your bets: Ridge's Monte Bello, from the Santa Cruz mountains, is considered a benchmark American Cabernet Sauvignon (that is, a wine that all other wines should be compared to) not just because it's delicious, but also because it's in more of a classic Bordeaux style, privileging finesse over brute strength. Prices start around $100; find an aged bottle to be especially dazzling.

3. Wine clubs: Lots of California star Cabernet Sauvignon wineries have wine clubs; typically, you sign up online and they send you rare bottlings a couple of times a year. Some top ones with good Internet sites: Flora Springs, Saddleback Cellars, and Duckhorn Vineyards.

4. The gift of meat: If the Cabernet lover in your life has a bunch of special bottles tucked away, give him an excuse to crack one open by giving really fancy steaks from New York City's premier meat market, Lobel's (www.lobels.com, 877-783-4512).

5. Stag's Leap Wine Cellars: Any American Cabernet lover is aware of the Judgment of Paris, the 1976 tasting during which a panel of critics judged California wines to be better than the most prestigious first growths of France. What was the red that won? Stag's Leap Wine Cellars' Cabernet Sauvignon. Get a bottle from their well-run Internet site, www.cask23.com, or a large-format bottle, and you'll make an unforgettable impression. One caveat: Don't be misled by a sound-alike winery called Stags' Leap Winery—that's something else. Though also something very good.

7

SYRAH
DARK AS NIGHT

Pronounced: Syrah (*sih-RAH*), Shiraz (*shih-RAZZ*).
Also known as: Shiraz, Côte Rôtie, Hermitage, Crozes
Hermitage, St. Joseph, Cornas

Dear Dara,

Let me tell you about my most traumatic wine mo-ment. I'm in the bar of this restaurant by my house, a place I go pretty often. I'm looking at the wines by the glass, they're all up on this chalkboard. I decide: I'll have the Shiraz. The waiter goes away. He comes back, he's like: I'm so sorry, we're out of the Shiraz, maybe you'd like the Syrah. So I say: No, I don't like Syrah— I don't even know why I said it really, I obviously know nothing. Which is proved because he says: You do know that Syrah and Shiraz are the same grape, don't you? D'oh! Ah, no, I didn't. Because you know what? I've seen those two on wine lists for years. For years! That's like learning the Who and the Rolling Stones are actually the same band. Syrah and Shiraz cannot be the same thing. I call bullshit on that. It's like they're trying to shoot themselves in the foot. It's like wine is trying to say to the world, "Don't like me." It's like some pretentious

*author who says, "I'm only going to answer interview
questions that are written without using the letter E."*
                                               —*Baffled*

I concur. You want to hear something even goofier? In
2008 this big wine company called Constellation commis-
sioned a study to find out what consumers thought about
wine. The result? 23 percent of frequent wine buyers—and
I emphasize *frequent*—core, frequent wine buyers, the main
consumer for wine, the biggest category identified in the
survey, described their wine buying experience as "overwhelming." The wine industry has a serious problem. But
don't hold that against the wine. Because Syrah, or Shiraz,
or Cornas, or whatever you want to call it (I prefer Syrah)
doesn't have a problem. It's pretty much perfect.

Really, you'll like it. Everyone likes it. Or rather, I should
say everyone likes some version of it. Some go head over
heels for Australian Shiraz, made soft, slippery, lush and
plush—like red wine's own special version of plum mocha
chocolate sauce. Meanwhile, others flip for French Syrah
from places like Cornas, which has some of that richness,
and more structure, but can layer a big animal bouquet of
tar, leather, and lovely forest floor on top of that. People who
like one tend to hate the other, at least at first. Often, people grow to like the opposite after some time with their preferred wine.

What's to Love About Syrah?

Syrah is the least confusing big red wine there is. In its important incarnations, from the Rhône and Australia, it's
usually bottled solo; in California and Washington when
single-estates bottle Syrah they typically bottle it solo too.
When it is blended, with Grenache and Mourvedre, in

southern Rhone versions or as so-called "GSM" blends it makes a textbook food-friendly table wine. It's easier to grow than most other wines, and because of that it's more reliable, at every price point, but especially at the lower price points, than every other red, and it is notably more reliable than Pinot Noir or Cabernet Sauvignon.

What's to Hate About Syrah?

Not much. The worst you could say is that it's not very fashionable—with everyone chasing fickle, impossible Pinot Noir and expensive, prestigious Cabernet Sauvignon, who cares about plain old hardworking Syrah? It's like that Tolstoy brushoff line that kicks off Anna Karenina, "All happy families are alike," and then he goes on to write about an unhappy one. Syrah is the happy family that gets ignored.

What's the Story with Syrah?

They call Syrah "the black grape" because it's really, really dark. How dark is it? It has so much pigment in its skin that sometimes you will get a glass of Syrah and hold it up to your chandelier and no light will come through.

The grape's native territory is the northern Rhône River—part of France, yes, but not the rolling, warm, olive-tree-growing France you usually think of. The Rhône actually comes out of the snowy Swiss Alps, and the northern Rhône is rockier, more mountainous, and generally a lot colder than you'd think. Of course it's not snowy year-round—they do grow wine-grapes—but it's a place where the locals drive a little north to spend weekends skiing.

The most esteemed area for Syrah in all the world is about a thousand acres of this alpine environment, on a place called the Côte Rôtie, or "roasted slope," which refers

Conversations with Bigwigs: Bob Lindquist

Bob Lindquist was one of the original Rhône Rangers, a small group of winemakers in the early 1980s who believed that the future of wine in America would depend on Rhône varietals like the red grape Syrah and the white grape Roussane. I called up Lindquist at his Santa Barbara winery, Qupé, which is both historically significant and one of the most reliable American producers of elegant French-style Syrahs.

When you look at where grapes are planted in Europe, you realize we don't really have to reinvent the wheel: The Europeans figured out a lot of things hundreds of years ago. If they wanted riper flavors in Pinot Noir they could have planted it in the Southern Rhône, but they didn't. Syrah was supposed to be the next big thing about ten times in my lifetime so far, but I'm still waiting. It's easy to grow well, and it's vigorous, it does well in a lot of different microclimates, plus winemakers like it. It delivers what Merlot promised so many years ago, a bigger, richer style of wine with balance and elegance. I say that with a certain amount of hesitation, because so many California Syrahs are over the top, and publications like Parker's [*Wine Advocate*] and the *Wine Spectator* have continued to reward that style, so people continue to make it. In blind tastings wines that are bigger and richer are going to stand out more, and because we have great weather in California we can get Syrah riper if we choose to get it riper. In Napa Cabernets the style made now bears no resemblance to the style made twenty years ago; wines used to be much more tannic and austere, now they're doing everything they can to make them plump, softer, and delicious. But you see that happening in Bordeaux now too. I guess eventually no one will even remember what they were supposed to be.

The biggest challenge in this stage of my career is the marketing—I started and the big question was how best to grow wine. How to get the vines to shut down at the right time so you can include whole clusters, if you want. Now I have that in hand, but the big question is: How to get people to try Syrah? Whenever I'm pouring Syrah at a big public event now, people come up and say, Can I taste your Shiraz? That's something I never saw coming when I started. I was looking at Europe; it never occurred to me that my big challenge was going to be getting people to switch from Yellow Tail to something more traditional. About half our production is our Central Coast Syrah. It's got a little more sweetness than my others but still has good acidity and spice; people love it, it's always winning best value awards. I'm hoping that people are moving from Yellow Tail to our Central Coast—if they are, that's a great sign for the future. There's a natural evolution that always occurs with wine. It takes a long time, but my guess is that over time the bigger jammier styles will find less favor and the more elegant styles will find more favor, just as they have in Europe.

to the vines on the steep southwestern side of the Rhône Valley that get blasted by morning sun. This slope is as much as 55 degrees in places—so steep it's hardly plantable at all. They can't get tractors, or even donkeys, on parts of it. The great wine educator Karen MacNeil writes of how some northern Rhône farmers have to form "human chains" to pass grapes down the mountains.

Needless to say, wine made by that many French hand laborers gets pretty pricey. The best easily cost $100 when they're released. But they're not even meant to be drunk when they're released; you're supposed to hold on to them for years so that their formidable tannins can settle down.

Really, formidable: Syrah from the northern Rhône is the most stereotypically masculine of all common red wines.

It's got scents of leather, tar, roasting meat, tobacco, bacon, and black pepper, and is generally described as stormy, brawny, tough, and untamable. It does everything short of ride up on a motorcycle and steal the virgin bride.

However, keep in mind that everything I just said applies to the northern face of the grape, and in this cold northern home, Syrah doesn't get very ripe. When Syrah is planted in hot places like Australia, Central California, and South

---

Chapoutier, Delas Frères, and Paul Jaboulet Ainé

When you're in the Rhône aisle you'll doubtless see the names above. They are all *négociants*—that is, large wineries that don't just grow their own fruit, but also purchase grapes or wine from other growers. This means that they put out a lot of different wines. Jaboulet, for instance, puts out dozens, from ultra-pricey Hermitage single-estate wines to southern Rhône Grenache-based wines like Châteauneuf-du-Pape to basic table wines made of Syrah, like their Le Petit Jaboulet.

Wine people who get big into collecting argue their nights away about whether *négociant* wines are as good as those of small *vignerons*—that is, grower-winemakers— such as Jean-Louis Chave, or Cornas' Jean-Luc Colombo and Domaine Clape. If you become a Rhône nut, this is something you will want to spend a couple of thousand dollars and a decade deciding for yourself.

Africa, it ripens thoroughly and so can come out quite differently. It gets jammy, plush, and sweet, and doesn't gain any of those rough and tough barnyard flavors. It's more like a fat, happy aunt than a burly motorcycle dude.

The fattest and happiest Syrahs come from Australia's Barossa Valley. If you put a northern Rhône wine next to a

Barossa Valley wine, you simply will not believe they are the same grape, but they are. One is lush, slippery, sweet, and glycerin-like in the mouth, buttery-feeling but without the taste of butter. The other is rough and tough and fierce.

All the other Syrahs of the world fall somewhere in between. In South Africa they'll tend toward a fruitier style, Australian ones not from the Barossa Valley but from Heathcoate, McLaren Vale, Margaret River, or Victoria can be lighter and fruitier, with more of a cherry or cranberry juice aspect to them. California ones will be all over the map, some fat, some tough, depending on where they're grown. Washington State ones will tend to split the difference, combining some of the meatiness of the Rhône with the lushness of Australia's Barossa Valley.

The "Holy Trinity" of Syrah

The Grape

Syrah is a very thick-skinned, almost black grape. The main problem that people have in growing it is that if they allow it to be too productive it will become watery and innocuous, and if it never gets ripe it may taste like sour water with lawn clippings and pepper.

Most of the time, Syrah is going to be all by its lonesome in a bottle labeled Syrah. That said here come the exceptions. Sometimes Syrah in its home, the northern Rhône, is blended with a bit of Viognier, a white grape that contributes aromatics. (Although on its own Viognier offers scents of orange blossom, jasmine flowers, peach, and apricot, when it's blended with overpowering Syrah it mostly just contributes the vague sense of aromatics, not actual orange blossom scents, as well as a general liveliness.) In Australia, Cabernet Sauvignon is sometimes blended into Shiraz for structure. While grapes are rarely blended into Syrah, Syrah

Petite Sirah

Think wine is confusing enough? Then consider skipping this sidebar, because it's only going to annoy you. Sometimes you'll see a wine bottle label reading Petite Sirah, Petit Sirah, Petite Syrah, or Petit Syrah. This is not Syrah! It's a whole other grape known in France as Durif, and while it originally was developed by mating Syrah with a sturdy but unremarkable grape called Peloursin, the child has very little in common with the father. Petite Sirah makes wine that's inky, peppery, highly tannic, and sort of brambly. Some people love it; many find it lacks fruit. Mostly it's used as a blending component to boost tannin, provide pepperiness, counterbalance sweetness, or extend finish in other wines such as Zinfandel, but some people really love it, so it's occasionally bottled solo as well.

itself is often used to plump up and deepen whatever a winemaker has in abundance. In the southern Rhône, Syrah is blended into light Grenache, but these wines will be called Côtes-du-Rhône, not Syrah; there's also a tradition of blending Grenache, Syrah, and tannic Mourvèdre—these are Châteauneuf-du-Pape and Gigondas in France, but called GSM or SGM blends when they come out of Australia and California. Lastly, in Australia they blend Syrah with *everything*—Cabernet Sauvignon, Merlot, you name it—and that habit has passed on to low-end American wines; nowadays you're quite likely to get a Cabernet with Syrah/Shiraz secretly blended in. Once you get familiar with the taste of Syrah, you may start detecting it in all sorts of places.

Terroir

Syrah grows wherever wine grapes can grow—South Africa, Italy, Switzerland, you name it. That said, its two most important growing sites are the northern Rhône in France and the Barossa Valley in Australia.

Northern Rhône

The northern Rhône is divided into two sections, each of which has the ultra-steep slopes that mark the alpine plunge down to the river, and each of which has its own lousy soil—lousy soil being, of course, the thing that makes concentrated fruit. The northern part, the Côte Brune, has iron-oxide-rich soils mostly made of schist; these wines are darker and more structured. The southern part of the northern Rhône is called the Côte Blonde, where they've got sandy, granite-based soil said to make wines of greater delicacy and finesse.

Barossa Valley

The Barossa is the leading wine region of Australia, and its excellent fruit is attributed to a combination of factors: the hot Mediterranean climate, dry farming (no irrigation), and deep, rocky, alluvial soils over limestone or ironstone that create good drainage. Grape vine roots in this dry, hot place have to seek perhaps fifty feet down to reach subterranean water. As is usual with grapes, the greater the suffering of the vines, the greater the final wine, and the vines in the Barossa suffer more than most.

Winemaking

Generally, what you're paying for in a more expensive Syrah or Shiraz is collectibility and hand labor: someone to drop fruit in the early part of the season so that the fruit at harvest is concentrated and good, someone to carefully hand-harvest the grapes, someone to examine every bunch and pull out the unripe or rotten grapes before they get fermented, someone to stir the crushed grapes and watch as

Conversations with Bigwigs: Stuart Bourne

Stuart Bourne is the winemaker for Australia's Barossa Valley Estate, and as such is responsible for E&E Black Pepper Shiraz, considered one of Australia's "First Growth" wines, one of the world's most prized, glossiest, richest, and thickest Shirazes. He's also the face of Australian winemaking in North America, because he comes here a lot and is charismatic, media friendly, and tireless. What does one of the kings of Australian wine want you to know about his world?

What I've really seen in the last ten years is that Australia started really making its name in the cheap and cheerful, good value critters. The critter brands really helped to demystify wine; the whole mystical concept of wine as this intimidating thing left people afraid to make a wine choice, and those critter brands with their bright labels took a lot of the wank-value out of wine and made it more approachable. But our challenge now is to get the North American market to accept that while Australian wine is a very good value, it's also a good value at the medium and luxury price point, not just the cheap price point. Just as everyone in the United States is comfortable with the difference between California state and Napa Valley, Australia does the same thing, so there's Southeast Australian appellation wine, and also individual appellation wines, like McLaren Vale. We're not just a generic amorphous blob of a country!

There is this perception in North America with Australian wine that it's all the same, no matter where you get it from it's going to all taste the same. When I hear that, I say: Wait a minute—it's a big country. We're the size of America's forty-eight states and have just as much variation in climate and topography. So the Shiraz you get from Barossa Valley is going to taste very different from the Shiraz you get down in McLaren Vale. In Barossa Valley we definitely see this depth of fruit, a great concentration of dark plums and dark cherries, and a wonderful sprinkling of pepper and spice, which has something to do with the greater variation between day and night temperatures. The soil in Barossa is fairly poor, the weather is quite dry, so it's a great region for growing grapes—if you can't grow decent fruit in the Barossa you really should find another job. The McLaren Vale Shiraz, though, it's very different, not quite as spicy, with a little more dark fruit, probably due to McLaren Vale having a maritime influence. Shiraz in general of course will tend to have some commonalities, it will always have cherries and plum with some spice and pepper, but that's nothing at all like it being generic—so don't look at all Shiraz as just being generic! There are more than two and a half thousand registered wineries in Australia, and while Australian Shiraz at the multi-appellation level [like Southeast Australia] will be good, an individual appellation [like Barossa Valley] will be better, and a single estate will be the best of all.

But whatever you think of us, don't think we're in the mountains next to Germany. I had one guy the other day ask me what it's like to live in Austria. I don't know, mate, I suspect it's bloody cold.

the juice macerates with the skins, and so on. Every time you take out a person and replace him with a machine the wine gets less expensive, but less exciting. Very old vines also make much less—but much more desirable—fruit. Younger grape vines mean less expensive wine.

Stop Reading, Start Drinking!

Now you'll learn about Syrah—what it tastes like, the different styles, the different terroirs, the different price points. You'll learn whether you're a spicy Rhône person or a silky Shiraz person. This will prove helpful in restaurants and wine shops, and will slowly turn you into the person who gets the wine list in restaurants, and when you get the wine list you'll know which one you want, and which you don't.

Syrah (and Shiraz) FIELD GUIDE

Most wine shops will have only a dozen or two Syrahs. Mostly you'll find mass-market Shirazes from Australia. Then there will be a handful of American West Coast wines. If it's a very good store, there will be a small handful of single-estate Australian Shirazes, with at least one Barossa Valley Shiraz. Hopefully there will be at least a corresponding handful of northern Rhône Côte Rôties, Hermitages, and maybe a single Cornas and St. Joseph. One of the nice things about getting to know Syrah is that it will immediately turn *you* into the wine-shop snob: "Really? Is this all you have?" you'll sniff. "I've had all these . . ." The other great thing about Syrah is that once you find the style you like, you'll probably like most everything you come across; consistency in style and quality is one of the many great virtues of Syrah.

Cheapie Australians, $10 and under

Most Australian Shirazes priced below $10 a bottle are sweet, jammy, and plush. Ubiquitous examples include Wolf Blass, Hardy's, Jacob's Creek, as well as the critter-label wines Yellowtail, Little Penguin, and Koala Creek. People who like them call them soft and approachable. People who hate them call them warm, flat Coke. You decide.

Inexpensive American, $12 and under

There are a lot of excellent under-$12 American Syrahs, especially from California's Cline Vineyards and also Washington's

Columbia Valley from vineyards like Columbia Crest, Snoqualmie, and Hogue. Inexpensive American Syrahs will ideally be peppery, bacony, lush, and well structured with abundant fruit; they're sort of a halfway point between Australian plush and French tough.

You'll sometimes see ultra-cheap American Syrah labeled Shiraz popping up in places like Trader Joe's or under fly-by-night labels. It's impossible to say what those will be like, or what's in them. Remember that only 75 percent of the wine in a bottle needs to be made of a particular grape for the label to call it by that grape name. So it's impossible to make generalizations about how these wines will be. However, chances are good they're aiming for a jammy Australian style.

That said, as a rule $4 American Syrah or Shiraz is likely to be better across the board than $4 Cabernet Sauvignon. It's an easier grape to grow, and when it goes wrong it goes wrong in more appealing ways than gone-wrong Cabernet.

Single-vineyard American, $18 and up

In the 1980s a group of California winemakers got to thinking that Cabernet Sauvignon was not the best wine California was capable of making, and that in fact the climate of the Rhône—mountainous and cold in the north, dry and Mediterranean in the south—actually had a lot more in common with California than did Bordeaux, the home of Cabernet Sauvignon. They called themselves the Rhône Rangers and got to planting the Rhône grape varieties like Syrah, Grenache (a southern Rhône staple), and Viognier.

Even today, the best American Syrahs pretty much all come from this initial group, especially those from Qupé, Bonny Doon, and Cline Cellars. What will you get in good domestic Syrah? Usually pepperiness, liveliness, muskiness, bacon, and fruit that's either red cherry or black fruit, depending on where it's grown. When things go well you should get all the power and aromatics of Syrah as filtered through American *terroir.*

Visit www.rhonerangers.org for more information on the many other American winemakers working with Syrah. But until then, if you're looking for sure things, those three wineries are as close as it gets. You can pretty much stick your hand out and grab anything labeled Syrah plus Qupé, Bonny Doon, or Cline and come back with a winner.

Tablas Creek is another great American Rhône producer; they're co-owned by southern Rhône Châteauneuf-du-Pape maker Château de Beaucastel.

Inexpensive French, $18–$50

Inexpensive French Syrah is not all that inexpensive by American standards, but there are quite a few in the $18–$50 range. The most affordable will tend to be those labeled Crozes Hermitage; look for producers like Alain Graillot, Paul Jaboulet Ainé, or M. Chapoutier. But be sure to look for the words "Crozes Hermitage" or you might end up with a Grenache blend from farther south on the Rhône.

If you are looking for Syrah, do not buy Côtes-du-Rhône; these wines are from the southern Rhône, and are usually blends with the Grenache and Mourvedre grapes. You'll occasionally see a French wine that just says Syrah on the label, but that's a pretty recent development. If you take a gamble on that you might get something Rhône-like, but it's hard to say.

These wines should be peppery, lively, and well structured and offer dimensions of black fruit, tobacco, hay, and leather (but not vanilla, because they use neutral old barrels instead of new ones).

Expensive Barossa Valley Shiraz, $20 and up

Barossa Valley Shiraz is quintessential critic bait: viscous, rich, lush, plush, and decadent. The standard bearers in this category are wines like Chris Ringland Shiraz, Torbreck's "The Factor," and E&E Black Pepper Shiraz, all cult perennial million-pointers.

Other Barossa Valley cult Shiraz stars include Grant Burge Meshach, St. Hallett Old Block, Rockford's Basket Press Shiraz, and Peter Lehmann Stonewell.

These wines will be viscous, sweet, sensual, lithe, profoundly fruity, and profoundly spiced, and will make many tasters swoon. Because their makers use plenty of new American oak, they have definite edges of vanilla and toast.

If you don't want to spend the money to get the super cult wines, there are a lot of $20–$50 Barossa Valley Shirazes that show the classic characteristics and style of the area. And by all means, if you decide you love the high-end ones, start buying the midprice Barossa Valley wines. They're made in the same style and, for those who love the cult Barossa wines, are considered great bargains.

Some bargain Barossa Valley names: Barossa Valley Estate, Barossa Valley Ebenezer, John Duval Barossa Valley Entity, Wolf Blass Barossa Gold Valley, and Yalumba the Signature Barossa.

Please note that not all of Australia makes these silk bombs: Shiraz from Southern and Central Victoria is typically more Rhône-like and spicy; McLaren Vale Shiraz is particularly balanced; Shiraz from Coonawarra and the Clare Valley is known for notes of red cherry and mint; and Shiraz from the Hunter Valley is said to be earthy and velvety. But it's the Barossa Valley that everyone talks about—it's their Napa Valley.

Expensive French, $35 and up
Hermitage, Côte Rôtie, Cornas, and St. Joseph: Hermitage is the most prestigious Syrah appellation in the world, and covers only 320 acres in its entirety, so, yeah, it's spendy. Like starting at $125 and going up from there. The Côte Rôtie is the other standard bearer and there are only five hundred acres of that, so it's nearly as costly. If you've got the bucks, try one of the "La La" wines from E. Guigal like La Landonne, La Mouline, or La Turque.

Cornas and St. Joseph are the little sisters of these regions:

less prestigious but certainly more affordable, starting at around $35. A lot of them are beautiful, especially Cornas from Domaine Clape, Jean-Luc Colombo, Thierry Allemand, or Domaine Vincent Paris. There are only 260 acres of Syrah in Cornas, so expect prices to shoot through the roof if anyone ever figures out what a good value they are. Cornas is distinct for its intensity, pronounced granite terroir, and stiff minerality. St. Joseph is cooler and makes lighter, more peppery aromatic Syrah.

Whichever one you end up with, these are the standard-bearers for Syrah, and you should taste one sometime in your life. Some more good names from Côte Rôtie include René Rostaing; for Hermitage, J. L. Chave or E. Guigal; in St. Joseph, Yves Cuilleron.

The rest of the story: Random Syrah and Shiraz from around the world, including but not limited to South Africa, New Zealand, Italy, Spain, and everywhere else

Because Syrah is so popular, and malleable, and reasonably easy to grow in sunny places there's a lot of it, and I couldn't possibly say what all those million random bottles are really like. However, I can get it out of your way by simply recommending you avoid it until you know where you stand in the French/American/Australian continuum, and what sort of Syrah you like. That said, most of the New World producers will make a jammier Syrah and not a French-style one.

Food and Syrah

Dry, peppery Rhône Syrahs are a consummate table wine, and go with most foods: Poultry, especially duck, goose, chicken, grouse, pheasant, quail, and other hearty birds; grilled or roasted beef, venison, veal, salmon, sausages, and other hearty meats. Basically anything that's not very light. Meanwhile, sweet, silky Shiraz goes better with foods with some sweetness to them—beef tenderloin with prunes in a Port reduction, say, instead of something plainer. Bottom-shelf Australian Shirazes, Yellow Tail and the other critters, are actually good pairs to dishes with both sweetness and spice: a Thai coconut milk curry, barbecued ribs, cheeseburgers, pizza, and so on.

Conversations with Bigwigs: Co Dinn

No one in America is doing more for the needs of budget-conscious, quality-obsessed American wine drinkers than Co Dinn, the winemaker at Washington State's Hogue. I called him up to find out what you need to know about Washington State, the wine lover's budget-healer.

The big difference between Washington and California is that we can't make bulk wines, box wines, or jug wines simply because of our tonnages. We can't get the amount of fruit out of a vineyard that California can, so we're forced to make better wine. Also, our winter comes in earlier and harder than theirs does—we have a door that just slams shut. So we are more likely to pick [the grapes] the second we think they're ripe, which means that with Washington you have less hangtime, and less raisiny and jammy flavors.

What makes our Bordeaux varieties so great up here is that we're in the rain shadow of the Cascades, so we get very, very little precipitation. This means that we can control almost all the water a vine gets, through drip irrigation. With your Bordeaux varieties, Merlot and Cabernet Sauvignon, a lot of the color and flavor come from the skin; with irrigation, we control how big the berries are, and a smaller berry makes more intense wine because of the ratio of skin to juice in a smaller berry. That's our secret weapon.

In Washington, because it's so cold we end up with the best of both worlds—good fruit flavors like in California but good structure like in Bordeaux, Burgundy, and the Rhône. I think Washington State will be seen as one of the top wine grape growing regions in North America; Brand California is going to keep promoting California, but we're gaining.

Conversations with Bigwigs: Randall Grahm

A larger-than-life force in American wine, Randall Grahm is an original Rhône Ranger, as well as a prophet, dreamer, and intellectual force whom most people in the world of wine regard as possibly crazy, certainly brilliant, and always worth listening to. I called him at his Santa Cruz, California, winery, Bonny Doon, to find out what he thought about Syrah these days, and I caught him in a melancholy mood.

My take on Syrah right now I should probably keep to myself. But my feeling about any wine that I make, or anyone else makes, is: If you can't do something really original and distinctive, why bother doing it? I'm so burnt out on Syrahs that are essentially generic. They're big, they're powerful, they're dark, they're heady—but they don't matter. Don't get me wrong, I have a couple Syrahs that I love, I think our Bien Nacido is truly great, and our Central Coast is very, very good, but I'm currently really over Syrah. Only in the sense that when you taste real Syrah, that is, wine from Cornas, they're so powerful, and mineral, and they have so much life force—it's depressing.

This feeds into my ongoing meditation: What can we do in California that is truly original? It doesn't make any sense to devote your life to making an imitation. Just because you can do something, should you? I'm beginning to have my doubts. So, how can I be the Rhône Ranger if I don't like Syrah?

Until recently no one in California has really thought about terroir and what it means, and taken the implications of terroir to its logical extension. Yes, the Rutherford Bench has certain characteristics, but those wines for me are generally banal, and the style of wine is so overwrought that winemaking has basically effaced terroir. Those wines are so alcoholic, so ripe, and contain so much new oak—they are so *manipulated*—that whatever terroir was there has been obliterated. You simply can't talk about *vin de terroir* that is so grossly manipulated. This is what I'm wrestling with.

And then take it a step farther: Does it make any sense to talk about a *terroir* grape that comes from irrigated grapes? I think what truly makes sense for American wine is to look at climates and soil types that are similar to what we've got, and in that case you're looking at warmer, drier areas—like Spain, Portugal, southern Italy, and southern France. So I think Grenache is a brilliant grape for California, and maybe Tempranillo, and the native grapes of Southern Italy and so on.

I think nobody can even try because you've got your marketing department saying: We need Chardonnay, Syrah, and so on. The popularity of wine, the success of wine, has been such a mixed blessing. The success of the wine business has also been its bane, and it's such an industry now, there's such self-consciousness, and a level of competitiveness that's mind-blowing.

Do more interesting wines emerge through competition? Most people are fighting over the same piece of meat, so you have a lot of people who are making the same wine, and a few people who are trying to make differentiated wines. The macro trend is always towards homogeneity, so the micro trend is towards the opposite. But anyone doing something else is basically out in the wilderness. They're out in the wilderness.

Is there even room for individual taste anymore? There was a study recently that showed there isn't prevailing taste, per se; individuals have many tastes; the same person can like something bitter or something sweet in the same meal at different times. Which means that if you like rich alcoholic wines it doesn't mean you don't like lean, crisp, low-alcohol wines. I think we do life a disservice if we try to anticipate taste.

But then it's really hard to express to a consumer what it is you're doing if you're trying to do something original, because anything original unavoidably becomes something expensive, and for expensive wines the desired message never is that it expresses an individual terroir. The message the marketing department wants to hear, the message people want to read is: This wine is expensive, and Parker gave it a 97.

So I'm just this mixed-up madman. Great wines are profoundly stimulating, and the challenge to make them is enormous. The challenge to drink great wines is great too. I think when you are confronted with a truly great wine you should ask yourself: Am I morally up to consuming this wine? Some great Burgundies are so rare, they make maybe fifty or a hundred cases a year, and if you're privileged enough to drink a bottle or a glass of it, doesn't privilege walk hand in hand with responsibility? You should ask yourself: What am I called upon to do here? I think the answer is, your responsibility is to deeply appreciate it, to pay profound attention to it. I don't think Parker asks himself that question, but it would be nice if he did. I think we should approach wine like the Native Americans approached food: To eat is to literally take the spirit of what you are eating inside of you. When you drink a great wine you want to take the spirit of the wine inside you and deeply incorporate it inside you, and into your *self.*

Tasting Syrah
Step by Step

1. A Brief Road Map to Our Upcoming Syrah Road Trip

It's going to take about five Syrahs/Shirazes to get a sense of what the grape and the wine really taste like. Your first task will be to try one of those ever-present sweet, jammy bottom-shelf Shirazes like Yellow Tail or Wolf Blass. Why? To get a sense of the ripe fruit of Syrah, and so that when you run into that wine in the future you'll know what about it is and is not Syrah-like. You'll compare that to a single-vineyard America Syrah, which will give you a dryer, more elegant expression, you'll see what the two wines have in common and what they don't. Next you'll move on to a Washington State Syrah, which will give you another face of the grape, this one aromatic but not sweet. After this you'll move on to the two highest expressions of the grape, one from the Barossa Valley and another from the place where it all began, the northern Rhône. The cumulative effect of these pairings will give you an unshakable sense of what Syrah tastes like, and whether you like it. You can either taste these five wines in a party with your friends, which makes it fun, spreads out the expense among your buddies, and contributes more voices; or you can do the tasting solo or with a friend, splitting the wines into two groups and tasting them on separate nights.

Notes on Tasting Syrah Solo or in Pairs

Even though Australian Syrah makes a good "cocktail" wine—that is, a wine suitable for drinking on its own—you'll learn more about Syrah generally and understand it better if you have some food with it, especially with the

French versions, which are meant as table wines. A take-
out burger or even a pizza (with sausage!) will do if you're
not a cook; if you are a cook, congratulations, you are getting into some fun dinner party territory. See the party instructions below for more ideas.

Notes on Tasting Syrah by Party

A dinner party is the ideal way to taste Syrah because the
French versions, and some American ones, are such high-
acid, food-friendly wines that just trying them cocktail-
party style may not showcase how magnificent they can be.
So, fire up the grill! Nothing goes better with Syrah than
grilled or wood-roasted meat: Lamb, beef, bison, elk, or
even chicken cooked over coals are dream Syrah pairings
because of the like-goes-with-like theory: Good Syrah is
gamy, a little bitter, and just a bit smoky, and the char of
the grill adds a bitterness and smoke to meat that put it in
utter harmony with Syrah. If you don't want to grill, a pot
of cassoulet, or some cassoulet-like stew, is good for big
groups; make it in advance and serve, after your initial
tasting, in mugs for people to eat as they wander and talk.
Vegetarians should think about rich, smoky bean stews.
Fish eaters could do roast salmon, swordfish, or ahi tuna.
Sweeter Australian Shirazes go well with desserts, especially chocolate things that aren't too rich, like a chocolate
Bundt cake.

2. Shopping

Whether you're alone or having a party, your first task is to
buy your Syrahs and Shirazes. You'll need five bottles, selected from the field guide above. The names provided here
are simply suggestions to help you in your shopping; whatever your local wine shop has should be fine. Just try to

match the categories, not the names. You want to end up with:

1. An inexpensive Australian jammy bottom-shelf Shiraz, like Wolf Blass or Yellow Tail. Under $12.
2. A single-vineyard American Syrah, like Bonny Doon's Le Pousseur or Qupé's Bien Nacido vineyard. $15–$30.
3. A Washington State Syrah like Hogue's Genesis. $10–$15.
4. A real French Syrah, from Hermitage, Côte Rôtie, Crozes-Hermitage, Cornas, or St. Joseph. Anything from those appellations will do; reliable names include E. Guigal, Domaine Clape, Jean-Luc Colombo, Thierry Allemand, J. L. Chave, Yves Cuilleron, or Domaine Vincent Paris. $40–$120.
5. A single-vineyard Barossa Valley Shiraz, such as E&E Black Pepper Shiraz, Barossa Valley Estate (BVE) Barossa Valley Ebenezer, John Duval Barossa Valley Entity, Wolf Blass Barossa Gold Valley Gold Label, or Yalumba the Signature Barossa. $20–$100.

3. Planning and Thinking About Tasting

Gather your wineglasses, dump bucket, and tasting markers. Make your life easier: Putting some of the following items in wineglasses will make comparing your various Syrahs and Shirazes much clearer. Try peppercorns in one wineglass, plums or plum jam in another, blackberries or blackberry jam in a third, and smoked sea salt, the tiniest dab of liquid smoke, or crumbled bacon in another.

Tasting Markers

Keep the following list handy so you can glance at it while you're tasting—it will help you name fragrances that seem just out of reach.

Above all		
Black pepper	Black raspberries or black raspberry jam	Chocolate or cocoa
White pepper		Coffee
Plums	Blackberries or blackberry jam	Black licorice
Smoke		Tobacco
Roasted meat (or smoked meat, like bacon)	Minerals	Boysenberry
	Leather	Iron
	Tar	Blood

Possible, but less likely		
Vanilla	Mint	Violets
Anise	Eucalyptus	Burnt rubber

4. Cool Things Off

Get your wine to cellar temperature! See page 10 for information on why. For Syrah that's around 55 degrees.

5. Pull the Corks!

6. Taste Your First Wine

Your basic Australian bottom-shelf Syrah is here to tell you what Syrah—or rather, Shiraz—is like when it gets fully ripe, as it does here. Pour an inch or so into each guest's wineglass and swirl. Sniff. Taste. Pass around your tasting markers if you've got them. Questions to consider: Pepper? Black pepper, white pepper, any pepper? Pepper is supposed to be one of the classic scents of Syrah. If not pepper: Plums? Do any of the other scents from the long list jump out at you? Be especially on the lookout for chocolate. Everyone likes chocolate. Moreover: Does the wine seem sweet, or balanced? Do you like it?

7. Taste Your Second Wine

We're on to the second wine, the single-vineyard American Syrah. Pour about an inch into a wineglass for each guest. Swirl. Sniff. Taste. It should be very different from the first wine: Drier, more structured, better acidity, more of a pull between different elements in the wine that make it feel taut and lively. Does any of that apply?

Time to move on. Make way for your next wine. If you feel as if you didn't totally get this wine, don't sweat it—you can always come back and try things again once the formal part of the tasting is done.

8. Taste Your Washington State Syrah

The point of this wine is to get another taste of Syrah, from another place. Washington State Syrah is good because the growing region is cold, like France, but sunny, like Australia. Pour each guest an inch of wine. Swirl. Sniff. Taste. How do you like it?

Questions to consider: Pepper? Plums? Blackberries? Does it seem well balanced? Does anything poke out and make it seem out of whack? Some winemakers talk about the goal of winemaking as getting rid of sharp elbows; if you notice any sharp elbows, that's bad. Tasted any? How is it different from the first two? More fruity? Less? More tannic? Less? Is it better knit? Pass the tasting markers if you've got them; do they help you notice anything? Consult your long list of tasting markers: Anything in this wine jump out at you?

Most important: How do you like it?

(Note to solo tasters, or those in tasting in pairs: You are now going to take a break. Pick up the tasting of the next two wines as soon as convenient.)

9. Tasting the Big Guns: The Rhône

Now we're moving into serious territory. Pour an inch of your Rhône Syrah into each of your guests' glasses. Swirl. Sniff. Taste. Tell people that despite the label reading Cornas or what have you, it's really Syrah. Tell them how much you had to shell out, and whether the people in the wine store treated you nicer because you were getting such an expensive bottle. Pass around your tasting markers. This wine should smell like bacon, smoke, pepper, leather, tobacco, and tar. Does it? More important: How do you like it? Taste it with some food. Does it improve the food? Does the food improve the wine?

10. Tasting the Big Guns: Barossa Valley Shiraz

Finally, pour your expensive Australian Barossa Valley Shiraz. Swirl. Sniff. Taste.

Welcome to the wine that remade wine in its time! Many people say that this is the style of wine that has inspired a generation of winemakers to craft "fruit bombs" in an effort to win 100-point scores and command corresponding high prices.

Questions to ask yourself: Plums? Blackberries? Chocolate? Pepper? Is this wine more like your first Yellow Tail–style wine, or more like the Cornas? And how do you like it? Do you feel that it has the structure and acidity to support the fruit?

What's your favorite of the tasting? At this point your group should neatly cleave into pro-French and pro-Australian camps, with a lot of people deciding they would buy the Washington State or domestic single-vineyard wines because they offer the taste people like at a price they prefer.

And that's it! Many people will try Syrah and move on to explore other grapes, and others never will and will simply stay with Syrah forever, like someone who went to a Grateful Dead concert and never came home. Because Syrah, be it silky or bold, has a way of seducing.

THE TAKEAWAY

Wine critics constantly talk about New World versus Old World wines, and nowhere is this contrast more vivid than in comparing Syrah from France's Côte Rôtie to the exact same grape grown in the Barossa Valley. You can, if you wish, extrapolate your taste from this: If you liked the Australian wine, you'll likely prefer American Cabernet Sauvignon to French Bordeaux, but if you flipped over the Côte Rôtie Syrah you're probably going to be a Burgundy person and not an Oregon Pinot Noir person. Isn't that pleasant? You learned what you think about Syrah and found out where you fall in the New World / Old World split as well.

Five-second cheat sheet for people who didn't read the chapter and are reading this on their iPhones in a farm-to-table bistro while they wait for a table

Syrah (*sih-RAH*) is the exact same grape as Shiraz (*shih-RAZZ,* rhymes with pizazz); and wherever you plant the stuff it grows inky black grapes that make inky black wine.

However, when it grows up in the northern Rhône, not too far from the French Alps, Syrah becomes rough, rugged, peppery, masculine, bacony, and intense, but when it grows in the dry, hot Barossa Valley in Australia it achieves another kind of intensity, a plush, lush, hedonistic, velvety, ripe one. All the other Syrahs on earth tend to fall between those two poles: California winemakers typically make peppery wines with good acid and structure, Washington State Syrahs usually develop more complex aromatics and a bit more silk because of their long days. No matter where you get your Syrah, though, it's the most reliable of red wines. If you happen to love Syrah your wine life is very easy because you have a much higher probability of finding a good wine than just about any other wine consumer. French Syrah, which goes by Côte Rôtie, Cornas, or St. Joseph, is a food-friendly wine that goes with every single meat on earth, from pheasant to beef. Australian Shiraz is sweeter and so goes best with sweet things—it's a great pair for cheeseburgers, or duck with cherries.

Knock-Their-Socks-Off
Gifts for Syrah Lovers

Because Syrah lovers fall into such different camps, and because the silky Aussie lovers and the smoky Rhone lovers often see each other's drinks as poisonous, I'm dividing the list into Barossa Valley and Other. If you don't know which one your Syrah-lover loves, skip it and buy them one of those grain-silo-sized cans of cheese popcorn—it's a safer bet.

Silky Aussie Shiraz Gifts
1. Penfolds Grange: Generally regarded as Australia's greatest wine, Penfolds Grange is hard to come by and expensive, and much of the stuff available on the Internet is probably a fraud.

They use Cabernet Sauvignon in the mix in many years, so it's not technically a Shiraz. No matter. If you could get a real bottle for the Aussie Shiraz lover in your life, they'd remember you forever and tell all their friends about you.

2. E&E Black Pepper Shiraz: A perennial Wine Spectator 90-something-pointer, this is a beautiful wine, and imported in big enough quantities that it is widely available.

3. Grant Burge Meshach: Another Barossa Valley cult star, this meaty, smoky Shiraz is not too hard to find in the United States. It's darker than midnight and comes from vines that are nearly a hundred years old, reflecting the Barossa Valley's happy avoidance many years ago of a worldwide vine blight called phylloxera.

4. Torbreck Barossa Valley: A tiny-production, boutique winery that uses all the latest Napa Valley hands-on, technology-off winemaking methods to produce painstakingly handcrafted Barossa Valley wine. They make many excellent Shirazes, including Run Rig, The Factor, and The Laird.

5. Greenock Creek Roennfeldt Road Shiraz: Famed critic Robert Parker has given this wine a perfect 100-point score three times, and has described it as "one of the greatest Shirazes I have ever tasted." If that's not good enough for the Shiraz lover in your life, nothing ever will be.

Rhône-style Syrah Gifts

1. E. Guigal's single-vineyard Côte Rôtie: La Mouline, La Landonne, and La Turque. These all-Syrah wines are released at around $400 each in the States and quickly get marked up on the resale market. They're the top of the top of the heap of Rhône Syrah, and a gift any Rhône nut would swoon over. How swoony are they? Rhône lovers call them the "La La wines," as in, "La la la, I can't hear you tell me this is a crazy price, I'm going to do what I'm going to do."

   For those not lucky or deep-pocketed enough to have tasted the La La wines, Guigal's Côte Rôtie Château d'Ampuis is a more affordable tippity-top-shelf option. It usually costs less than $150 on release and is pretty widely available.

2. Domaine Jean-Louis Chave Hermitage: This ancient family-owned estate has been producing wine since before the Americas were discovered. Seriously, this same family has been growing wine on this land since 1481. Not a typo: the year 1481. Needless to say, a product that has had a steady market through all the European wars, all the world wars, all the Depressions, and the birth, death, and rebirth of New Kids on the Block is pretty darn good. It's also a nice gift for people celebrating the birth of a baby, as it is supposed to be cellared for a good ten years before you open it, and could last a hundred.

3. Jean-Luc Colombo: This rebel winemaker from Cornas is credited with turning a once-sleepy, though well-respected, wine region into the new hot thing. His most sought-after wines are his Cornas wines Terres Brûlées, Les Ruchets, and La Louvée.

4. Michel Chapoutier La Mordorée, Les Bécasses, or any of the Hermitages: Chapoutier is one of the great wineries of the Rhône, and the firm controls about a quarter of all the prime land there. Their most prestigious bottlings, like the Les Bécasses, are worldwide standard-bearers for Syrah.

5. Le Cheval Fou: Translated as "Crazy Horse," this is the first ever American-made real Hermitage wine. It's the product of a partnership between a few Americans, including cult winemaker Heidi Peterson Barrett (Screaming Eagle) and local French legend Michel Chapoutier. It gets released at $125 and would be a feather in the cap of anyone who loves Syrah and reads *Wine Spectator* enough to care about Heidi Peterson Barrett.

8

SANGIOVESE

PREFERRED BY PIZZA PREPARERS
AND PRINCES

Pronounced: *san-zho-VAY-zeh.* Also known as: Chi-
anti, Chianti Classico, Chianti Riserva, Chianti Su-
periore, Chianti Rufina, Sangioveto, Carmignano,
Morellino di Scansano, Super Tuscan, Brunello,
Brunello di Montalcino, Prugnolo, Vino Nobile di
Montepulciano

Dear Dara,

Italian wines are a mystery wrapped in an enigma
wrapped in a restaurant. I mean, I certainly get why
Italian restaurants have Italian wine lists, but it all
looks like Greek to me. Should I even bother?

—Baffled

Hell, yes, you should bother! Italy is one of the world's
greatest wine nations, and the riches that await anyone
who falls in love with Italian wine are considerable. That
said, you have to be smart, even ruthless, about starting
your life in Italian wine, because otherwise you'll drown.

Italy has more wine, more different grapes, more different wine styles than anywhere else on earth. About four
thousand years ago when the ancient Greeks sailed their
ancient boats over to ancient Italy they took a gander

around and immediately dubbed it Oenotria, or Land of Wine. I recommend that you think of it that way, too, and, at first, don't get too hung up in the details.

Because the details will just kill you. The place has twenty official wine regions (like American states, if all the states were the size of Rhode Island) and at least five hundred varietals of grape under cultivation. Winemakers are allowed to mention a mere 350 on labels. In her estimable *Wine Bible,* Karen MacNeil says there are currently 900,000 registered vineyards, any of which could potentially slap their name on a bottle.

Worse, the infinitely confusing Italian wine bureaucracy has four alphabet-soup designations of quality—VDT, IGT, DOC, and DOCG—which are supposed to tell you something, but some winemakers skip them, and a lot of them are meaningless. Want to be an Italian wine authority? Start today, and in twenty years you'll understand what you've bitten off. Which of course is why some very brilliant and interesting people devote their lives to Italian wine: it's deep, rich, endless.

It's the sort of deep, rich, endless joy that can make you gouge your eyes out with dry spaghetti, if you know what I mean. My advice? Ignore every other wine authority on the planet—high-end Italian reds like Barolo and Barbera are nothing you need to know about until you already have long experience with Italian reds. Ditto for the high-end whites from the top of the boot, from Piedmont and the Tre Venezie.

Instead, start with Sangiovese, the great grape of Tuscany, and an increasingly popular varietal to plant on American soil. If you learn this one Italian red grape, you'll be able to make sense of Italian wine lists, talk to Italian restaurant sommeliers, and generally get around the world of Italian wine pretty competently.

What's to Love About Sangiovese?

Sangiovese makes really delicious wine, and, unlike lots of other varietals, it does this both at the high end and low end of things—it makes great $10 wines to join you and your pizza on your couch, and great $90 wines for when you and Giorgio Armani want to go out and celebrate your mutual successes. What's not to like? It's the perfect place to start with Italian wines if you want to enjoy life.

What's to Hate About Sangiovese?

It doesn't have the snob appeal of the most expensive, most collectible Italian wines, like Barolo and Barbera, and it doesn't confer the punk-rock, I-know-more-than-you bragging rights of obscure grapes from the heel and toe of the boot, so Sangiovese is not going to inoculate you from all attack by Italian wine nerds. But screw 'em. It's still delicious.

What's the Story with Sangiovese?

Americans love Tuscany. What do we love about it? Absolutely everything: The rolling hills, the olive groves, the picturesque vineyards, the terra cotta roofs, the bread, the tomatoes, the olives, the wine. We love it so much that in off hours we are given to imagining ourselves there, sitting at a big outdoor table full of people who like us, laughing and downing carafes of wine. In fact, we love it too much, and our love goes in crazy directions, resulting in a whole Tuscany casino in Las Vegas, which is home of Tuscany Gardens, the self-proclaimed "restaurant with a touch of class." Sigh. Speaking of class, Infiniti cars can be ordered in Tuscan Pearl. And if that's not classy enough for you, "Tuscan" is currently one of the leading design styles for bathrooms.

And let's not even consider Arby's *and* Subway's Tuscan chicken sandwiches and Olive Garden, which maintains a culinary academy in, yes, Tuscany.

Isn't it embarrassing? However, the good news is that if you learn to truly respect and appreciate Tuscan wine, the Italians will forgive you the sins of your countrymen. So here we go.

Sangiovese: The name of the main red grape of Tuscany, and in fact of everywhere in Italy outside the cold north, actually means "the blood of Jove," and is so named because it harks back to Italy's ancient pre-Christian past of Jove worshipping. Italy's old! Now, in the tradition of Europe, the Italians don't traditionally call their wines Sangiovese, they call them something else, after the regions where they grow, so while Sangiovese is the grape, the wines are Chianti (*kee-AHN-tee*), Brunello di Montalcino (called Brunello), and Vino Nobile di Montepulciano.

In addition to being the grape of those ancient and classic wines, Sangiovese is also a primary component of the very popular, sometimes expensive "Super Tuscans," and increasingly shows up as a varietal label on Italian wines. Finally, Sangiovese, because it doesn't need a lot of water to grow and is delicious, has been planted up and down the American West Coast, where it's usually called a "Cal-Ital" (pronounced *cal-ee-tal*), even if it comes from Oregon or Washington.

Why does it make up the basis for so many wines? Because it's *tasty tasty tasty*. It's tasty in its profound, complex versions, and it's tasty in its juicy budget versions, which can be like some sort of cherry-strawberry juice shot through with a bit of smoke and cocoa. These uncomplicated versions can be not just quaffable, which is a word people use to connote "easy drinking" (unlike a "hard-to-drink" very tannic complicated French wine that requires your full attention), but it's full-on gulpable, like strawberry lemonade on a hot day. When critics put down uncomplicated Chianti they'll say it's "grapey," but I actually enjoy the way the down-on-the-farm Sangioveses seem to have something in common with grapes: I always picture them coming from a mixed-use family farm, the kind that has a flock of chickens and a single milk cow and a couple of rows of vines growing near the tomato plot. I know in my brain that this is absurd, and that Italian vine growers live in the twenty-first century with the rest of us, with chickens flocking in poultry factories, not backyards, but my heart tastes what it tastes, if you know what I mean. You know, I think I'll redo my bathroom into something classy . . .

Where was I? Right. I also love how Sangiovese is such a natural part of Italian food. Pasta and pizza, eggplants and cheese, salami and olives all simply taste better in the company of Sangiovese, and Sangiovese tastes better in the company of food. The technical reason for this has to do with the fact that Sangiovese is high in acid—and by the same logic that a squirt of lemon improves a crabcake, a squirt of acid, in the form of a high-acid wine like Sangiovese, improves everything you eat it with.

Generally, I find that most people who like Sangiovese or other non-northern Italian wines tend to explain their liking it in terms of the Italian lifestyle, the way that food and wine there are so seamlessly integrated, and if you yourself are prone to thoughts like "Wine *is* food!" then welcome home, you have found your varietal. You are a Sangiovese/Chianti/Brunello lover.

So why does Sangiovese have all those names? Short answer: to drive you nuts. Real answer: Italy is mainly what Americans would think of as mountain foothills. For thousands of years, transportation was as far as you, or you and your donkey, could walk, and so the difference between your

Conversations with Bigwigs: Joseph Bastianich

Mario Batali may be the famous face of Italian food right now, but he has a publicity-shy counterpart when it comes to Italian wine—that's Joseph Bastianich, Batali's partner in and director of wine service for Babbo Ristorante e Enoteca, Lupa Osteria Romana, Esca, Casa Mono, Bar Jamón, Otto Enoteca Pizzeria, and Del Posto.

But that's not all! Bastianich is also a partner in New York City's greatest Italian wine shop, Italian Wine Merchants. And that's not all! He wrote the book on Italian wine in America. It's called Vino Italiano: The Regional Wines of Italy. *Also, he's Lidia Bastianich's kid and pops up on her TV shows. And he makes wine in Italy, and blogs about it. I called him up to ask him what someone new to wine should do once they have gotten a handle on Sangiovese.*

What you have to understand is that wine is food and food is wine in Italy. The culture of the Italian table is such that you don't have one without the other. Wine is everywhere in Italy; if you want to understand it, just decide you're going to understand it. You can conquer Italy by understanding twenty areas. You have to study the geography and the topography of all of them, and learn the two most important varietals in each region. Taste as much as you can. It can seem complicated, but it isn't. You probably already know 20 cocktails, it's not that hard.

hill and the world six hills away was big. Therefore the difference between the wine of your hill and the world six hills away was big. And that's where all the names came from.

Morellino di Scansano, for instance, is what the people on one particular hill called their Sangiovese for thousands of years, and so they're going to keep on calling it that. Wine critics can go on about the different "clones" of Sangiovese—

that is, spontaneous mutations in the field that allow some particular plant to thrive in its particular soil, light, or moisture conditions—but worrying about these "clones" is distracting and useless. All Sangioveses are more similar than they are different, and the various end qualities of the wine, say, a dark concentrated one versus a light vapid one, often have as much to do with the winemaking as the clone.

What you really need to know about Sangiovese is this: It's the most planted, most popular red in Italy, and it is significantly represented on 99 percent of the world's Italian wine lists. Knowing Sangiovese is the same as having a single semester of Italian under your belt: if you know Sangiovese, you know enough to get around.

The "Holy Trinity" of Sangiovese

The Grape

A red grape used to make still red wine, Sangiovese has a thin skin and needs a long time to get fully ripe, which leads to big alcoholic wines in warm years, and thin wines in cool years. Because of that thin skin, where all the coloring pigments and most of the grape tannins are, Sangiovese sometimes needs additional grapes to deepen the color, which is where the blending partners come in.

Traditionally Sangiovese has had quite a few blending partners, including Trebbiano, an easy-to-grow white wine (called Ugni Blanc in France) prized mainly for its ability to make grape growers' lives easier. Some Chianti and other producers still use Trebbiano when the Sangiovese of the vintage is big and alcoholic, to give it a lighter, more food-friendly quality. However, just as many winemakers today blend in traditional Bordeaux varietals like Merlot and Cabernet Sauvignon to give the wine greater tannin, color, depth, and power. For the sake of historical accuracy it may be helpful for you to know that, in addition to Trebbiano, the traditional Chianti blending partners are Canaiolo (to add sweetness and thus alcoholic strength), Malvasia Nera (for color and perfume), Mammolo (for perfume, especially of violets) and Colorino (for, yes, color).

Terroir

Sangiovese's main *terroir* is, of course, the classified areas in Tuscany that were first identified as superior Sangiovese territory in the thirteenth century. The most important regions are today called Brunello, Rosso di Montalcino, Chianti Classico, and Chianti Rufina. The best vineyards are generally thought to be those at high elevations with clay and limestone soils where grapes can't suck up too much water. The yields of these vineyards are also controlled by Italian wine laws. Lower yields result in more concentrated, and thus better, fruit.

Winemaking

Sangiovese responds well to oak, so one of the choices a winemaker makes is how long to age the wine, and in what sort of oak. When you see "Riserva" on a Chianti bottle it means the grapes were the best that were harvested, and so were treated to a long stay in oak.

Stop Reading, Start Drinking!

Sangiovese in all its forms—Chianti, Super Tuscan, Brunello, and so on—is a wine arranged in a more predictable stairstep of ascending quality than any other wine on earth. By doing this tasting you will learn three invaluable things. One, you'll learn whether you like Sangiovese, Chianti, and Brunello, which will help you forevermore. Two, you'll learn how to use Italian wine laws, which seem arcane and peculiar to American eyes until you taste the difference between Chianti and Chianti Riserva, at which point you will say: *Hey, it's totally worth the extra eight bucks for the Riserva!* Or: *Hey, it's totally not worth the extra eight bucks for the Riserva!* Third and finally, you'll see what people mean when they talk about wine as a food, or as an inextricable part of the Italian table, because Sangiovese just makes food so much more delicious than it is on its own.

Sangiovese FIELD GUIDE

A good wine shop should have a dozen Sangioveses. They'll probably have a single run of Chianti, Chianti Classico, and Chianti Classico Riserva from a big producer like Antinori, and a couple of other Chiantis, a couple of Cal-Ital Sangioveses, and maybe one or two Super Tuscans and Brunellos. However, if you live in a smaller city, finding the "good wine shop" for Italian wines might be tricky. Here's the way to do it: The Brunello is going to be the hardest one; call around to your likely liquor stores before you leave the house, asking if they have a Brunello. Find the Brunello, and that will also be the store where the rest of the Sangioveses are. Read the section below for more exhaustive detail on what you're looking at when you're looking at all those bottles in the wine shop.

Plain old Sangiovese, $7 and up

You'll occasionally see an Italian wine labeled "Sangiovese"; these tend to be wines that have labels specifically designed for the American market, and will be co-op products or private label wines for big American chains like Trader Joe's. They'll usually be fruity and innocuous.

Chianti, $10 and up

There are a lot of different labels reading Chianti Something in the wine shop. What's the deal? Since the Middle Ages the area in the high hills between Florence and Siena has been known as the Chianti Mountains. Today Chianti refers to any Sangiovese-based wine from that pretty big area of mountains. The least prestigious and expensive Chiantis are the just plain Chiantis—Chianti with no second name. Chianti Something is always supposed to be a little better than plain old Chianti.

What's the difference between Sangiovese and Chianti? A matter of degree: A Chianti must contain at least 80 percent Sangiovese. (Remember, a California or Australian bottle labeled, say, Pinot Noir need only be 75 percent Pinot Noir, so the 80 percent requirement is meaningful.) Chianti may contain other grapes, like the helpfully acidic white Trebbiano, but it doesn't *have* to have them. A lot of good Chiantis are wholly Sangiovese. So if you just see the word "Chianti" on a wine label, it means mostly or entirely Sangiovese, from a pretty big region.

Cal-Ital and other American Sangioveses, $10 and up

What do you call Sangiovese grown in California? Cal-Ital. What do you call Sangiovese grown in Washington State? Cal-Ital or Sangiovese, depending on your mood. Sangiovese grown in the United States has a middling reputation, which probably has to do with the fact that the vines tend to produce exuberantly in their early years in a sort of fit of toddler energy, though what they produce isn't too great.

However, as lackluster as the reputation for American Sangiovese is, I've personally found that it's often both underrated and underpriced. I'd recommend it to anyone seeking a red wine bargain. Of course, American Sangiovese's great problem is that basic Chianti is also both good and cheap, but has name recognition.

Top California producers: Seghesio, Atlas Peak, Valley of the Moon, Unti Vineyards, Ferrari-Carano, Monte-Volpe, Rutherford Grove, Benessere Vineyards, Chariot, Bonny Doon, Eberle Winery,

Muscardini Cellars, Pietra Santa Winery, Flora Springs (including a remarkable rosé made of Sangiovese), Coturri, Silverado Vineyards, Swanson Vineyards, Sterling Vineyards, Palmina, Uvaggio, Vino Noceto, and Altamura.

Leonetti Cellars, Maryhill, Stella Fino, and Naked Winery in Washington State and Eola Cellars in Oregon also make Sangiovese.

If you fall in love with Cal-Ital wines, you can keep up with whatever's going on in the group through cal-italia.org; they also post a lot of recipes designed to go with particular wine varietals.

Chianti Classico, $15 and up

Chianti plus prestige equals Chianti Classico. Chianti Classico is from a small, highly esteemed region inside the bigger Chianti region. In addition to being from better sites, by law these wines must come from fields with smaller yields and are, broadly speaking, made with more care than basic Chianti. You'll spend more for Chianti Classico, but it will usually be worth it.

Chianti producers who want to stand out from the regular Chianti pack but aren't in the Classico area can get government approval to call themselves Chianti Superiore, which means, roughly, "as good as Chianti Classico, darn it!" As of this writing very few wineries had taken this option; you may well never see one.

Chianti Riserva, $15 and up

Chianti plus time equals Chianti Riserva. Stick your Chianti in a barrel for thirty-eight months instead of the standard four to twelve months and you've got Chianti Riserva. Stick your Chianti Classico or Chianti Superiore in a barrel for two years plus another three months in bottle, and you get Chianti Classico Riserva or Chianti Superiore Riserva.

Super Tuscan, $25 and up

Here's an anecdote the libertarians in the crowd will appreciate. In the old days, by law, Chianti had to include both Sangiovese and some number of other grapes, such as the white grape Trebbiano. Some were basically included as a sort of farm support program, because there were a lot of people growing, say, Trebbiano, and they wanted a guaranteed market for their product. Again, by law, non-Italian wine varieties, like Cabernet Sauvignon, were forbidden.

This pissed off Italian winemakers who wanted to make excellent wine. They felt their wine was being hamstrung by these antiquated laws. So they told the government to jump in a lake and started making wine called Super Tuscan. It was Tuscan because it was Sangiovese, and Super because it was considered better than Chianti. Most Super Tuscan wine was upwards of 80 percent Sangiovese (often 100 percent), and the balance could be French grapes like Cabernet Sauvignon or Merlot.

These wines commanded cult superstar prices, and so eventually the government changed its laws and now Chianti can contain up to 20 percent of whatever the Chianti maker wants to include, including varietals like Cabernet Sauvignon. Today the decision to call your Sangiovese-based wine a Super Tuscan is largely a marketing one, though some Super Tuscans are made with 100 percent French varietals.

Since Super Tuscans are geared toward the American or international market, they'll tend to say what they are on the label. The most famous Sangiovese-based Super Tuscans are Antinori's Tignanello (*tin-ya-nell-o*), Fontodi's Flaccianello, Felsina's Fontalloro, and La Brancaia's Il Blu. Half-Sangioveses include Argiano's Solengo and Ornellaia's La Volte.

All the Super Tuscans tend to have trademarked proprietary names because when they were born their options were either to be called Chianti or "table wine" and they wanted a third path. Later they had a brand to sustain, and now it's just how Super Tuscans are done.

Vino Nobile di Montepulciano, $15 and up

No one can remember the name of this one. Use this to your advantage: Vino Nobile is Tuscan Sangiovese at half the price of its Tuscan siblings. This isn't a Sangiovese to seek out for your first tasting, but one to know about as you explore the grape. It tends to be warmer, fruitier, and richer than Chianti because it's grown in a warmer place. Because of this it goes particularly well with tomato-based dishes and even spicy foods from other cuisines, like Szechuan or Mexican.

Carmignano, Morellino di Scansano, and Sangioveto, $20 and up

Also Nielluccio, Sanvicetro, Morellino, Torgiano, and San Gioveto. These are all just more Sangioveses you may run into, but probably won't. There are also some more from Umbria and the Marches. I put them in here so that wine nerds can't email one another about how I don't know anything about Sangiovese because I didn't mention Morellino di Scansano. If you're not one of those, feel free to spend a few moments thinking about how ridiculous it is that Europeans want to sell us a product yet refuse to do the most elementary translating on the label.

Brunello di Montalcino, popularly just called Brunello, $50 and up

Considered the most wonderful possible expression of Sangiovese, Brunello fetches the sort of prices that usually only attend to French superstars. Top bottles easily rank with Château Margaux and other goods you only buy if you have a yacht.

Why do people love Brunello? Because it's a sort of super-Chianti, warmer, richer, more concentrated, more powerful. Classically it should be lush, rich, well structured, resonant, and chocolaty, with flavors of sour cherry and wood smoke. It always ages, and it goes wonderfully with food; it's arguably the world's greatest wine to have with dinner.

Good bottles cost upwards of $50. If you see a $20-something bottle, skip it, as there's bound to be something wrong with it. By law all Brunello is 100 percent Sangiovese, though some producers call their Sangiovese by other names, like Sangiovese Grosso. Also by law it can't be released until years after harvest, which partly accounts for the price. But mostly it's pricey because of all the passionate collectors.

Top names: Biondi Santi, Case Basse di Soldera, Col d'Orcia, Cerbaiona, Il Poggione, Fattoria dei Barbi, Emilio Costanti, La Poderina, Poggio di Sotto, Ciacci Piccolomini d'Aragona, Il Palazzone, Lisini, Uccelliera, Camigliano, Il Greppone Mazzi, Fanti, Casanova di Neri, Caparzo, Castelgiocondo, Mastrojanni, Tenuta di Sesta, Antinori, Frescobaldi, Argiano, Ruffino, and Castello Banfi.

If you can't find a decent Brunello in a wine shop near you, try italianwinemerchant.com, New York City's excellent Italian Wine Merchants, or Vino Italian Wine and Spirits, vinosite.com. Both offer impeccable Brunellos.

Food and Sangiovese

Because of its mouthwatering acidity, Sangiovese is considered not just a great food wine, but exclusively a food wine. No one ever mills around a patio watching the sunset with a big glass of Chianti. Or they shouldn't, unless there's a buffet present, because it's a wasted opportunity. While hunger may be the best seasoning, Sangiovese is a runner-up: Eat a bite of pizza, lasagna, cheese, olives, bread, or what have you, add a sip of Chianti—whammo! Your food is suddenly 20 percent better.

Speaking of pizza, Sangiovese is the ultimate pair for all things with tomato sauce: pizza, pasta, you name it. The acidity of the wine harmonizes with the tomatoes, but then clears your palate, resetting it so that you don't get palate fatigue and can enjoy the next bite as much as you did the first.

Tasting Sangiovese
Step by Step

1. A Brief Road Map to Our Upcoming Sangiovese Road Trip

Whether you're tasting alone or by party, you're going to need about five Sangioveses to know what the stuff tastes like. Your first task will be to identify the basic taste of the fruit, the cherry, strawberry, black cherry of it, the pepper and spice; you'll do this by comparing the two most inexpensive versions of the grape, domestic American Sangiovese and entry-level plain old Chianti. You'll compare these to your Chianti Classico or Chianti Classico Riserva, which will be the same grape but from a better territory and with more careful winemaking. In them you'll see what the cherry essence of Sangiovese is like when it's honed. Then you'll try a Sangiovese-based Super Tuscan, which will show you what the basic fruit of Sangiovese is like— supercharged, with more structure and more indefinable oomph. Finally, you'll try the highest expression of Sangiovese: a Brunello. This should be the rough equivalent of putting a super-amplifying echo effect on the wine: It won't just be a Sangiovese, it will be a Sangioves-*ay-ay-ay-ay* that stirs your soul. Or it won't, and you'll decide plain Chianti is good enough for you. But either way you'll come out of this tasting a master of the universe (of Italian restaurant wine lists), which is a good thing to be! You can either taste these five wines at a party you'll throw with your friends, which will spread out the costs and lend other voices to the drinking, or you can taste them alone or with a buddy, in which case you'll simply break the pairing into two separate nights.

Notes on Tasting Sangiovese Alone or in Pairs

If you're tasting your Sangioveses solo, plan to do your tasting with some food. Sangiovese is a food wine, period. If you like to cook, anything Italian will do, especially anything with a tomato component. If you don't like to cook, pizza or a meatball hoagie will do just fine.

Notes on Tasting Sangiovese by Party

Sangiovese is above all a food-friendly wine, and since it goes with all the easiest Italian foods this will be the simplest dinner party you'll ever hope to throw. Simply gather everything your nearest upscale grocery store loves to sell you: salami, lasagna, pizza, olives, Parmigiano-Reggiano, and so on, and get out the good china. Or cook, if you're a cook! Anything Italian, from *pasta puttanesca* to meatballs and spaghetti to steak *pizzaiola*. The only thing not to cook are northern Italian white-wine-sauce things, such as veal in a butter sauce. But osso bucco would be fine! Heck, if you want to get off the Italian theme, Sangiovese also goes with steaks on the grill, Italian sausages, grilled vegetables, and pretty much anything else you want to eat. But the Italian thing is fun, so do that. Tell some of your friends to get olives and bread, others to bring cheese and salami, and make a large serving of something with a tomato-based sauce. It's almost time to party.

2. Shopping

Whether you're alone or having a party, your first task is to buy your Sangioveses. You'll need five bottles, selected from the field guide above. The names provided here are simply suggestions to help you in your shopping; whatever your local wine shop has should be fine. Just try to match the categories, not the names.

1. A domestic Sangiovese, like one from Seghesio, Monte Volpe, Atlas Peak, or Ferrari-Carano. $10 to $25.
2. One bottle of basic Chianti; any will do. Some names: Antinori, Felsina, Fontodi, Frescobaldi, Querciabella, or Ruffino. $15 to $25.
3. A Chianti Classico or Chianti Classico Riserva, ideally from the same producer as your basic Chianti; see item 2 above for names. $20 to $30.
4. A Sangiovese-based Super Tuscan, like Antinori's Tignanello, Fontodi's Flaccianello, Felsina's Fontalloro, or La Brancaia's Il Blu. The words "Sangiovese-based" are very important here—you do not want to end up with an all-Cabernet one. $50 and up.
5. A good Brunello. Some names: Biondi Santi, Il Poggione, Castello Banfi. $50 and up.

3. Planning and Thinking About Tasting

Gather your wineglasses, dump bucket, and tasting markers. Make your life easier: Put some cherries or cherry jam in one wineglass, some tobacco in another, and some spice, like cinnamon sticks and whole allspice berries, in a third, and you will get an instant idea of how your different Sangioveses differ from one another.

Tasting Markers

Keep the following list handy so you can glance at it while you're tasting—it will help you name fragrances that seem just out of reach.

Above all

Red fruit (especially cherry, but also strawberry and cranberry)	Black pepper	Truffles
	Spice (cinnamon, nutmeg, allspice)	Cedar
		Blueberries
	Tea	Violets
Plums	Tobacco	Licorice
Black fruit (blackberry and black cherry)	Earth	Tar
	Chocolate	Roses
	Leather	Raisins
		Dried flowers

Less likely, but still possible

Toasty oak	Coffee	Dried green herbs
Vanilla	Green herbs (sage, basil, parsley, etc.)	Black olive
Orange peel		
Gingerbread		

4. Cool Things Off

Get your wine to cellar temperature! See page 10 for why. For Sangiovese that's around 55 degrees.

5. Pull the Corks!

6. Taste Your First Wine

Your basic American Sangiovese will tell you what Sangiovese's fruit is like. Pour an inch or so into each guest's wineglass and swirl. Sniff. Taste. Pass around your tasting markers if you've got them.

Questions to consider: Cherries? Strawberries? Anything darker, like raisins, tobacco, or tea? How do you like it? Does it seem watery, or concentrated enough?

Try the wine with a bite of food: Does it make the food taste better? Does the food make the wine taste better?

If you've got only one wineglass, dump your wine. If you've got two, now is time to bring forward the second glass and put some of the basic Chianti in it.

7. Taste Your Second Wine

We're on to the second Sangiovese, the basic Chianti. Pour about an inch into a wineglass for each guest. Swirl. Sniff. Taste. You should experience similar fruit to the first one, and hopefully some point of contrast. What is different? Does it seem richer? Thinner? More acidic? More balanced?

More questions: Cherries? Strawberries? Cranberries? Altogether, these red fruits are called: red fruit! If you feel you are experiencing something that's almost cherries, almost strawberries, and almost cranberries, congratulations! You have successfully put your finger on what wine critics blithely call red fruits. When you see "red fruits" on a wine label forevermore, this is what they're talking about. Do you get it? Do you like it?

More questions: Anything dark, like raisins? Mouth-watering acidity is one of the basic characteristics of Sangiovese: Do these two wines have that? Do they make you want to eat something? What happens if you do eat something? Does it improve the wine?

8. Taste Your Chianti Classico or Chianti Classico Riserva

Pour an inch of your Chianti Classico or Chianti Classico Riserva in each guest's glass. Swirl. Sniff. Taste. It should be noticeably different from the other Sangioveses, it should have more structure, more tobacco, more dark sensations—olives, tea, maybe even chocolate?—and less red fruit. Does it?

Remember, the same grape is in all the wines you have tasted so far. The only difference between Chianti Classico or Chianti Classico Riserva and basic Chianti is better soil, better *terroir,* and more careful winemaking. That's why it costs more. So, what do you think? Does the taste difference justify the price difference?

(Note to solo tasters, or those tasting in pairs: You are now going to take a break. Pick up the tasting of the next two wines as soon as convenient.)

9. Tasting the Big Guns: The Super Tuscan

Pour an inch of your Sangiovese-based Super Tuscan in each guest's glass. Tell them how much money this one set you back—they will enjoy the wine more with this information. Seriously. They'll also enjoy your house more. It's been scientifically proven that people who were served what they thought was complimentary expensive wine actually rated restaurants more highly than those served what they thought was complimentary cheap wine. And who are you to block your guests' pleasure?

Okay. Swirl. Sniff. Taste. You should now be moving well away from the cherry-juice personality of Sangiovese and into its velvety, intense, chocolaty personality. Are you? Questions to consider: Do you like this wine? Love it? Are you swooning over its intensity? Does it have a more cohesive structure to support the fruit? Does it feel bigger and weightier in your mouth? If you've got two glasses going, use one of them to backtrack to the fruity, simple Sangioveses. Does this Super Tuscan have anything in common with the early, fruity ones? If so, what?

Try your Super Tuscan and the simpler one with some food. Does each seem to improve the food to the same degree? If all you're getting from it is that the Super Tuscan is more than the Chianti—more weight, more structure, more power, more interest—that's enough. All wine critics try to do is put that "more" into more words.

10. Tasting the Big Guns: The Brunello

Holy cow—you're going to drink Brunello, one of the most esteemed Italian wines on the planet! This is some serious wine drinking. Get ready. Brunellos are the most noble, the most regal, the most expensive Sangiovese wines on earth. Pour. Swirl. Sniff. Taste. What do you think?

This wine should have the exotic, bewitching scents of black truffles and chocolate, should be both elegant and velvety, both lush and well structured, and should seem pure, profound, and ennobling. Also, it should be delicious. Is it? Is it more subtle, quieter than the Super Tuscan?

Now it's time to ask yourself the big questions. Which wine was your favorite? Which ones were worth the money? Which do you want more of in your life?

Having tasted these five wines, you now have a bona fide grounding in Sangiovese. Try another dozen this year and you'll be a stone cold American Sangiovese expert, which is pretty rare.

THE TAKEAWAY

Italian is one of the great cuisines of the world, and Tuscan food is most Americans' favorites— we love the big earthy flavors, the ingredient-driven freshness, the honest simplicity. And now you know what wine goes best with it! Tart, deliciously acidic Sangiovese. You tasted it in its uncomplicated, juicy guise, in its finely textured American version, and in its highest Italian forms, in a good Chianti and a cult superstar Super Tuscan. You learned whether you like it, and you laid the foundation to be happy in Italian restaurants for the rest of your life.

Five-second cheat sheet for people who didn't read the chapter and are reading this on their iPhones while they watch the artisanal pizza guy shove delicious-looking things into wood-fired ovens

Sangiovese (*san-zho-VAY-zeh*) has been the favorite table wine of central Italy since before recorded history. It's the ultimate food wine; its mouthwatering acidity improves everything it touches, the same way a squirt of lemon improves everything from lettuce to fish. The cheap, simple versions like basic Chianti (*kee-AHN-tee*) and Sangiovese grown in the United States are like smoked cherry juice, a little sweet, a little tangy, great to wash down pizza, chicken parmigiana hoagies, and all your red-sauce favorites. The midprice versions, the Chianti Classicos, are perfect nice Italian restaurant wines: They are the best possible version of Sangiovese's basic cherry juice, now well structured, with black-fruit tastes and scents. The most expensive Sangioveses on earth, Brunello and Sangiovese-based Super Tuscans like Tignanello and Fonsalloro, take Sangiovese's food-friendliness and give it velvety intensity, echoing oomph, and profundity.

Knock-Their-Socks-Off
Gifts for Sangiovese Lovers

1. Biondi Santi: Despite its status as one of the greatest wines of Italy, Brunello is actually pretty new. It was invented by a guy named Ferruccio Biondi Santi in the 1880s. If you want an iconic Brunello, get one from the still-going-strong Biondi Santi estate. Sure, it's pricey—new releases start at over $100 and the Riserva costs more—but it's also history.

2. Case Basse di Soldera Brunello: One of the greatest Brunellos in the world, the Soldera wine is also made in the most traditional way, using old neutral Slovenian casks instead of new French barrels so you taste only the Sangiovese and not the vanilla of oak. If you want to impress someone, and you've got $200 or $300, here's a surefire way to do it.

3. Antinori's Tignanello: One of the original Super Tuscans and a perennial critical darling, the giant winery Antinori's signature wine Tignanello is bold, ripe, peppery, and powerful. It's one of those wines that is so intense, fruit-forward, and well balanced it gives American wine lovers an understanding of why Italian wine people are so gaga for Sangiovese, and makes Sangiovese lovers say "I told you so." It's also very widely distributed; you should be able to find it for $80 to $100.

4. Felsina's Fontalloro: Lots of critics feel this is the textbook, benchmark example of what Sangiovese from Chianti can be. Their regular Chianti, the Riserva Rancia, is considered one of the world's most reliable. But their Super Tuscan, the 100 percent Sangiovese wine Fontalloro, is one of my favorites. It's raspberry-bright, gracefully smoky, and tightly knit, and often sells for around $40.

5. Castello di Ama's single-vineyard Chiantis, Vigneto Bellavista or La Casuccia: What's the best Chianti on earth? Chances are it's one of these two single-vineyard offerings by Castello di Ama, a Tuscan winery in the heart of the Chianti Classico appellation. They only make these wines in years they deem worthy of a vintage. For how good they are, they're surprisingly affordable.

9

TEMPRANILLO

SPAIN'S GREATEST GRAPE

Pronounced: *tem-pra-NEE-yo*. Also known as: Rioja, Red Rioja, Rioja Alta, Rioja Alavesa, Ribera del Duero, Tinto Fino, Tinta del Pais, Tinto Toro, Tinto de Toro, Cencibel, Ull de Liebre, Ojo de Liebre

Dear Dara,

I'm not even sure I want to know about Spanish wine. I mean, I know it's something I'm supposed to know about to be a hipster today. I know that the wine geeks at my local hip wine shop (that I never go to because it makes me feel like an idiot) always suggest I drink it. However, the two times I've trusted them I've ended up with something that tasted like barbecue ashes, and my wife looked at me like I took our money to the store and came back with magic beans. I guess what I'm saying is, give me any excuse and I will never touch Spanish wine again as long as I live.

—Baffled

Ah, it pains me to hear you say that. Because Spain is weird, in the coolest way, and cool in the weirdest way. You get into it and you can't help but be enthralled: All these scorched vineyards where grizzled old farmers have been making intense wine for thousands of years, like Europe's own Galápagos Islands with the freaky big tortoises. I mean, there Spain is, stuck onto France like a fist on a wrist, but that wrist is covered with spiky, almost impenetrable mountains, the Pyrenees. So whatever people wandered down into Spain got cut off from the rest of Europe and had to make a go of it in that hot, hot place. Consequently they developed all sorts of indigenous unique wine styles—the first records of Spanish wine culture date back to 1100 B.C., and today they grow more than six hundred varieties of wine grape! And they love wine. They have the most land under vine in the entire world, almost 3 million acres. If you wanted to, you could drink a different bottle of Spanish wine every night for the next twenty years and never repeat one! You might get bored with Chardonnay, but if you get bored with Spain you are bored with life. So, I am very sorry you got a barbecue-ash wine, and I apologize on behalf of all wine geeks everywhere. But don't let the gargantuanness of Spain get you down—the same thing that you find off-putting about it now, its vast, ancient, endless depths and billion idiosyncracies, is the same thing you'll find appealing in twenty years when you are bored with life.

But where to start? Most wine books will give you five leading areas and a couple of dozen leading producers—but I know you don't have time for that. So let's not consider all the wines of Spain, just its biggest one. Its big gun: Tempranillo. Even more than Sangiovese in Italy, Tempranillo is the most significant grape in Spain. It's the one that the biggest cult wines are based on. It's the one the Spanish consider the best. It's the one that, if you ask any sommelier or wine shop guy about, he will have some common ground to have a conversation with you.

What's to Love About Tempranillo?

Tempranillo is earthy, dry, meaty, and lively at the same time. If you like dry red table wine but find that many dry reds today are in fact too sweet and alcoholic for your taste, Tempranillo is the wine for you, for two big reasons. One, it's rarely one-dimensionally sweet; instead, delicious non-fruit characteristics like leather, tobacco, and spice dominate, leading it to read to the palate as especially dry. Two, Tempranillo is a high-acid wine, meaning that it improves food in the same way that a squirt of lemon improves crab cakes or a splash of vinegar improves salads. High-acid, very dry, affordable red table wines are a rarity, but Tempranillo is one. I like Tempranillo because to me it tastes elemental and farm-driven. It tastes like something a farmer in a hot, high area would make to go with bread and olive oil and cheese, to nourish and feed him during meals. To me it tastes honest and real.

What's to Hate About Tempranillo?

All those names? Hate them. I've stood in wine stores and had clerks insist to me that Tinto Fino and Tempranillo were totally different; they're not. Why is it that wine names are sacred and untranslatable? Not that Spain is the only offender here—I'm looking at you, France! Italy, stop smirking. Do we have to call German shepherds "hunds" and Mexican chihuahuas "perros"? No. Every other object on the planet crosses a border and gets a new name. When it was in France it was an *horloge,* but by the time it got to America it became a clock. Please. Pull it together, Spain. If you were trying to sell lightbulbs over here would you call them *bombillas* and refuse to translate the packaging? Spend a couple pesetas on some stickers reading "Tempranillo" and help a sister out.

What's the Story with Tempranillo?

Tempranillo is the major grape of Spain, and can be found at every price point: in basic bottom-shelf Spanish cheapies, in exceedingly expensive Spanish cult wines, and as the major component of the wine from Spain's most famous region, Rioja (*ree-O-ha*), another region that critics adore, Ribera del Duero, and others.

About those regional designations: Like wine from the French regions of Bordeaux and Burgundy, a wine can *be* a Rioja—"Sir, I recommend the $45 Rioja"—or come *from* Rioja—"Sir, if you turn to page six you'll see our wines from Rioja." Ditto for Ribera del Duero. Rioja itself is pretty big, about the size of the state of Delaware, and it's in the north central part of Spain, not too far from the Pyrenees that separate France from Spain. Ribera del Duero is just southwest of it.

There are white Riojas, and white Ribera del Dueros, but unless you're hanging out with sommeliers and wine writers they won't much come up. They're not Tempranillo. Ignore them for now.

Technically, careful wine critics don't talk about Tempranillo on its own because it's usually blended with something else. It's not unusual for a Rioja to be, say, 85 percent Tempranillo, with another 10 percent Grenache (*Garnacha* in Spanish) added for body, and another couple percentages of the red varieties Mazuelo and Graciano for fragrance. Alternatively, some winemakers use international varieties like Syrah, Cabernet Sauvignon, or Merlot to round out the Tempranillo.

But I don't care about being a careful critic in this case. The main thing you taste in Rioja and Ribera del Duero— the main point of difference between the Spanish wine aisle and the French one—is Tempranillo. So I think it makes sense to focus on Tempranillo as an entry point into Spanish wine. The second point of difference between Spain and the world is: oak. Now, oak—everybody uses oak. But for Americans and people coming out of the French tradition, one of the primary concerns about an oak-aged wine is whether the fruit is appropriately showcased by the oak. In Spain, I get the sense that that equation is flipped.

For instance, one day I was talking to Paul Draper, the godfather of American Zinfandel, and he was telling me about oak. Specifically, he was telling me about cleaning out an oak barrel and preparing it for use. He had put in boiling water and was getting it on every surface, trying to swell up the inside of the barrel and check for leaks. He was about to dump the resulting barrel-cleaning water when he had a second thought. "It was just a beautiful amber color," Draper told me, "and I had a thought. I took a wineglass and trapped the water that was flowing out, and walked around the winery asking people what they thought of this wine. They were saying: Oh, it's beautiful, all that butterscotch. What is that wine?" He went on to explain to me the difference between falsely tarting up a wine with oak and using oak as what he felt it should be—a sort of beautiful picture frame to set off the main thing; the grapes.

I wonder what they would make of this anecdote in Spain. I suspect it would be more like *Why did you waste those lovely oak molecules wandering around the winery like that?* The Spanish really, really love oak. Why? Probably for the same reason that the French love anise, people from New Orleans love the roasted flour taste of roux, and the Thais love cilantro: They just do. Of all the world's peoples, do the Spanish love the taste of oak the most? I'd say yes. So much so they organize their Tempranillo classifications (both Rioja and Ribera del Duero) around it entirely. There are four levels:

The first has no oak and is called *joven,* or young, or simply noted to come from a guaranteed place by the phrase *Denominación de Origen,* or *Denominación de Origen de Calificada,* abbreviated as DO or DOCa. You'll rarely see this on a Spanish red wine in America, as they're not really considered good enough to export. If you do find one and it's from a well-respected importer like Jorge Ordonez, Eric Solomon, Kermit Lynch, or Dan Kravitz, who runs Hand Picked Selections, give it a whirl, it should be pretty good.

The second level is *crianza,* which spends one year in oak and one year in the bottle before being released. These are the simplest Spanish wines Americans tend to see.

Reserva wines are at least three years old, and have spent at least one year in oak, though usually more.

Gran Reserva wines have a heck of a lot of oak! They are only made in the best vintage years, and because they're such beautiful grapes the Spanish do the nicest possible thing they can think of for them: They age them for two years in oak, then keep them for another three years in the bottle. This means that if 2010 happens to be a banner vintage year, the wines won't be released until at least the December of the fifth year after harvest. But wineries often choose to hold on to them longer. Famously, one Rioja producer didn't release its 1942 Gran Reserva until 1983!

Ridiculous? Kind of. But also very hospitable and loving to mankind: Since oak is meant to preserve wines for long aging, a young wine with a lot of oak may well be undrinkable for years, and since most wines Americans drink are consumed within 48 hours of purchase, there's a lot of people who think that Americans are, by and large, getting swindled because we keep getting sold wine that's not ready to drink.

Will you like all this Spanish love of oak? You'll only know by tasting. There's an argument to be made that the Spanish approach to aging (we age them till they're ready for you to drink) is more honest and consumer-friendly than the French one (buy 'em—but don't drink 'em!). Till you actually do taste, just keep in mind that oak + Tempranillo = the basic taste of Spain. Also keep in mind that if you're looking for a new name for your punk rock band, you could use "The Law of Oak," which is actually a chapter heading in a book the Spanish Trade Commission once sent me. Grapes cower when brought before the Law of Oak!

In addition to the cheapie Tempranillos and the Tempranillo in Rioja and Ribera del Duero, there's an unofficial fourth category of Tempranillo in Spain: the expensive cult superstars. There are winemakers who feel that their wines are better than mere Rioja, mere Ribera del Duero, and so put proprietary names on them like Pingus, Pesquera, and Calvario. If you read about the Super Tuscans in the Sangiovese chapter, this will seem very familiar to you; the fact of the matter is that Americans, British, and Japanese collectors are simply more prone to collect things they can pronounce and understand. Try to wrap your head around that one for a bit.

The last part of the Tempranillo story is about those wines that have been planted in the New World—or as we call it, *here*. As I write this, the American West Coast is being planted with all sorts of new Tempranillo vines. Why? It was illegal for many years in dry, arid Spain to irrigate Tempranillo. That should give you a sense of how much water the vines really need: not much.

When you talk to California winemakers they'll often mention that France has a "Continental" climate, which is totally meaningless until you realize that what they mean is that in France, it rains in the summer. On the American West Coast it doesn't. It rains in the fall, winter, and early spring. So planting French grapes on the West Coast generally means they have to be irrigated. And then, because it's so much sunnier there than in France, the vines have to be aggressively trimmed back lest they bear too much fruit, because too much fruit means watery wine.

Tempranillo, though, can be "dry-farmed"—that is, grown without irrigation. Since water is so precious, especially in California, and because it's kind of silly to have to both irrigate and fight the effects of water on your vines, a lot of the cutting-edge, visionary, more intellectually inclined California winemakers such as Randall Grahm, Bob McCrea, and Bob and Louisa Lindquist are saying that Tempranillo is the true vine of the American future. Will it be? Thousands of years of hardscrabble Spanish history say: Could be.

So, we're off. The plan is to try Tempranillo in its various manifestations, young and fruity, old and oaky, young and oaky, expensive and fancy, to get the measure of Spain's greatest grape, and generally to figure out where you stand in relation to it.

The "Holy Trinity" of Tempranillo

The Grape

Tempranillo is a thick-skinned, dark grape used to make dark still wine. Spicy, leathery Tempranillo can lack sweetness and fruit, which is why it is frequently blended.

Ribera del Duero Tempranillos typically aren't blended, but Rioja ones are, especially with Garnacha, known to the rest of the world as Grenache. Grenache is mostly famous for making the spicy red wines of Châteauneuf-du-Pape in France. In Spain, Garnacha plays a costarring role in the spicy red wines of Rioja, stands alone, or is used in the dry rosé (pink) wine called *rosado*. The distinguishing characteristics of Grenache are that it grows well in hot, dry locations and it produces quite a lot of sugar as it does so, which creates a fair amount of alcohol. It has the basic flavor profile of "fruity"—think cranberries, strawberries, cherries—in its fresher incarnations, and black cherries, plums, and jam in other ones. When Garnacha and Tempranillo are blended, you get the spice and weight of Tempranillo brightened by the acid and fruit of Garnacha.

Tempranillo also has other blending partners. In Rioja it may also be colored with Carignan, a lean, spicy, cherry-accented, and acidic grape; lightened with Graciano, an intensely fruity one; or cut with Viura, a white wine used to lighten a blend. In Spain's Penedès region, Tempranillo is blended with Monastrell, a spicy grape offering lots of black fruits. While most Ribera del Dueros aren't blended, some are; the most famous wine in Spain, Vega Sicilia, contains Cabernet Sauvignon.

Why does so much blending go on with Tempranillo? Chalk it up to the long-standing growing traditions of Spain. Each of those blends reflect a particular microclimate and the historical wisdom of the grape growers who have been dealing with it for generations.

Terroir

Tempranillo grows in Spain, and a little is planted on the West Coast of the United States and in South America. Tempranillo grape vines are hard-trained, which means they grow into plants that resemble bushes that are free-standing and far apart; to seek water, their roots may shoot thirty to fifty feet underground. Generally speaking, these vines do their best work in temperate, sunny, dry places, particularly the regions of Rioja and Ribera del Duero.

Ribera del Duero wines are typically denser, darker, and more powerful than Riojas.

Winemaking

See "What's the Story with Tempranillo" above. Also know that the Spanish favor new American barrels, which impart a toasty vanilla flavor.

Stop Reading, Start Drinking!

You'll be tasting five different versions of Tempranillo, and thus you will learn what Tempranillo tastes like to you. You'll taste what it's like when it's being cheap and cheerful, when it's being traditional and straitlaced, when it's made in America, when it's newly emerged from a lot of oak, and when it's made so carefully it comes out all big, brawny, powerful, and plush. You'll also see what the Spanish wine laws can do for you, and whether you will be using them as a lifelong guide (if, say, you think the upper-level wines as designated by law are in fact better) or ignoring them. Finally, you'll taste the difference between old-fashioned winemaking, in terms of the straight-ahead Riojas, and newfangled winemaking, in the cult wine.

Tempranillo FIELD GUIDE

You're going to need to find a wine shop with a decent Spanish selection, which might take some doing. Most really good wine shops should have at least ten or twelve Tempranillos, including inexpensive bottom-shelf under-$12 ones, at least a couple of Ribera del Dueros and Riojas, and a Spanish cult wine or two. To find a store with a good Spanish selection you might just have to start calling likely suspects and asking: I need a Flor de Pingus and a Crianza Rioja for a wine tasting . . . anyone who knows what you're talking about will be the wine shop you're looking for. If you live in a rural place you may have to turn to the Internet for these wines, but then again, you probably realized that before I did.

Just going to the wine shop and sifting through what they've got as you hunt for a few Tempranillos will teach you quite a bit about the wine. First, you'll notice that the wines are older than what you're used to seeing. You'll commonly find five- and six-

year-old bottles, or even older ones, that are newly released. If you find any encased in a wire net, know that those were traditional on high-end Rioja for decades. They're meant to prevent unscrupulous merchants from refilling expensive bottles with cheap wine.

Miscellaneous bottom-shelf Spanish and Argentinean cheapies, and Joven wines, $6 and up

Tempranillo is Spain's most planted wine, and much of it is grown outside the famous Rioja and Ribera del Duero areas. What to do with it all? Why not send it to the States! Some bargain Tempranillos I've seen in my day are Manyana, Heretat Vall-Ventós' Vina Belldaura, and Senorio de Valdehermoso Joven, but basically, if you see a wine label reading Tempranillo and it costs less than $12—eureka! You've found the bottom shelf. *Joven,* of course, means "young," and these Riojas and Ribera del Dueros should be on the cheaper side. When you're starting out try to avoid the bottom-shelf Tempranillo that is blended, usually with Grenache or Cabernet Sauvignon, but by all means try it once you have a handle on the grape.

Crianza Rioja or Ribera del Duero, $15 and up

Crianza wines are the lowest tier that Rioja and Ribera del Duero producers take seriously. Some people prefer them to the pricier, older Reserva and Gran Reserva wines because they are fresher. Some people prefer the older wines because they're more complex. Which is better? There really is no right answer, which is why the Spanish make all the different styles. You may find in your tasting that you strongly prefer one to the other, or that you prefer them situationally, a Crianza for summertime grilling, a Gran Reserva for winter dinner parties. You'll never know till you try them. Expect to pay $10–$20 for most Crianzas.

Top names: Campo Viejo, Campillo Reserva, Conde de Valdemar, Cosme Palacio y Bermejillo, Alejandro Fernandez, Raimat,

CVNE, Vina Real, Bodegas Muga, R. Lopez de Heredia, La Rioja Alta, Marques de Murrieta Ygay, Marques de Riscal, and Sierra Cantabria.

Reserva Rioja or Ribera del Duero, $18 and up

Reserva wines seem like they'd be second best, and sometimes they are, but sometimes because these wines are kept for so much longer in new oak, they're less approachable on release than the Crianza wines. Sometimes they're even drained out of new oak and moved to *newer* oak.

Sometimes the winery will hold them back and let them age in bottle for a while, meaning your new Reserva will actually be three years old and perfect to drink. Hard to say what you're going to find. However, you'll never be able to talk authoritatively about Tempranillo if you don't try a Reserva or three, so get drinking! Expect to pay $15 to $30 for most Reservas.

Top names: same as above for Rioja.

Gran Reserva Rioja or Ribera del Duero, $20 and up

Gran Reservas are supposed to be the best of the best, thoroughly mature wines from the best grapes. They should be deep, rich, and thoroughly balanced, which means that the fruit, structure, and oak are all in proportion. Don't be surprised to see ten-year-old or even forty-year-old Gran Reservas on the shelves; the winery may well have just released them.

If you become fond of Gran Reservas and decide there are not enough in your neighborhood, the San Francisco Bay Area wine shop K&L (klwines.com) has extensive selections and can ship to about 18 states; Schaefer's (schaefers.com) in Skokie, Illinois, has the best Spanish wine selection in Chicagoland; New York City's PJ Wine (pjwine.com) has the best Spanish selections in Manhattan. Expect to pay $20 to $100 for a good Gran Reserva; most are between $20 and $50.

Top names: same as above for Rioja.

American West Coast, $8 and up

Depending on whom you ask, Tempranillo is either the next big thing out of California, or was supposed to be the next big thing twenty years ago and never will be. For my money West Coast Tempranillo, be it from California, Oregon, or Washington, is one of the world's most underrated wines. It can be meaty, fruity, and tightly graceful in the most appealing way. Some of the best Tempranillo in America is being made by Verdad, Bonny Doon, Gundlach Bundschu, Artesa, Clos du Bois, Abacela, St. Amant, Boeger Winery, Truchard, and Bokisch Vineyards.

When buying American Tempranillo expect more fruit—that is, lots of strawberry, cherry, blackberry, and chocolate—and less oak. If you fall in love with American Tempranillo yourself, keep up to date through the website of TAPAS, the Tempranillo Advocates, Producers and Amigos Society (tapasociety.org).

Cult Spanish, $50 and up

The hottest, most expensive wines out of Spain over the last twenty years have tended to be the wines by Rioja and Ribera del Duero producers who threw off the shackles of the traditional Spanish wine laws and made their own rules—and, of course, invented their own wine names, because then they couldn't legally use Gran Reserva and such. Happily, for those of us uninterested in spending as much on a bottle of wine as we could on a vacation, all the cult wines have little-sister, second- and third-label wines so you can taste the skill and vision of the winemaking team behind the big guns without shelling out the big bucks.

A few to watch for:

1. Flor de Pingus: Peter Sisseck, a Danish winemaker, started the Spanish cult wine revolution in 1995 with his wine Pingus, made from sixty-year-old Tempranillo vines in Ribera del Duero. Critics loved it, and a legend was born. Flor de Pingus, Pingus's little sister, usually is released at around $50, and is

deeply plummy, layered, and dense, with scents of barnyard, coffee, chocolate, raspberries, and rich wet earth. Or is it a too-powerful show-off? You decide.

2. Roda I and II: The legend behind cult wine Cirsion is this: One grapevine in a thousand offers fruit of such stupefying greatness that the wine is beyond mere mortal comprehension. The people at Bodegas Roda figured out how to find these grapes—bada boom bada bing, *money!* Or something like that. Whether you believe the legend or not, Cirsion's little sisters Roda I (from about $65) and Roda II (about $50) remain two of the best Tempranillo-based wines you can easily buy. Both are pretty and offer a nose of roasted meat, cinnamon, and raspberry pie.

3. Tinto Pesquera, Alion: Alejandro Fernandez makes cult superstars Pesquera Janus and Millennium Reserva, but unless you're reading this on your private jet you'll probably be more interested in the Pesquera second wines, like the $60 Reserva, $40 Tinto Pesquera, or $40 Alion.

4. Atalayas de Golban: The 100 percent Tempranillo little sister of superstar Dominio de Atauta, this $25 Ribera del Duero wine is a phenomenal value, concentrated, cherry-bright, and velvety.

The Rest of the Story

What if you run into any wines that don't fit in the above categories? Keep in mind that Tempranillo-based wines are made all over Spain. Occasionally you'll run into an all-Tempranillo wine from Penedès, Cigales, or another Spanish region. The usual angle on these is that they're as good as Rioja or Ribera del Duero without the price tag; you be the judge. Tempranillo also tends to grow everywhere that's hot where the Spanish have traded, so it's all over Portugal (where it is called Tinta Roriz), Argentina, and Chile.

Food and Tempranillo

A spicy, smoky, medium-weight, dry red wine, Tempranillo goes with anything spicy or smoky: sausages, salami, and other charcuterie, anything salami is on (like pizza or a sandwich), any char-grilled meat, including beef, lamb, pork, veal, venison, bison, chicken, pheasant, grouse, goose, and duck. It even goes with grilled fattier fish, like fresh sardines, mackerel, or bluefish. Of course it goes with all the classic Spanish dishes: paella, albondigas meatballs, or Pincho Moruno marinated pork skewers. The only things that Tempranillo doesn't go with are the same things no big reds go with: light foods, like sole in a butter sauce, hamachi crudo, and so on.

Tasting Tempranillo
Step by Step

1. A Brief Road Map to Our Upcoming Tempranillo Road Trip

You're going to taste five Tempranillos, from bottom-shelf cheapies to the most sought after expensive Tempranillos on earth, to get a sense of the personality of Tempranillo. First, you'll be trying to nail down the basic taste of the grape Tempranillo, that is, its plummy, leathery, smoky essence. To do this you'll try a bottom-shelf generic Spanish Tempranillo. Then you'll try a Tempranillo from the most important Tempranillo growing territories on earth, Rioja and Ribera del Duero; this is your Crianza Rioja or Crianza Ribera del Duero, depending on what you found in your local shop. Next, you'll try an American Tempranillo to get a sense of what the grape tastes like grown elsewhere; it should be lacier and lighter but still recognizably Tempranillo. The cumulative effect of these three bottles—bottom-shelf cheapie, Crianza, and American—should be to nail down for you what Tempranillo tastes like. It tastes different from every other red wine on earth—right? Right. Now, you will move on to sample what a Tempranillo plus time tastes like—you'll try a Reserva or Gran Reserva of Rioja and Ribera de Duero. If you can find the Crianza and Reserva or Gran Reserva offering from a single producer, snap them up; this will really aid your comparing-apples-to-apples cause. Generally, Tempranillo from an esteemed area plus time should equal a more magnificent wine than the previous three. But how great can Tempranillo really get? You'll find out in your final bottle, when you sample an all-Tempranillo Spanish cult star like Flor de Pingus, Finca Allende's Calvario, or Roda II. This will tell you about the vibrant, plush, velvety, international face of Tempranillo. And then you'll really truly once and for all know what it tastes like!

Notes on Tasting Tempranillo Solo or in Pairs

If you're tasting your Tempranillos solo, plan to do your tasting with some food. Tempranillo is a table wine, a food wine, and you won't totally get it if there's not food around. If you're a cook, see the dinner party suggestions below for ideas. If you're not a cook, a take-out burrito, barbecue, or even pizza will do just fine—maybe add some salty green olives. Tempranillo does really well with brined and salty foods.

Notes on Tasting Tempranillo by Party

Do you like tapas? Those little plates of Spanish finger foods? Of course you like tapas. Everyone likes tapas. They're very *now*. So, welcome to your tapas and Tempranillo party!

You'll need olives, and plenty of them. Big green ones are particularly Spanish, as are littler green ones flavored with lemon zest, hot peppers, or herbs. And *jamon*. Spanish ham is a star of every tapas bar. It's like Prosciutto—in fact, if you can't find it, substitute Prosciutto. You'll also want some Spanish cheese: Manchego, Cabrales, Mahon, or whatever else you can find. If you can't find any Spanish cheese, set out an American smoked cheese, a good Gruyère, a Dry Jack, and a soft cheese like Brie or Camembert.

Mine the Internet for some tapas recipes, and grill some kind of meat. Lamb is especially good, but steak, pork, or herb-marinated chicken are also considered perfect Tempranillo pairings. (Tempranillo goes with everything except the lightest foods, like sashimi.) Grilled vegetables are also a good choice; add garlic to their marinade.

For dessert, get anything you want. Chocolate is a natural pair, or anything mocha, perhaps chocolate cake, or coffee ice cream with chocolate sauce. So is anything with cinnamon, like churros, bread pudding, coffee cake, or flan. However, you'll probably no longer have the heart for strict wine tasting by the time dessert rolls around, so just get whatever will make you happy.

2. Shopping

Whether you're alone or having a party, your first task is to buy your Tempranillos. You'll need five bottles, selected from the field guide above. The names provided are simply suggestions to help you in your shopping; whatever your local wine shop has should be fine. Just try to match the categories, not the names. You want to end up with:

1. One bottle of basic bottom-shelf Spanish Tempranillo, which will be labeled Tempranillo, Joven Rioja, or Joven

Ribera del Duero. Some names: Manyana, Heretat Vall-Ventós' Vina Belldaura, and Senorio de Valdehermoso Joven. Try to avoid blends with lots of Grenache (Garnacha). $8 to $18.

2. One bottle of Crianza Rioja or Ribera del Duero or any producer. Some names: Campo Viejo, Conde de Valdemar, Muga; see above in field guide for more, but any will do. $15 to $25.

3. An American single-estate Tempranillo like Verdad, Bonny Doon, or Gundlach Bundschu. $18 to $30.

4. A Reserva or Gran Reserva Rioja or Ribera del Duero from any producer; it's extra nice if you can get one from the same producer as your basic wine in item 2 above. $20 and up.

5. One cult Spanish wine such as Flor de Pingus, Roda II, or Tinto Pesquera; see field guide above for more names. $30 to $100.

3. Planning and Thinking About Tasting

Set out your wineglasses, dump bucket, and tasting markers. Make your life easier: Put some tobacco from a cigarette or cigar in one wineglass, strawberry jam in a second wineglass, and a bit of leather, such as a shoelace or a bit of suede from a craft store, in a third wineglass. Pass these glasses around during your tasting, and you will leap light-years ahead in your understanding of the scents that emanate from a glass of Tempranillo.

Tasting Markers

Keep the following list handy so you can glance at it while you're tasting—it will help you name fragrances that seem just out of reach.

Above all

Leather	Spice (cinnamon, nutmeg, allspice)	Blackberries
Tobacco		Black cherries
Red fruit (especially strawberry, but also raspberry, cherry, and cranberry)	Black pepper	Plums
	Smoke	Raisins
	Vanilla	Prunes
	Earth	

Possible, but less likely

Licorice	Green herbs	Dried herbs
Cedar	Tomato leaf (greenish and tart; if you have an actual tomato leaf, break it and sniff)	Mushrooms
Cigar box		Tea
Mocha		
Chocolate		
Mineral, like a wet rock		

4. Cool Things Off

Ideally your Tempranillo will be around 55 to 60 degrees. (See page 10 for why this is important.)

5. Pull the Corks!

6. Taste Your First Wine

Your basic Spanish bottom-shelf Tempranillo will tell you what the Tempranillo fruit is like at its most basic. Pour an inch in each guest's glass. Swirl. Sniff. Taste. If you were in a tapas bar in Madrid, the house wine would probably be something very much like this. You're hoping to notice scents of strawberry, cinnamon, and leather. Do you? Pass around the wineglasses with the tasting markers in them if you've got them. Try a bit of food. Does the wine improve it? Does it improve the wine?

7. Taste Your Second Wine

We're on to the second wine, the Crianza Rioja or Crianza Ribera del Duero. Pour about an inch into a wineglass for each guest. Swirl. Sniff. Taste. You should experience similar fruit to the first one, a strawberry-cherry quality, but this time filtered through oak, which you should perceive as vanilla and smoke. Do you taste any difference between this wine and the first?

Questions to consider: Do you like this more than the first? Does the greater oak give the wine more structure, or seem extraneous? Are the two wines the same age? Do you think the additional age changed anything?

8. Taste Your American Tempranillo

Pour an inch of your American Tempranillo into a wineglass. Swirl. Sniff. Taste. It should be wildly different from the first two; it should be lighter, lacier, less oaky than the Reserva, less rustic than the first one. Is it? Do you like it? Other questions to consider: Do you get more fruit from the American one? Fruit like figs, blackberries, cherries, plums—ideally, there should be lots more fruit than you've seen in any Tempranillo up to now. Try this one with food: Is it different than the Spanish ones were? Better or worse?

Do you have a favorite wine so far?

(Note to solo tasters, or those tasting in pairs: You are now going to take a break. Pick up the tasting of the next two wines as soon as convenient.)

9. Taste Your Reserva or Gran Reserva Tempranillo

Pour an inch of your Reserva or Gran Reserva Rioja or Reserva or Gran Reserva Ribera del Duero. Swirl. Sniff.

Taste. Pass tasting markers if you've got them. The conventional wisdom with Reserva or Gran Reserva wines is
that you're starting with better quality fruit and then
treating it more opulently. You should get loads more
structure in this wine, and more tannin. Does your mouth
feel prickly inside? Does the structure seem to sweep the
fruit into a more complicated presentation, or does it overwhelm the fruit and dwarf it? Take a gander at the vintage: How old is this wine? Much older than the others
you've tasted? Does the fruit seem less fresh—or more? It
might seem more fresh and vibrant if it was better fruit to
begin with. If you have a Gran Reserva, good for you—producers only make it in good years, so theoretically it's
guaranteed to be a good vintage. Either a Reserva or Gran
Reserva wine should be well structured, that is, no part of
the wine should seem out of balance with the rest of
it, nothing should seem to poke out. More questions: black
pepper, tobacco, leather, or licorice?

10. Taste Your Cult Spanish Tempranillo

You are now moving into costly and prestigious territory, a
real bona fide Spanish cult Tempranillo, so be sure to tell
your friends how much you spent. Are they impressed? If
not, consider getting new friends. Till then: Pour. Swirl.
Sniff. Taste. What do you think? These cult wines are supposed to have the concentration and character of Tempranillo raised on its perfect home turf, while also being
livelier than the mere Reservas and Gran Reservas. Do you
think this is true? Does your wine feel fresh and lively? Vibrant and exciting? Deep and powerful? How about layered,
intense, earthy, and velvety?

Do you feel like it's something special, and you'd like to
spend quality quiet time with it, or does it feel like just an-

other glass of wine? Try it with food. Pass around the tasting markers. Do you detect anything new? Chocolate? Plums? Tea? Glance at the long list to see if anything leaps out at you. Take another sip. You did it! You're done.

Questions to consider after tasting these five Tempranillos: Which was your favorite? Which was worth the money? Which do you want more of in your life? Is Tempranillo different than you thought it would be? If you used the tasting markers, were they helpful?

And that is that. Congratulations! You now know enough about Spanish wine to consider yourself well launched on your Spanish wine life. Picture yourself standing on a Spanish highway holding a driver's permit and a certificate saying you finished your driver's ed course. Where you go now is totally up to you.

THE TAKEAWAY

Now you know what the people drink in Spain, a country with one of the longest, deepest wine cultures on earth. They drink smoky, spicy, sometimes cherry-berry Tempranillo, a food-friendly wine that marries well with oak. Through your tastings you found it comes in basic, unadorned rustic versions, and velvety intense ones. You know whether you like it, and you know that because of various levels of grape quality and winemaking, the wine can be simple, or quite complex.

Five-second cheat sheet for people who didn't read the chapter and are reading this on their iPhones in a tapas bar while they wait for a table

Tempranillo (*tem-pra-NEE-yo*) is the most important grape in Spain. Ask any sommelier in a Spanish restaurant to recommend a good Tempranillo and she'll think you know your stuff. Better yet, any Tempranillo that shows up will go well with the food you order, because Tempranillo is a great food wine; it's a spicy, smoky, dry, medium-weight red that is a natural match with all things Spanish, but especially any and all grilled or cured meats, from steaks to salami. Really, all of them. Rabbit, pheasant, bison, duck, pork, veal—try to find a meat Tempranillo doesn't go with, I dare you. In addition to all the meat, cherry-and-smoke-scented Tempranillo goes well with all tomato-based or cheese-based dishes, and the oilier varieties of seafood such as fresh sardines or grilled mackerel. Tempranillo is sometimes labeled as Tempranillo, but it is usually named after the two famous areas it grows in, Rioja (*Ree-OH-ha*) and Ribera del Duero. Rioja is made mostly of Tempranillo with some light sweet Garnacha (Grenache) or other grapes blended in; Ribera del Duero is more likely to be bottled solo. A few of the biggest, best names in Tempranillo and Rioja that you're likely to run into: Marques di Caceres, Conde de Valdemar, Muga, Marques de Riscal, La Rioja Alta, Palacio, and Contino. The most expensive, most highly sought after form of Tempranillo is what are called cult wines, so named because they have a cult of passionate collectors who buy them every year. These wines take the plum/cherry smoke of basic Tempranillo and combine it with weight, structure, elegance and grace. Some names? Flor de Pingus, Roda I or II, Tinto Pesquera, Alion, or Atalayas de Golban.

Knock-Their-Socks-Off
Gifts for Tempranillo Lovers

1. Vega Sicilia: In case you were wondering what the Hope Diamond of Spanish wines was, this is it. I hope you can afford it, and then I hope you give me some. Personally, I'll probably go to my grave never having tasted it, but that's not for lack of reading about it. I read it's amazing. If you gave a real bottle of it to someone who cared about Spanish wine, they would fall over in a dead swoon.

2. Pingus: The quintessential cult wine. Fewer than five hundred cases a year are made, and it regularly scores 96, 98, and yes, even 100 points in critics' ratings. It's all Tempranillo, and if you want to know what Tempranillo is capable of, by all means sell your car and see if you can't come up with a bottle. Alternatively, its little-sister wine Flor de Pingus, also Tempranillo, can be had for around $50, is widely distributed in the United States, is reliably lovely, and, in a good year, can be stupendous.

3. Pesquera: Alejandro Fernández, the founder of Bodegas Pesquera, is called "the Master of Tempranillo" and is credited with making Ribera del Duero the hot commodity it is today. Not bad for a onetime machinist who made his living designing beet harvesters and then turned his attention to developing new winemaking equipment. Pesquera Janus or Millennium Reserva is released in tiny quantities at stratospheric prices, but this wine has two little sisters, a Reserva wine that's released at about $60, and a Tinto Pesquera released at about $40. Either one should make any Spanish wine nut's day.

4. Finca Allende's Calvario: An unusual single-vineyard bottling from Rioja producer Finca Allende. The plot it comes from was entirely planted in 1945; it's 90 percent Tempranillo and is famous for its grace and elegance. It usually costs about $50 on release. Better yet, Finca Allende makes a whole line of regular Riojas, Crianzas, Reservas, and so on. There's a good argument to be made that if you want the best of the new producers and the best of the old majesty of Rioja, you want Finca Allende.

5. Verdad: Bob Lindquist is famous as one of the original Rhône
   Rangers, the first American winemakers to bring Rhône varietals like Syrah to these shores. Well, he was right about
   Syrah, and now Bob and his wife, Louisa Sawyer Lindquist,
   have got to thinking that Spanish varieties with their low
   water needs are the new future. Their newish Spanish varietal
   winery Verdad makes an impressive Tempranillo, one that's as-
   tonishingly meaty, fragrant, and graceful all at the same time,
   and costs less than $20.

10

PINOT NOIR

THE HEARTBREAK GRAPE

Pronounced: *pee-no nwa* or *pee-no nwahr*. Also
known as: Red Burgundy

Dear Dara,

*I love Pinot Noir. It's my favorite. But I kind of feel
like the fat kid that fell in love with the princess: Sometimes Pinot Noir smiles on me, I get one that's terrific
and I float on air. But most of the time she's, um, busy.
Instead of something terrific what I get is sour, or kind
of weird and thin, or really black and alcoholic and not
Pinot Noir–like at all. How can I make Pinot Noir love
me back? Or barring that, at least find the $12 Pinot
Noir of my dreams?*

—Baffled

I've got some good news for you, and some bad news. The
good news? You have more or less hit on the central
dilemma in wine—winemaking, wine criticism, wine education, wine marketing, all things wine. They can put a man
on the moon, why can't they make great $12 Pinot Noirs?

More good news: The $50 Pinot Noir buyers aren't actually
having that much better a time of it. While a $12 Pinot Noir
buyer finds a great wine maybe one out of twenty times, the
$50 gamblers are getting at best one out of two good wines.
It ain't you, babe.

The bad news is that there is no magic bit of insidery information that's going to make terrific $12 Pinot Noirs ap-
pear before you. Everything you don't like about wine—the
variability, the unknowability, the fickleness of what's in
the bottles versus what you hope is in the bottles—is
quadrupled, even quintupled for Pinot Noir.

Frankly, the insider's secret to outfoxing Pinot Noir is to
fall in love with Champagne. Champagne—try to find a bad
one. You can find an unthrilling one, sure, but a bad one? A
real French Champagne that you sip and think, "Nah, that
ain't right, they shouldn't have made Champagne this
year"? Doesn't really happen—which is funny, because
blanc de noirs Champagne is in fact made of Pinot Noir.

So why is still red Pinot Noir so variable and Pinot Noir
Champagne so reliable? Winemaking. Champagne is a fid-
dler's and improver's art. To make it they add sugar (chaptalization), blend multiple vintages, and do all sorts of
things to create, above all, consistency. You want consistency? Buy Champagne. You want the erratic beauty of
fickle nature? Pinot Noir.

The key to instant happiness and the secret to success
when shopping for Pinot Noir is more or less the exact same
secret to success that one must employ when approaching
puppies or toddlers: Accept that they are not driven by logic
and love them for what they are.

Because if you go into it any other way you'll just be mis-
erable. That said, you can find happiness, even bliss in your
relationship with Pinot Noir; you just have to understand
what it is, and what it isn't.

What's to Love About Pinot Noir?

At its best, Pinot Noir is nothing short of sensuous and
thrilling. It's like a first kiss from someone you've admired
for years. It's a thunderbolt of blackberries and chocolate
shot through with pepper. Or it's raspberries arranged into
architecture. Either way, it's as electrifying as the thick air
on a stormy summer night. It's as concentrated as a code.
It's a song you heard in a dream and suddenly hear again.
Sound fabulous? It is!

But that's not all! It's also the food-friendliest of all
wines. In fact, if you want to be a flawless, peerless food-
and-wine pairer for the rest of eternity, just do this one
thing: Always order Pinot Noir. It goes with fish, with shellfish, with lamb, poultry, game, pork, even beef. Even *cake*.

What's to Hate About Pinot Noir?

Brother, pull up a stool; they don't call it the Heartbreak
Grape for nothing. Pinot Noir is notoriously difficult to
grow, harder than any other wine grape. As a plant it's frag-
ile, and given to mutating in the field. (Wine grapes are reproduced by grafting vines onto roots, not through grape
seeds.) If it mutates, it can create flavors you don't want.
When it doesn't mutate, it is prone to viruses, mold, and
fungi, and just plain dying.

When it doesn't die, things are still tricky. It buds early, so
spring frosts, a normal thing in cold Pinot Noir territory like
Burgundy or Oregon, can be deadly. It's prone to "coulure,"
which is what growers call it when baby grapes drop off and
die before they grow or ripen. When Pinot Noir does ripen, its
skins are very thin, so a big rain, especially around harvest
time, can cause the grapes to swell and burst.

Pinot Noir skin isn't just thin, it's lightly colored, and

just as fair-skinned humans are more likely to burn in the sun than people with darker complexions, Pinot Noir is prone to sunburns, which can make the grapes taste like burnt plums or burnt cabbage. If it's not burning, it might just over-ripen—fast. A single hot day can turn Pinot Noir from underripe to overripe, which means the difference between an elegant wine and a pot of jam.

Because of its fragility, there's really no ideal climate for Pinot Noir. In cold, cloudy areas it is prone to coulure, rot, and mildew, and may never ripen. In hot sunny areas it is prone to death and sunburn, and all but guaranteed to become overripe.

You know that image of an American corn farmer, a single guy on a tractor tending plants as far as the eye can see? Growing Pinot Noir is the exact opposite. Some years Pinot Noir growers have to be in their vineyards just about every day fussing over their plants to make them grow right. Occasionally even that will come to naught because it rained too much, or wasn't sunny enough at the end of the season, or was too sunny. Because Pinot Noir is so infernally difficult to raise, growers charge a lot for the grapes, and winemakers charge a lot for the wine. However, in a good year in a cool, alternately foggy and sunny place, like Burgundy or Oregon, Pinot Noir becomes blissful.

What's the Story with Pinot Noir?

You can't really talk about Pinot Noir in America without mentioning the movie *Sideways,* the surprising art-house hit about a sad sack who equates the fickle, often disappointing, yet in its best moments fleetingly sublime and ecstatic nature of life with the fickle, often disappointing, yet in its best moments fleetingly sublime and ecstasy-inducing nature of Pinot Noir.

Quick and Dirty Pinot Gris Guide

Fads, fashions, and trends are a major driver of all things wine—for instance, the preferred drink of swashbuckling pirates in the time of Shakespeare was "sack," the strong wine known to us today as Madeira or sherry. Yes, the wine of people shooting cannons and swinging on ropes with their swords drawn is now popularly conceived as the best drink for demure old British ladies. Fashion. Go figure. So it shouldn't come as a great surprise that Pinot Gris (*pee-no gree*), or, in Italian, Pinot Grigio (*pee-no greezh-ee-oh*), roared into fashion in the last twenty years, going from one of the most obscure grapes in the world of American wine to the number two most popular white. Only time will tell if Pinot Gris, a spontaneous, natural mutation of Pinot Noir, remains popular—but if it does, here's what you need to know about it.

Pinot gris is a golden-green white wine that is grown primarily in Oregon and California domestically, and in France's Alsace region and in Italy. At its best Pinot Gris is both flesh and bones, offering scents of pear, apple, and a bready richness as well lush texture (the flesh) over a nicely acidic structure that provides the wine with nervy, racy excitement. At its worst Pinot Gris/Grigio is just bone, and not much bone at that; it can be the wine equivalent of lemon water with a teaspoon of vodka.

If you want to improvise a Pinot Gris/Grigio tasting like the longer ones here for other varietals, gather at least four wines.

1. A cheap Italian Pinot Grigio.
2. An Alsatian Pinot Gris (Domaine Zind Humbrecht, Domaine Weinbach, and Trimbach are good names).
3. A Willamette Valley (Oregon) Pinot Gris—King Estate is the American benchmark Pinot Gris, but there are lots of good ones, like those from Chehalem, Eyrie, or Ponzi.

4. A nice, over-$20 Pinot Grigio from northeastern Italy, from a place like Alto-Aldige or Friuli-Venezia Giulia.
5. If you want to be absolutely comprehensive, find a fifth, a late-harvest or, if it's Alsatian, "vendanges tardives" wine to give you a sense of what the Pinot Gris grape is like in its fruitiest state.

Alongside, pair either a dinner of a lightweight protein (any white fish, shellfish, salmon, pork, or chickenlike poultry) or a cheese and appetizer spread similar to the one suggested for Sauvignon Blanc.

Open your wines. Taste them!

You should find that the cheap Italian one is thin, the Alsatian one fatter and more complicated, the Oregon one someplace between the two, the expensive Italian different in that it offers lots of structure and a mineral nose. If you've got the late harvest, you should have a fruit bowl of fascinating apple-pear complexity. And that's Pinot Gris slash Grigio!

The lead character, Miles, is an intolerable schlub, but Pinot Noir came through *Sideways* with flying colors, and ever since the movie came out, sales of the wine have increased up to 30 percent a year. Pinot Noir, already the world's most in-demand heartbreak grape, got even more in demand, and thus heartbreakier. Prices rose across the board, and because the economic incentives were so great, people who shouldn't have been planting the stuff did, making a complicated grape even more complicated.

How complicated is it? Oh, bother, it's just nuts. Here's your background info: During the Dark Ages the Duchy of Burgundy, a quasi-independent French nation in the middle of France, was the wealthiest and most stable part of northern Europe. One of the things they used their stability for was to nurture groups of monks to go on out there and make wine. Make wine they did, Pinot Noir and, eventually, Chardonnay, the wines known as red and white Burgundy.

To make this wine they scrupulously examined the more or less continuous series of limestone and chalk slopes that make up the important wine-growing area of Burgundy, the escarpment we now call the Côte d'Or, the "golden slope," to determine which vineyards made the best wine. The system they established survives, more or less, to this day, filtered through hundreds of years of Napoleonic inheritance laws, which specified that vineyards weren't to be passed down through families whole, but had to be split among all the heirs.

Today, Burgundy looks like a crazy quilt of thousands of vineyards and tens of thousands of producers. A single vineyard in Burgundy called Clos de Vougeot is, as of this writing, split among eighty owners. Burgundy is only thirty-odd miles long, but contains around seven hundred appellations and some thirty thousand producers. How many individual wine labels are there, then? Who knows! There are whole vineyards in Burgundy the size of an American dining room.

It gets worse: Burgundy changes dramatically from vintage to vintage, and even individual bottles can change from week to week. Are you scared off yet? If wine connoisseurship is snowboarding, Burgundy connoisseurship is snowboarding naked, on your hands, through exploding land mines of manure.

What's a wine lover to do? Hire a critic. If you want to know why wine critics have traditionally been so stuffy, brainy, arcane, weird, and necessary, look to Burgundy. Whom can you trust? Who has tasted the stuff, who understands the weird geography, the zillions of labels? You may as well trust a critic. If you yourself fall in love with Burgundy, my best advice is to get yourself to burghound.com and buy a subscription. Its critic, Allen Meadows, is the best Burgundy authority in the business, and while at first you may think, "I don't want to pay $125 a year for a quarterly journal and a database of tasting notes," once you buy a couple of lousy $40 Burgundies, you will.

Another option is to find an importer whose taste jibes with your own. A lot of longtime Burgundy drinkers shop for Burgundy by simply walking into the aisle and turning bottles around until they see the names Kermit Lynch, Martine's Wines, or Robert Kacher. This is an insider's secret that a lot of wine critics won't tell you, because for one thing it doesn't confer any intellectual bragging rights (my secret? I lean on others!), and for another, most critics see it as their job to critique importers like Lynch, Martine Saunier, and Kacher as much as they would any winery or winemaker, because Lynch, Saunier, and Kacher act as sort of co-winemakers (more on that in a second).

But I don't feel that way. While Burgundy is nigh impossible, I've found I have a 90 percent chance of predicting my happiness with what's inside a bottle if one of those three names is on the outside. And that's as much as a guarantee as you are ever going to get in the world of Burgundy.

Of course, there are certain high-maintenance hassles in life, like dogs, horses, babies, and vintage cars, that are, to the people who love them, worth every high-maintenance moment. Pinot Noir has two attributes that forever and inalterably will outweigh the hassle: the ecstasy of the great ones, and the food-friendliness of them all.

Speaking of food-friendliness, now is as good a time as any to demolish one of the central tenets of wine writing: Pairing wine and food is no big deal. Why do people think it is? Let me tell you about something called the news hole. Every newspaper, every magazine, operates with some

Conversations with Bigwigs: Kermit Lynch

Berkeley, California–based wine importer and wine shop owner Kermit Lynch is one of the most reliable names in French wine in this country. If you see his name on the back of a bottle, it's a guarantee that the wine inside has personality and distinction. Whether it's a personality you yourself will like is something you'll only know once you fit the key of that wine into the lock of your own taste, so to speak. I asked Lynch about the differences between Pinot Noir and Burgundy.

It's a cultural difference. Compare a French movie to an American movie: The French movie feels no need to end in a giant explosion. French actresses haven't had boob jobs.

In France there is a much greater diversity of styles, and this of course comes from the winemakers, who can be stubborn, or even strange, but each winemaker has a vision, which comes from knowing their soils, or their grapes, and from these different visions come different things. That's why I ended up concentrating on France.

I think a lot about [pioneering California chef] Alice Waters and what she's done with Chez Panisse: By supporting and publicizing small farmers all of a sudden we have small farmers again. That's huge! It's huge for our food, and our world. In the old days [French] farmers would sell their wine to *négociants* and you'd lose all character. Now there's a change, and small winemakers can find people who appreciate what they do, even if they're half a world away. So this allows them to keep doing what they do—that's huge too.

I'd say the wine marketplace is divided in pieces today, into real wine and pop wine. "Real" wine is probably not the right word, but you've got the soil, you've got the grape, you've got the sun, you've got the winemakers, and that's what comes out in the bottle. Then there are pop wines, like

pop music, designed to satisfy the popular taste, to catch
the trend, the spirit of the day. Some people will only like
the pop wine, the same way some people only like pop
music, or movies that end in explosions. And some people
will say, "Wow! This has no explosions! Fantastic."

ratio of advertising pages to editorial content. When editors
are planning their publications they often refer to the pages
allocated to editorial content as the "news hole." Part of
their job is to figure out how to fill it. Some days the problem is that there are too many good stories fighting for too
little space; other days, like, oh, Thanksgiving, the problem
is that all the writers are on vacation and there is not
enough to fill the news hole. I attribute the entire genre of
"what wine to serve on Thanksgiving" stories to the horrible confluence of the holiday news hole crisis, newspaper
editors' cluelessness about wine, and wine writers' great desire to collect a paycheck.

I know because I have gotten these calls myself. When an
editor says, "Do you want to write about what wine to pair
with Thanksgiving?" writers hear, "Do you want some
money?" The answer is always yes. And because wine writers have written the story eight times in the past, and because they've read their friends' and frenemies' stories on
the subject eight times, the temptation is ever stronger to
be ever more baroque.

But you know what? Everything pairs with Thanksgiving. Thanksgiving has just about every food known to man
in it, and so a case can be made for whatever wine you feel
like writing about. Chardonnay? Sure! It goes great with
roast turkey! Syrah? Sure! Goes great with cranberry
sauce, and turkey! Cabernet Sauvignon? Why not, it goes
great with sausage stuffing—and turkey! Riesling? Sure, a

good crisp Riesling goes perfectly with sweet cranberry sauce, rich stuffing—and turkey! Now where's my check?

Seriously, there are really only a rare few wines that don't go well with Thanksgiving, and these are the same wines that don't go well with any food, because they are very oaky. So consider this your free pass to never reading another one of those articles again: Everything goes with Thanksgiving except fruity New World oak bombs meant to be drunk as cocktail wines, or astringent old-world oak bombs that are meant to age for five years before you drink them, at which point they will go with Thanksgiving.

Oh, and ditto for Easter, Christmas, and New Year's. Yes to practically everything; no to oak bombs.

In fact, if editors asked, "What wine *shouldn't* you pair with Thanksgiving?" the genre would have much more quickly exhausted itself, because there would be only one answer, oft-repeated, and it would soon seem as self-evident as "Should I park my car in a lake?"

"No" is actually the most important part of wine pairing. When wine writers tell you a delicate yellowtail hamachi appetizer goes well with Riesling or a Burgundian Pinot Noir, what they're really doing is eliminating things it *wouldn't* go well with: It wouldn't go with heavy, rich reds because the fish would be overwhelmed. It wouldn't go well with heavy whites for the same reason. If they tell you pot roast goes well with Cabernet Sauvignon, they're really thinking, "It can't go with Riesling because the roast would overwhelm the Riesling." The only meaningful idea behind food-and-wine pairing is that neither partner should overwhelm the other, which is where the idea of "like goes with like" comes from.

Pinot Noir goes with everything because it's the medium grape. It's thin-skinned, like a white, but red, like a red. It makes a light-colored red wine, halfway between a white and a red. When it's used to make Champagne, it makes a fuller-bodied sparkling wine that has weight and depth. If you want to know the insider's no-brainer secret to appropriate wine-food pairing forever and ever, it's simply: Pinot Noir.

The "Holy Trinity" of Pinot Noir

The Grape

A thin-skinned grape primarily used to make a still red wine, Pinot Noir makes such a varying and complicated wine that some critics devote their whole lives to understanding it. This variation may in part be due to its many clones. Wine grapes are not reproduced by seed, like corn, but by grafting parts of one plant onto other rootstock. Because spontaneous mutations can occur in the fields, a number of distinct Pinot Noir clones have arisen, and Pinot Noir geeks are happy to spend years comparing the difference between, say, Dijon clones (from Dijon, in Burgundy) and Wadenswil clones (from Switzerland; popular with some in Oregon).

High-end Pinot Noir is always bottled alone, and whatever blending is done is combining grapes from different vineyards, say, one that is more tannic with another that is candied with a third which is more acidic. Bottom-shelf Pinot Noir may sometimes be blended with anything handy, like Merlot or Syrah, which is why some cheap Pinot Noirs don't taste very much like Pinot Noir.

Terroir

Pinot Noir *can* grow anywhere. It is very difficult to grow in hot climates because it burns, but people grow it there anyway because it is so easy to sell and commands a high price. However, Pinot Noir's great homes are invariably cold. There's Burgundy, of course, where it is grown in the same

limestone that makes Chablis and Sancerre what they are
and gathers similar mineral notes from the rocky soil. Certain pockets of California, such as the land occupied by the
vineyards Calera or Chalone, also have limestone soils.
Other parts of California, most notably Santa Barbara, the
Russian River Valley, Santa Maria Valley, and the Anderson
River Valley, have cold weather fog, and intermittent sunshine. Oregon is cold, like Burgundy, and foggy, but has
longer days, so fruit has more "hang time" on the vine,
which allows the grapes to develop great nuance and flavor.

Winemaking

Pinot Noir's often commanding prices also reflect the
amount of hand labor that goes into making the wine. Typically, high-end Pinot Noir grapes are hand-harvested, not
machine-picked, in the cold of night and transported to the
winery not in dump-truck-size bins, where the bottom grapes
get bruised, but in small bins. Rotten, bruised, or broken
grapes are removed, sometimes all the stems are too, though
sometimes not. The grapes are then lightly pressed, and the
grape juice is allowed to sit with the skins to absorb color and
flavors. Fermentation will proceed using either wild yeasts
or more predictable commercial ones. Enzymes may be used
to extract more color. Top-shelf Pinot Noir is then typically
100 percent barrel-aged in French wood for somewhere between ten months and two years. Winemaking in Pinot Noir
is less obvious to a wine drinker than it is in Chardonnay, but
just as much tinkering goes on with Pinot Noir as does with
Chardonnay, its Burgundian sister.

Stop Reading, Start Drinking!

In this chapter you'll learn about Pinot Noir—what it
tastes like, the different styles, the different *terroirs,* the
different price points. Most important, you'll figure out

whether Pinot Noir is your own particular brand of heartbreak, or whether you think the hassle outweighs the love. Whatever you decide, it will help you for the rest of your life.

Pinot Noir FIELD GUIDE

A good wine shop should have at least two dozen Pinot Noirs, including some French *vin de pays* (pronounced *vahn deu pay*) or country wine, under $10, some basic domestic Pinot Noir from producers like Gallo, some basic *village* or *négociant* Burgundy, and some single-vineyard wine from California and the Willamette Valley in Oregon, as well as real classified-growth red Burgundy. Nice Pinot Noir, on average, costs more than the nice versions of most other wines because it takes so much work. If your store doesn't have at least six wines priced $50 and up, you're not where the Pinot Noir heads near you shop.

Bottom-shelf French: *Vin de pays* Pinot Noir, under $12
France makes a lot of wine, and one place where it makes a lot of it includes the Languedoc (*long-dock*), an area south of fancy Burgundy territory in France. Bright, cherrylike, uncomplicated Pinot Noir from this part of the world floods the bottom shelves of every big liquor store in America, some of it bottled under French labels, and some, interestingly enough, bottled under American ones. If your wine bottle, box, or Tetra Pak says *Vin de Pays* or *Vin de Pays d'Oc,* what it's trying to tell you is: This is quaffable, basic, simple Pinot Noir from a place where vines grow the way corn does in Iowa. Possible names: Red Bicyclette, French Rabbit, Barton & Guestier, and many more.

Bottom-shelf domestic: California, under $12
Cherry-berry or cherry-cola Pinot Noir from the big, sunny, happy heart of unspecified California is never profound, but will

usually give you a sense of what the fruit of Pinot Noir tastes like in its simplest form. Names? The usual suspects: Gallo, Mondavi, Beringer, Beaulieu, Fetzer, and Turning Leaf.

Village and *négociant* Burgundy, under $25

Négociants are French people who buy wine grapes, crushed grapes, or wine from growers and make and market, or just market, the wine under their own name. Big ones include Drouhin Boisset, Bouchard Père & Fils, Louis Latour, Louis Jadot, and Chanson. Sometimes the *négociant*'s name will be the biggest thing on the label, and sometimes the village from which the wine comes will be; village names include Vosné Romanée (*vone rome-a-nay*), Gevrey-Chambertin (*jeh-vray sham-bear-tan*); Chambolle-Musigny (*sham-bowl mu-sin-yee*); and Nuits-Saint-Georges (*nwee sahn zhorzh*). Any under-$40 wine with one of these venerable names will, ideally, deliver some classic Pinot Noir fruit, as well as some earth and complexity.

Single-vineyard California, $20 and up

California is big, and Pinot Noir grows well just about everywhere in it that has poor soil where the Pacific Ocean works to keep things cool. Stand in the California Pinot Noir section and you'll see single-estate bottles from the Anderson Valley, the Russian River Valley, the Sonoma Coast, the Carneros region of Napa Valley, the Santa Cruz Mountains, Mount Harlan, Mendocino County, Santa Barbara County's Santa Rita Hills, and the Maria Santa Valley. Prices are always over $20, almost always over $30, and frequently over $40. What do you get for your money? Sometimes you'll get red fruit like cranberries and strawberries built on a lacy, elegant structure. This is especially true for wines from California standard-bearer Calera, famed for their Burgundy-like limestone soils. Sometimes you'll get intense, dusky currants like the hard-to-find wines of critical lightning rod (some adore it, some despise it as overripe) Kosta Browne.

Are they *all* worth the money? Nah. Some are just thin cherry juice, others so overripe they might as well be Merlot, Syrah, or a flat vodka-Coke. But they're *often* worth it enough that prices and demand stay high. Some good names to tilt the odds in your favor: Calera, Goldeneye, Williams Selyem, Fess Parker, Kistler, Flowers, Failla, Gary Farrell, DeLoach, La Crema, Siduri, Au Bon Climat, Château St. Jean, MacPhail, Londer, Tandem, Lynmar, Pisoni, Vision Cellars, Morgan, Sanford, Clos Pepe, and Sea Smoke.

Single-vineyard Oregon, $20 and up

Oregon is the land of Pinot Noir in America: Three-fourths of its vineyards are planted with Pinot Noir. The grape does wonderfully there, responding beautifully to the longish days and soils heavy with volcanic and marine sediment. The most esteemed wines come from the Willamette (rhymes with "damn it!") Valley, a hundred-mile-long valley south of Portland with distinct sub-regions, like Yamhill-Carlton, the Dundee Hills, and the Chehalem Mountains, all of which you will enjoy exploring if you fall for Oregon's signature dense and supple, but typically not overripe, lush, dark fruit and spice Pinot Noirs. Some names to look for: Eyrie, Adelsheim, Argyle, Cristom, Erath, Soter, WillaKenzie, Beaux Frères, Patricia Green, Brick House, Ken Wright, Domaine Serene, Panther Creek, Rex Hill, Elk Cove, Domaine Drouhin Oregon, Sokol Blosser, Archery Summit, and St. Innocent.

Good Burgundy, $75 and up

By good Burgundy I mean the stuff you get dressed up for: the Premier Cru wines, or, if you're rich, powerful, and lucky, the Grand Cru, or at least the wine from the surrounding villages. (Quick refresher course: In Burgundy, Grand Cru are the best wines, as classified by French wine laws, Premier Cru next best.) How much should you spend on good Burgundy? That's up to you and your God, but my experience is you're not going to touch the hem of greatness for less than $75. However, even an entry-level good Burgundy should give you a pretty good sense of what all the fuss is about: You should taste and smell red and black fruits, but also get good structure and at least a hint of earth, mineral, aged beef, or something that kicks off a little switch in your brain that asks, "What is that? It's wonderful. Let me smell that again. What is it? Let me taste that again. Hey, that's my bottle, back off, people!"

The labels will have the names of the villages on them; listing them all would fill a separate book, but here are a few biggies: Vosne-Romanée (*vone rome-a-nay*); Volnay (*vohl-nay*); Pommard (*po-mar*); Morey St. Denis (*mo-ray sahn duh-nee*); Aloxe-Corton (*ah-lohss cor-tohn*); Gevrey-Chambertin (*jeh-vray sham-bear-tan*); Chambolle-Musigny (*sham-bowl mu-sin-yee*); and Nuits-Saint-Georges (*nwee sahng zhorzh*).

The rest of the story: New Zealand, Chile, Argentina, South Africa, Italy, Washington State, Australia, and elsewhere, $8 and up

Because it's so far south, closer to Antarctica than any other major wine growing area, New Zealand has a cool climate and has been widely touted as the next big place for Pinot Noir. Also cool, Chile is increasingly a player when it comes to under-$20 Pinot Noirs. Australia puts out some well-regarded Pinot Noirs, especially from the Yarra Valley. South Africa's leading grape, Pinotage, is a cross between Pinot Noir and the grape Cinsault, and some think Pinot Noir should be a bright part of South Africa's future.

What do I think? Once Pinot Noir in its major French and American West Coast personalities is concrete in your mind, the world is your oyster. But if you try these first, they'll just confuse you.

Conversations with Bigwigs: Bobby Kacher

What exactly does a wine importer do? A lot more than you'd think. I called up Bobby Kacher, a man who has transformed the French wine scene in America in his lifetime, to find out.

I spent my first summer in France when I was nineteen and trying to figure out if I was a college person. I was working for an importer who said: Can you build France for me [as a source to import wine from]? Live there as long as you want. They paid me practically nothing, and I took an apartment in Gigondas. You're driving down the road, you see twenty miles of rocky riverbed vineyards, you say, look at this old Grenache, old Carignane, growing on a slope with a lot of limestone. I wonder whose it is? You start knocking on doors. Eventually I would find the grower, taste his wines. Often the wines were fifty, sixty, seventy percent of what they could have been. So I would say: If you crop thin, if you go for more maturity before harvest, if you transport your grapes carefully in ten-kilo trays instead of truck-size bins, if you triage grapes and de-stem half the fruit, I think you could make a classic wine. Triage is where you sort through the grapes on a big table, you throw away 10 to 15 percent of the fruit, everything that's overripe, underripe, rotten, or broken. You throw away anything you wouldn't put into your mouth to eat. The whole concept of producing less was a little foreign. Their dad or grandpa had told them: Always produce more. Yeah, it's not going to be very good, but you're selling by the ton to a négociant, so who cares?

Before these changes a lot of wine was made like this: Near the door of the winery would be a big bin, all the fruit got dumped in there, some rotten, some unripe, and a thing like a big corkscrew would bear down on it all, pushing it through pipes towards tanks. To make wine with rotten fruit in it you have to add chemicals—tartaric acid, sulfur—to arrest the rot. A lot of people were using chemicals instead of cleanliness.

So I would tell them, if they did all those things, if they cared for the fruit, if they were careful in their winemaking and would commit to letting the wine clarify naturally and not by filtering or other manipulations, and after that if they made sure the wine was bottled in good form, I'd honor my side and make sure it got sold in America. Once people saw this happen two or three times, they became very interested. Suddenly their neighbors were making much better wines and getting much more money. You have to show them that all that work is worth it, because the consumer will pay more for good wine. I don't like selling sizzle; if my name is on the bottle I have to believe in what's inside.

What is the difference between Domaine de la Romanée-Conti and their neighbors? It's not the terroir that made it good; they had the money to buy everything they needed to make the best possible wine from their terroir. The guy next door was a peasant farmer, he was using every grape that came out of his fields, and finally putting the wine in filthy old barrels. In Burgundy it used to be considered a virtue to keep your money close to your mattress and reinvest nothing in the business. Now things have gone the other way. I'm going to write my own book one day—but the book I'm going to write, I won't be able to sell wine after that. It will be called *Fiddlers in the Cellar,* and it won't be about violinists.

The beginning of my year starts in November, because it's really the first look at the new harvest. I taste the wine in tanks and do a little triage for myself: Let's keep this apart, I think this tank is for me. I return in January, to relook and re-taste everything I saw in November, to see if I'm still on track. Some things will be in barrels, some are only ever in tanks—our rosés from Provence, for instance. The rosés and fresh whites are bottled in February and March, and I make final selections for those in that January trip. You learn right away not to take your opinion too seriously. The first trip the grower may say, I think these are the best for making rosé. I'll say, I think this is a little overripe for me, because I know that overripe in November is really overripe in May. But then in January I may taste it again and say, You were right. This hasn't moved at all, it's just as it was in November, I think it should be blended with the ones I chose. You have to have an open mind; there is no room for ego in a tasting room.

I go back in May to reexamine wines that are still in barrel, and taste everything I already tasted twice earlier, and eliminate or adjust as necessary. You have to have a good taste memory for what the wine was like in every stage, and back over the years. My reputation is good because of that hard work, and maybe that's why people follow our wines. You've got one life to live, I always thought you should do everything as well as you could. However, there's a limit to what I can personally vouch for, and that's why Robert Kacher selections is so small—we import about 100,000 cases from eighty winemakers, which is nothing compared to a Georges Duboeuf or some of the California wineries. But in Burgundy you only get six to eight bunches of grapes per plant—in California you can get twenty bunches per plant. That's why they say in Burgundy you make Pinot Noir, but in California you can make money.

Food and Pinot Noir

To find a food that *doesn't* go with Pinot Noir, you have to really stretch into crazy territory and start messing with foods that essentially have no pairing, like herring braised with cinnamon red-hots. Rest assured, there will be a blowhard or two on the Internet—or, if you're very unlucky, in your actual life—who will labor hard and come up with an exception. There are blowhards in the world of baseball stats, tax law, and above all in wine, but ignore them, because the exception is not the rule. The rule is: Pinot Noir–based

Champagne (blanc de noirs) tastes fabulous with 99 percent of foods, and the red wine Pinot Noir with 95 percent.

Tasting Pinot Noir
Step by Step

1. A Brief Road Map to Our Upcoming Pinot Noir Road Trip

Whether you're tasting alone or by party, you're going to need about six Pinot Noirs to get a sense of what the grape tastes like generally, and what it is capable of in the right hands. First, you'll compare the basic taste of the grape, strawberry-cherry-earth, as found in bottom-shelf French Pinot Noir, called *vin de pays,* and bottom-shelf American Pinot Noir. Next, you'll try a well-known California Pinot Noir and compare it with one from the Willamette Valley; this pairing should create concrete extremes in your mind of what Pinot Noir tastes like in America. Then you'll try a basic village Burgundy and the most expensive Burgundy you feel comfortable buying, which will give you a sense of the magnificence Pinot Noir is capable of achieving in its native soil.

You'll come out of this tasting with a definite idea of what Pinot Noir tastes like, which style you like, and which is worth your money. This will give you a firm enough foundation in Pinot Noir that you can embark on a lifelong journey, or skip it, albeit from an informed perspective.

Notes on Tasting Pinot Noir Solo or in Pairs

If you're tasting your Pinot Noir solo, plan to taste with some food. Pinot Noir is a food wine and you might lose some of the beauty if there's not food around. Not a cook? A grocery store rotisserie chicken will do nicely, or pick and choose from the foods in the party plan below.

Notes on Tasting Pinot Noir by Party

This is a perfect tasting to arrange around a dinner party. Since you'll be drinking six bottles of wine, you could serve ten people or so—why not roast a whole salmon or leg of lamb, or cook a whole turkey on the grill? In winter, beef Bourguignon is classic; buy an extra bottle of *vin de pays* for the pot. Vegetarians, think about earthier foods (truffles, mushrooms, grilled eggplant, grilled fennel, braised chard, beets, and such) and fruit flavors that emphasize Pinot Noir's cherry, plum, and blackberry scents, and of course all the nuts—walnuts, hazelnuts, pignoli, and the rest. Risotto with truffle oil, dried cherries, and pignoli, perhaps?

If you'd rather host a simple wine, cheese, and appetizer tasting, focus on hard, well-aged, nutty cheeses like cave-aged Gruyère or Parmigiano Reggiano. Some people like to add a young goat cheese like Chèvre or an aged one like Garrotxa. If you like, add more substantial splurges like pâté, or even truffled foie gras.

For dessert, go for medium-weight options like pound cake, madeleines, or Italian pignoli cookies.

2. Shopping

Whether you're alone or having a party, your first task is to buy your Pinot Noirs. You'll need six bottles, selected from the field guide above. The names provided are simply suggestions to help you in your shopping; whatever your local wine shop has should be fine. Just try to match the categories, not the names. You want to end up with:

1. A fruity California bottom-shelf Pinot Noir like ones from Gallo, Mondavi, or Fetzer. $5–$12.
2. A fruity French bottom-shelf *vin de pays* Pinot Noir—this may have an American winery's label on the front, or

a French one. Key words: *vin de pays* and Pinot Noir. Names: French Rabbit, Red Bicyclette, Barton & Guestier. $5–$12.

3. A single-vineyard California Pinot Noir. Some names: Calera, Hanzell, Château St. Jean, Goldeneye. $20–$40.

4. A Willamette (Oregon) Pinot Noir. Some names: Eyrie, Adelsheim, Erath, WillaKenzie, Domaine Serene. $20–$60.

5. A *village* or *négociant* Burgundy: You're looking for something like Joseph Drouhin's Laforet, basic good but not crazy expensive real Burgundy. Names of *négociants*: Drouhin, Bouchard Père & Fils, Louis Latour, Louis Jadot, and Chanson. $15–$40.

6. Real Burgundy! Something from a Premier Cru vineyard, if you're particularly blessed in the bank account, or, if you're merely well off, from a real Burgundian village. Some names: Vosne-Romanée, Volnay, Pommard, Morey St. Denis, Aloxe-Corton, Gevrey-Chambertin, Chambolle-Musigny, and Nuits-Saint-Georges. Some producer names: Georges Roumier, Dujac, Dugat, Armand Rousseau, Faiveley, Jean Chauvenet, Louis Jadot, and Denis Mortet. Expect to pay $75 or more.

3. Planning and Thinking About Tasting

Gather your glasses, dump bucket, and tasting markers. Make your life easier: Put some fresh raspberries, frozen raspberries, or raspberry jam in a wine glass. You will instantly understand the so-called red fruit that emanates from a glass of Pinot Noir. For black fruit, go for fresh blackberries or black cherries, or their frozen or jam equivalent. For spice, cinnamon sticks and peppercorns work well. If you have any actual dirt handy—from the garden? from a houseplant?—put it in a wineglass and you'll know immediately what earth smells like in this context.

Tasting Markers

Keep the following list handy so you can glance at it while you're tasting—it will help you name fragrances that seem just out of reach.

	Most common	
Red fruits (Raspberry, cherry, strawberry, cranberry)	Black fruits (black cherry, blackberry, plum) Currants	Spice Roses Earth Tar Mushrooms

	Less likely, but still possible	
Chocolate	Leather	Licorice
Mocha	Barnyard	Violets
Herb	Roasted meat	Minerals
Cola	Forest floor	Truffles

4. Cool Things Off

Get your wine to cellar temperature! (See page 10 for why this is important.) For Pinot Noir, that's around 60 degrees.

5. Pull the Corks!

6. Taste Your First Wine

Your basic American bottom-shelf Pinot Noir should tell you what Pinot Noir is like in its ripe, uncomplicated cherry-berry guise. Pour an inch or so into each guest's wineglass and swirl. Pass around your tasting markers if you've got them.

Questions to consider: Red fruit? Cranberry? Cherries? Strawberries? Raspberries? Black fruit? Black cherries, blackberries, plums? Usually Pinot Noir will be more one or the other, either more red fruit or more black fruit. Sometimes you'll detect both; this is a good thing, and indicates a more complicated wine.

Does the wine seem bright or deep? Does it seem sweet or balanced? Do you like it?

Try the wine with a bite of food: Does it make the food taste better? Does the food make the wine taste better?

If you've only got one wineglass, dump your wine. If you've got two, now is the time to put forward your second glass and put some of the French bottom-shelf Pinot Noir in it.

7. Taste Your Second Wine

We're on to the second Pinot Noir, the French vin de pays. Pour about an inch into a wineglass for each guest. Swirl. Sniff. Taste. You should experience fruit similar to the first one, but more acid. This should be a brisker, lighter wine. Is it? How else is it different from the American wine?

Try some food with it: Does the wine improve the food, or vice versa?

(Note to solo tasters, or those tasting in pairs: You are now going to take a break. Pick up the tasting of the next two wines as soon as convenient.)

8. Taste Your California Single-Estate Pinot Noir

Pour an inch of your California single-estate Pinot Noir into a wineglass. Swirl. Sniff. Taste. It should be very different from the others. Ideally it will have a more unified structure, and offer some other benefit. More lively fragrances? Depth and a mushroomy intensity? A better structure that gives the wine more oomph?

Questions to consider: Does it have anything in common

with the first two you tried? Remember, any differences are almost entirely because of where the wine was grown. Isn't that astonishing? Again, try the wine with food.

9. Taste Your Willamette (Oregon) Pinot Noir

Pour an inch of your Willamette Pinot Noir. Swirl. Sniff. Pass tasting markers if you've got them. Typically, Oregon Pinot Noirs are more on the black-fruit side of the Pinot Noir spectrum, and might even have some chocolate or mocha intensity. Do you get that from yours? Does it feel lusher, softer, silkier in your mouth? Or more shrill and taut? Go back and try one of the bottom-shelf wines; they should feel lighter and less substantial than the Oregon wine. Check the back label of your wine: Does it note any particular scents? Do you get them, or does it seem like mere marketing-speak?

(A note to solo tasters, or those in groups of two: Another break! Pick up the tasting of the next two wines as soon as convenient.)

10. Taste Your *Village* or *Négociant* Basic Burgundy

Pour an inch of your village or *négociant* Burgundy. Swirl. Sniff. Taste. Typically, this wine will be rougher, tougher, brawnier, and offer mushroomy, beefy, forest-floor, and other indelicate notes. How do you like it? Some people find France's less polished Pinot Noirs wonderful, and other people find them off-putting. Which camp are you in? Other things to consider: Black fruit, red fruit, or neither? Try it with food. How do you like it?

11. Taste Your Real Burgundy

On to the big-dollar wine! Real Burgundy. Tell everyone how much you spent—you want them to really enjoy it, right? (Consider the neuroeconomist who put electrodes on people's heads and watched their brains light up with pleasure as they drank wine they were told was expensive.) Pour. Swirl. Sniff. Taste. If things have gone well, this should be a whole order of magnitude above everything else you've tasted. It should unite the acidic structure and fruity qualities of the bottom-shelf wines with the silk and intensity of the Willamette wine and the funkiness of the basic Burgundy into something much greater than the sum of its parts. Does it? Or do you feel ripped off? Try your wine with food. Let it sit in your glass and evolve; it should change over time, releasing new aromas, gathering in intensity, or becoming more approachable.

Now it's the time to ask yourself the big questions: Did you have a favorite among the half-dozen Pinot Noirs? Which would you buy again? Which were worth the money? Is Pinot Noir what you thought it was? Go back and compare the various wines. If you're tasting by party, whichever bottle gets finished first wins!

And that's it! You now have a basic familiarity with what Pinot Noir tastes like. Taking into account that this is the most difficult wine on earth, having a basic familiarity is no small thing. Spend the next six months drinking Pinot Noir and you should be able to drink it, order it, and know it better than just about anyone outside the food and wine business. But if you start selling your family's fine antiques in pursuit of Premier Cru Burgundy, don't come crying to me; I told you they call it the Heartbreak Grape.

THE TAKEAWAY

Pinot Noir is a thin-skinned dark grape used to make red wine called Burgundy or Pinot Noir, a sparkling white wine called Champagne, or rosé wine. It is grown all over the world, though most people agree its highest expression is in France and in pockets of California and Oregon. It's considered the most food-friendly of all wines, and the most vexingly difficult of all wines to make and buy well, which is why Pinot Noir drinkers are the most critic-dependent of all wine drinkers.

Five-second cheat sheet for people who didn't read the chapter and are reading this on their iPhones in a wine bar

Pinot Noir (*pee-no nwahr*) is one of the world's greatest reds—and one of its greatest whites, when made into Champagne. However, it's very, very tricky to make, and therefore the prices for the good stuff are invariably very high.

Whenever possible, ask for a taste of the Pinot Noir you're thinking of ordering before getting a whole bottle or glass; more than any other wine, there's a very good chance you're not going to like it. Good Pinot Noir tends to fall into two styles: plush, ripe, and deep, epitomized by the Pinot Noirs of the Willamette (*willAM-it*) Valley in Oregon, and Burgundian, which is both lighter and earthier than American wine.

Knock-Their-Socks-Off
Gifts for Pinot Noir Lovers

1. Domaine de la Romanée-Conti: This is kind of akin to saying: You know what would be a great gift for someone who loves architecture? The Empire State Building! But I thought I'd throw it out there anyway, because a DRC wine wouldn't just knock the socks off a Pinot Noir lover, it would throw most of them into a dead faint. DRC makes lots of different single-vineyard offerings, like La Tâche, and you'll typically pay upwards of $600 a bottle for them, but if you're sitting around trying to figure out what all-family gift to get your dad for his sixtieth birthday or how to impress Steven Spielberg, now you know.

2. Domaine Serene: Down at prices for mere mortals, Domaine Serene, the Oregon winery, makes a wine called Evenstad Reserve that generally sells for around $75 and is one of America's most esteemed wines. Expect it to be black-cherry rich and stormy.

3. A Wine Club Membership: Calera, Eyrie, Williams-Selyem, Au Bon Climat, Sea Smoke Cellars, and many other prestigious American Pinot producers have wine clubs or special mailing lists you can join to get exclusive chances to buy in-demand wines. Some operate such that you sign up for a certain price level, say $150, and they send you wine twice a year. Others send out emails giving you a chance to buy. Either way, that's how you get wine with big bragging rights in the world of American Pinot Noir.

4. Something Old: Aged Burgundy is one of the most intense pleasures that a wine person can ever experience. Or so I've read. Sadly, the truth is that most wine lovers never get a chance to taste twenty-year-old Burgundy, even though it's not necessarily that expensive. Specialty wine merchants like Morrell (morrellwine.com), K&L Wine Merchants (klwines.com), Haskell's (haskells.com), and Addy Bassin's MacArthur Beverages (bassins.com) all can put their hands on good ten-year-old or older Burgundy for under $200, or even under $100.

5. Pinot Noir Camp: Okay, technically, it's really known as the International Pinot Noir Celebration, or IPNC, but "Pinot Noir Camp" captures the spirit of it. Sign up and you'll spend a three-day summer weekend in Oregon's Willamette Valley having fancy dinners, touring wineries, going to seminars, and *tasting tasting tasting* Pinot Noirs till your teeth turn purple. You'll also hobnob with lots of Oregon Pinot Noir bigwigs. You can stay in a dorm room at Linfield College, where IPNC takes place, and experience college as it should have been, or rent a room in a nearby B&B. But if you stay in the dorms, you don't need to designate a driver. Why not have your best friends from college meet you there? Or make it your bachelor party—you'll drink a lot better than you will in Las Vegas.

11

MONEY, MONEY, MONEY

Dear Dara,
See if you can answer this in one sentence: What's the difference between an $8, a $25, and an $80 bottle of wine?

—Baffled

A lot.

Okay, actually, you got me. I can't answer it in one sentence. But I can answer it. Assuming we're looking at $8, $25, and $80 bottles of the same wine (all California Chardonnays, or all Italian Chiantis), the difference between the bottom two represents incremental bits of winemaking cost. The difference between the top two is more complicated.

First, lets look at the easier one. Why is one California Chardonnay $8, and another California Chardonnay $25?

To start, let's dial it back and look at the absurdly big picture: Why does anything cost anything? You buy a box of two-inch nails and you're basically paying for the metal that went into them, plus a little bump to pay for the machinery and people who made them, plus a little more for shipping, plus a little bump for profit for the maker, and a little more for profit for the retailer. So, for argument's sake, let's say a $3 box of nails has $1 worth of metal in it and $2 worth of everything else.

What's the equivalent for a bottle of wine? Does a bottle of wine you pay $30 for have $10 worth of grape juice in it and $20 worth of miscellaneous labor, transport, and whatnot?

Not even close.

Here's a little informed, back-of-the-envelope calculating for what goes into a bottle of wine.

1. There's the cost of land, which can be low, if your family has had it for thirty generations or it's just cheap farmland, like a lot of that in Australia, central California, or South America, or high, if you just bought well-regarded land, say, in Napa Valley, where good land can go for upwards of, not kidding, $300,000 an *acre*.

2. The cost of harvesting, which can be low, if you're harvesting by machine, or high, if you're harvesting by hand, or, in the case of some sweet dessert wines, even grape-by-grape, hand-harvesting the same row of vines over many weeks.

3. The cost of the grapes, if you're buying them, or the costs of farming them and raising them, if you did that. Again, these can be low, if you buy bulk grapes from people who have always raised them and who themselves have low overhead, like people in parts of Italy, Argentina, Australia or the central valley of California, or high, if you buy highly sought after, expensive grapes from prestigious growers.

What's the dollar figure per bottle for land, harvesting, and grapes? It would be a book in itself to do this for every winegrowing region on earth, so let's skip every winegrowing region on earth and look just at how much California growers got for their grapes in 2007. On average, most good wine grapes went for between $1,000 and $6,000 a ton. In Napa Valley grapes for premium varietals like Chardonnay and Cabernet Sauvignon sold for a little more, from about $2,000 to $6,000 a ton. One ton of grapes yields about sixty cases of wine, or 720 bottles. So, at $1,000 a ton (that is, wine on the low end), grape juice (and, folded into that, land and harvesting costs) run about $1.40 for grapes, per bottle; on the average high end, you're looking at $6,000 a ton for grapes, which is about $8.30 a bottle. The most common price, though, the one that holds for most prestigious American wines like Napa Valley Cabernets and Oregon Pinot Noirs, is around $3,500 a ton; that's a grape-cost-per-bottle of about $5. We'll use that $5 as the average grape juice cost for a nice bottle of wine.

Of course, there are exceptions to this $1,000 to $6,000 range; wine grapes selling for $100 to $300 a ton are not uncommon—that's what you can assume is ending up in bulk-wine jugs and boxes. On the high end? Hold on to your hat: The top price for a single ton of grapes in California in 2007 was $37,000 dollars a ton—insiders speculate that was for Cabernet Sauvignon from Beckstoffer Vineyards. Never heard of it? It's a privately owned grape grower that sells its grapes to various wineries and tiny labels that make single-vineyard, highly collectible, and yes, exceedingly expensive wine. Do the math and you'll see that even the most expensive grapes in all the world run only something like $50 a bottle—and the wine made from them will retail in the $300 range. (For more on grape prices, check out the USDA's National Agricultural Statistics Service: nass.usda.gov.)

So we've got one key chunk of the price of what goes into a bottle of wine, the land, harvesting, and grape juice. Figure your bottle of wine holds anywhere from a few cents worth of land, harvesting, and grape juice, when you're buying bulk, to at the absolute most around $50 a bottle; but your average nice bottle, your $18 to $35 wine, holds around $5, $6, maybe $10 worth of grapes and land.

Now let's add in some other costs that go into a bottle of wine:

4. The costs of winemaking, which can be low—if you're using a lot of machines, make your wine in cement or steel tanks, and spread your winemaking costs between hundreds of thousands of cases—or high, if you're using lots of expensive new barrels and hand labor, and need to support a large, or any, staff on a small production of a few thousand cases.

   Figure in that in 2009 prices, a new French oak barrel costs about $800 to $1,000; one made of eastern European oak, like that from Slovenia or Hungary, costs about $600 to $800; and one made of American oak runs about $400 to $600. A winemaker might choose to put all his wine in new barrels, which people call 100 percent new oak; he might even choose to put all his wine in new oak and keep it there for a while, and then transfer it to another set of brand-new barrels, called 200 percent new oak. This is rare. More likely is a winemaker who chooses to put, say, 30 percent of her harvest in new oak, and age the rest in older barrels or tanks, blending it all together before bottling. Now, while there are different shaped barrels that hold slightly different amounts (Burgundy barrels, for Pinot Noir, hold 228 liters), for our purposes we're going to focus on the most popular barrel, the Bordeaux barrel, for Cabernet Sauvignon and Merlot, which holds 225 liters, or 300 traditional 750-milliliter bottles. At 300 bottles per barrel, oak can cost as much as three dollars per bottle, but frequently will cost maybe half a dollar.

(How do cheap wines get oak? Maybe by throwing oak boards into winemaking tanks. Maybe by putting little oak pellets made with sawdust and glue into giant plastic-mesh bags and dunking them in the wine. There are a lot of cheap shortcuts.)

In addition to costly barrels, winemaking requires all sorts of expensive machines, like crushers, destemmers, forklifts, tanks, pumps, chillers, and whatnot. It also requires laboratories, salaried winemakers, assistants, electricity, water, and so on. How to estimate those costs per bottle? It's impossible to compare places that make a million cases a year with those that make ten thousand; but let's do it anyway, knowing that this exercise is just informed back-of-the-envelope penciling. So, guess $4 a bottle for winemaking costs, not counting oak, for a small operation, and fifty cents a bottle for a big one.

Now back to the running costs of a bottle of wine, on top of land, harvesting, grapes, barrels, and winemaking equipment. You've also got:

5. The cost of storing the wine, which can be nil, if you're releasing it soon after harvest, for instance in the case of almost all whites and most reds, or substantial, if, say, you're a Port or Rioja producer paying the costs associated with storing something a decade or more after harvest. (Storage includes the cost of evaporation; a typical barrel might lose a couple bottles' worth

of wine every year, which is much the point, as it leads to concentration of flavors in the remaining wine.)

6. The cost of bottles, closures, and labels. Believe it or not, there's a spread in what wineries pay for bottles. In the United States, a bag-in-box costs less than half a dollar, a cheap bottle runs about sixty-five cents, and a single heavy bottle meant for long cellaring costs around two dollars.

As for closures, corks, corklike things, and caps range widely in price. Figure five cents or so for the cheapest

---

Wine Boxes: Smart Bargain or True Sign of a Loser?

Wine writers have been hailing boxes, Tetra Paks (like juice boxes), and other alternative packaging for so long that the question would seem to be why all wine isn't in these eco-friendly containers. They are much lighter than wine bottles, so they take less petroleum to transport. At some point Tetra Paks will probably overtake wine bottles on the lower end of the market. They're fine for fresh wines meant to be drunk young, but wine stays good in them for only about six months and starts to decay rapidly after that. My advice? I wouldn't buy a case of Tetra Pak wine that was on sale without tasting it first, as it might have turned.

Another inexpensive way to package wine is in bags inside boxes. The bag shrinks around the wine as it is dispensed, preventing air from getting in and oxidizing the wine. A bag-in-box wine can stay fresh for maybe three weeks after it is opened, a feat no bottle can match. Boxed wine is not meant to be aged; wine you plan to keep around the house for even a year should only be bought in bottles.

Your takeaway? Wine boxes are just wonderful for fresh, inexpensive wines, but never buy more than you plan on drinking in the next few months.

possible closure, synthetic corks; a couple cents more for "agglomerated cork," that is, chipboard cork made of ground-up cork or cork chips and food-grade glue; ten to fifteen cents for the most basic solid-cork corks; and about 20 cents for all the metal involved in screw caps. The most expensive corks for regular wine bottles are actually the all-cork, super-high-grade ones you'll find in first-growth Burgundy, Bordeaux, and the world's most collectible top-shelf wines, which cost winemakers about fifty cents. (The most expensive closures, like the whole cork-cage-foil combo on top of a Champagne bottle, might run toward a dollar.) Needless to say, all the machinery to put foil on or corks in bottles costs something too.

The actual cost of a front-and-back paper label can be next to nothing, if it's very plain paper, or as much as half a dollar if it has a lot of engraving, embossing, gold foil, and so forth.

In total, figure that the cheapest bottle of wine comes inside seventy-five cents' worth of bottle, closure, and label; the most expensive wine has maybe five or six dollars' worth of non-grape-juice paraphernalia keeping it from spilling onto the floor.

7. The cost of label design and marketing. Obviously you could spend nothing on marketing, or millions, if you're managing, say, the Veuve Clicquot brand. There's too much variation to truly consider here, but, interestingly, in 2008 the Napa Valley label designer Jeffrey Caldewey said he typically charges $35,000 to $75,000 for design services to come up with the labels for a new line of wines.

8. The cost of transport. Wine bottles are heavy, gas costs money, and on top of that wine is supposed to be transported in refrigeration to prevent it from deteriorat-

ing—this can add anywhere from a few cents to half a dollar to a single bottle's price, depending on where it started, where it went, and how it got there.

9. Taxes, tariffs, and subsidies. Alcohol is more heavily taxed than just about any product in America, a tradition that dates all the way back to the Civil War, when alcohol taxes were one of the main ways the Union government raised money for the Northern army. Today, any bottle of wine you buy is subject to both federal and state taxes, and imported wines are subject to those and also import tariffs.

When the states get into the game, taxes can soar: Alaska is the worst place to be a wine connoisseur, as all wine is subject to a $2.50 per gallon excise tax. Another terrible place to be a wine lover? Florida ($2.25 per gallon, $3.50 per gallon on sparkling wine.) To find your state's tax rate, check out the website of the Federation of Tax Administrators: taxadmin.org. Lots of states have special sales taxes for alcohol in addition to the excise taxes. Some states, like Pennsylvania and Utah, keep complete monopolies on alcohol sales. In his book *Wine Politics,* Tyler Colman describes how a "case of wine that the Pennsylvania Liquor Control Authority buys for $100 is subject to a 30 percent mark-up, a $10.80 'bottle handling' charge, and an 18 percent Johnstown Flood Tax (enacted in 1936 and never repealed), plus a 'rounding up' to the nearest 99 cents and a local sales tax of 6 or 7 percent, depending on the county. The case might sell to the consumer for $166.42." Do the math and that means for any $14 bottle of wine you buy in Pennsylvania the state gets almost six bucks. Calculating average markups on wine is nearly impossible because all the states do things differently; the reason Trader Joe's famous Two Buck Chuck is two bucks in California and three or four bucks in the rest of the country has to do almost entirely with state regulations and taxes.

If you want to calculate the real-dollar impact of government on your bottle of wine, things get even more impossible. Various governments around the globe subsidize their grape growers, provide grape price supports, subsidize irrigation, or give tax shelters to people starting new vineyards, any of which can take a dollar or three off what would have been the free-market price of any given bottle.

10. Distributor's and retailer's cut. After Prohibition the United States established what is known as the three-tier system, meaning that the producer (a winery) and retailer (your store or restaurant) must be separated by a distributor or wholesaler. Think of it as an hourglass, with wineries at the top, you and everyone you know at the bottom, and a distributor in the middle. Why is it like this? Our system was supposed to aid in tax collection (a big concern after the years of bootleggers) and prevent crime. However, today many people see the distributor system as a state-granted monopoly. What does this mean to you? Figure any bottle price has between 15 percent and 35 percent added to it by this distributor middleman, and of course the retailer must make his profit. Some states even stipulate what that profit must be; for instance, in Ohio, wine retailers are required by law to mark bottles up a minimum of 33 percent. (Some states, notably California, allow a retailer to also hold a distributor's license; this is why the cheapest wines in America are the "Private Label" wines of big-box stores like Trader Joe's, Target, and Sam's Club.)

11. Currency value. Because wine is global, we have to take currency into account. The same bottle of Italian wine the maker sells for 10 euros might cost you $8

one year and $12 the next, due to nothing except the
way the dollar and the euro are valued against each
other.

So is that enough variables for you? For pure academic
interest, let's use the above to extrapolate: What's the absolute lowest possible price for a bottle of wine in the
United States?

Your cheapest possible domestic wine is going to be in
California, which has the least stringent separation re-
quirements between retailer and producer:

$300-a-ton grapes: 40 cents per bottle

Cheapest possible bottle, closure, and label: 75 cents per
bottle

No barrels, no aging, maybe a few dollars here and there
for oak-dust tea-bags: zero

Machine-harvested winemaking costs averaged over millions of bottles of wine: 30 cents

Lowest likely taxes: 40 cents

Total cost: $2. There is never going to be a One Buck
Chuck, unless California starts handing out free glass bottles and ends taxation. (This scenario assumes almost no
distributor or retailer cost, because it's a private-label wine,
and the store, say, Sam's Club or Trader Joe's, is making
their money on other things in the store.)

But what if you buy average or excellent grapes—that is,
not the one-in-a-million, $37,000-a-ton ones, but the typical
excellent ones that brand-name wineries on the West Coast
buy, those costing $1,000 to $4,000 a ton?

For oak-free average-to-excellent whites:

$1,000 to $4,000 a ton grapes: $1.40 to $6 per bottle

Nice bottle, closure, and label: 90 cents a bottle

Winemaking: depends, let's guess $2 to $5 a bottle

Lowest likely taxes: 40 cents

Our running total so far, doing some rounding, is wine costing $4.50 to $13. Wholesaler/distributor: costs could be as little as 10 percent or as much as 50 percent, but for the sake of argument let's say 25 percent. The wine now has a wholesale cost of $4.75 to $16.25. Retailer profits: depends, but let's guess 30 percent, so average-to-excellent wine is going to cost $6 to $21.

So a nice, oak-free white is going to have a lowest possible price of around $6 to $21. The $6 bottle will have been machine-made from the cheapest possible grapes and will have had as little hand-labor invested in it as possible; sometimes this is totally appropriate and not a bad thing, for instance, in the case of steel-tank fermented Riesling or Sauvignon Blanc.

If you want to calculate the basic costs for an average-to-excellent red, you need to add a couple of bucks both for grapes, because they cost more, and for winemaking, because oak barrels, aging, and evaporation come into play. You even might add more for taxes, as some municipalities tax wine that's over 14 percent alcohol much more highly than other wine. Figure an average excellent red will run from $10 to $35.

So what's the difference between the $8 white and the $25 one? Or the difference between a $10 red and a $35 one? Usually, incremental bits of winemaking cost and investment.

Finally, of course, there's the price the winery decides to set. Winery A may price a wine with $15 of costs sunk into it at $20, while Winery B may have the same $15 cost and price its wine at $22—because their wines have gotten high scores in the past, or they are more famous, or they are competing with their ex-wives at Winery C, which prices its wine at $22, or for any number of human reasons. When that base cost is amplified by distributor, retailer, and shipping costs, the two wines might end up next to each other on a shelf near you at $30 and $37.

In another example, Winery A and Winery B might use the exact same $6,000-a-ton grapes, the same painstaking winemaking, and so on, but because the owner of Winery A inherited his winemaking facilities and the owner of Winery B just built a brand-new winery, Winery B has to charge more. Again, you might end up looking at a shelf with $30 and $40 wines sitting right next to each other that are, qualitywise, identical.

So what about $80 wines? Now you're purely into issues like reviews, collectibility, and price positioning—that is, a wine doesn't want to be too low-priced in comparison to its competition, because then people won't think it's any good.

In case you're wondering, winemakers aren't just being shallow in setting high prices so that people think they have made good wine, they're using good science. In 2008, Dr. Antonio Rangel of the California Institute of Technology published the results of a study about whether people enjoy more expensive wine more in the journal *Proceedings of the National Academy of Sciences.* Here's how he did it. He took twenty volunteers and rigged them up to a magnetic-resonance imaging machine that would study the parts of their brains that register pleasant experiences, their medical orbitofrontal cortexes. Then he gave them sips of what he claimed were five different glasses of Cabernet Sauvignon and he told them the price of the wine, from $5 to $90, before each sip. They said they liked the more expensive wines more, and as he watched their brains on the screen he could see that yes, indeed, their brains were showing that they were much, much happier when drinking the $90 wine. Better yet, Dr. Rangel actually used only three wines, not five, and people trying the exact same wine enjoyed it more when they thought it was more expensive. Best of all, when people were given a $90 wine and told it was $90 they loved it, but when they were given that same $90 wine and told it cost $10 retail, they rated it only half as highly—and their brains showed they didn't enjoy it as much. Dr. Rangel did this experiment twice, once on wine novices and again on people who presumably knew a couple of things about wine, because they were members of a Stanford University wine club, and he got the same results every time. To recap: People don't just think they enjoy $90 wines more than $10 wines, they *do* enjoy them more. No one has ever done this study, but I'd bet money that you could do the same thing with 100-point and 70-point wines, and you'd find medial orbitofrontal cortexes lighting up like Christmas trees over the higher-point wines.

Why? It's probably evolutionary. Study after study has shown that no matter what culture they live in, women prefer high-status mates, presumably because high-status mates make it more likely that offspring will thrive. So, the thinking goes, our brains are hard-wired to enjoy high-status experiences, like $90 wines, because they bring us reproductive advantage.

So the next time you see someone ordering a $400 wine, you'll know it's really their monkey-brain trying to get them laid. Or it's a really good wine.

A scientist from Cornell University, Brian Wansink, did an experiment to study how the status of wine makes us feel about our dinner as a whole. He went to a restaurant and offered subjects a free glass of wine to go with their prix fixe, multicourse French dinners. Everyone got a Two Buck Chuck red, but half the diners were told it was from "Noah's Winery, in California" and the other half were told it was from "Noah's Winery, in North Dakota." You probably see where this is going, but not only did people rate the "California" wine more highly, they liked the food they had with it better, ate 11 percent more of it, and were more likely to make return reservations to the restaurant.

To recap, what's the real difference between an $8, a $25, and an $80 bottle of wine?

A lot, but, generally speaking, an $8 wine is made by machines, the $25 wine is a handmade wine reflecting some inherent expense in the grapes and winemaking, and the $80 wine confers reproductive advantage.

Truly, you can assume that everything $80 and up is priced that way because of some kind of bragging rights that come with it—it's gotten great scores, it's highly collectible (meaning that people are buying it not to drink but speculatively, because they think it will increase in value), or it does something for someone's self-esteem. And if you don't know what those bragging rights are, and if it doesn't do anything for your self-esteem, skip it, because really it's not worth it to you.

And now here come the exceptions. I'm going to hedge my bets and say that my broad generalizations only cover *most* of the wine you'll find. Every so often, for instance, you will find a $12 handmade wine that's spectacular. Why? Usually because it's unpopular, or worse unknown. Unpopularity— of varietal, of region, or whatever—invariably dictates a lower price. Gruner Veltliner (*grooner velt-leener*) is an Austrian wine that no American wanted twenty years ago, so it was very cheap, but then it got very fashionable, and expensive, very quickly. There are also inequalities of currency or land price that can push wines outside of my rule-of-thumb guidelines. There are new Napa Valley Cabernet Sauvignons made from old vines on newly purchased land that have to sell at $150 to make back their huge debt costs. There are some European wines that have exceptionally high labor costs because they're Champagne, or their vineyards are planted on slopes that have to be harvested by human chains, or the grapes are harvested not just by hand but berry-by-berry over many weeks. Still, excepting the exceptions, you can use as a rule of thumb that wine under $80 is priced roughly like a box of nails—the final price reflects some multiple of what it cost to produce it, plus a lot of taxes—while wine over $80 is priced more like a Rembrandt—it's in the eye of the beholder.

Hopefully that clears up the mystery of the $8, the $25, and the $80 bottle of wine. I find the other seemingly simple but actually ungodly complicated question that bedevils wine drinkers is how to pick a cheap pizza wine. People always ask me how to do that, how to find that perfect

---

The Feel-Good Conspicuous Consumption Story of the Millennium

In his 1899 work *Theory of the Leisure Class,* the economist Thorstein Veblen laid out the idea of conspicuous consumption, namely that people devote a lot of time, thought, and money to buying things to signal our status to the rest of the group. Any wine drinker must reckon hourly with conspicuous consumption, because it informs so much of the world of wine. However, it's not just wine shoppers who have to deal with conspicuous consumption—birds do too! When birds do it, it's called "the handicap principle." This principle was first hypothesized by the biologist Amotz Zahavi and runs something like this: It's hard for animals to tell if their potential mates are being truthful about their reproductive fitness. If you're a lady peacock, how can you tell if any particular male peacock is truly strong, healthy, and possessing good genes? The answer: You can tell by looking at his crazy tail. The logic runs as so: If this peacock is fit enough to lead his life and also carry around and keep up this insane, and insanely useless, tail, then clearly he has resources to burn. Another example of resources to burn? Drinking a $300 bottle of Bordeaux.

Thursday-night-on-the-couch wine, nothing too fancy, just something good and interesting to make life with a movie and a pizza better than average.

The unfortunate long answer is this: The best way to find your pizza wine is going to be to go through the tastings in the prior chapters and find out where you yourself stand with the various varietals and wine styles. I could tell you that the best pizza wine in the land is Santa Cristina Sangiovese, or Snoqualmie Syrah, or Cline Cellars Zinfandel, all of which are great choices, but since wine shops are so individual, and taste is so individual, I can't possibly say which is the right wine for you.

If you invest the time in figuring out your own taste, if you systematically drink Sangiovese for a few months, and Zinfandel for another few, and Syrah for a few past that, you will hold the keys to the kingdom. You will walk into the wine shop and see teaser bins, shelf talkers, end caps, and other bits of merchandising and you will know the only thing that matters: your own taste. You will be able to find your pizza wine, you will know the difference between the sale bin full of bottom-shelf Chardonnay and the shelf in the back of the store with the Chianti as well as you know the difference between *Top Chef* and *Sesame Street*.

To find the price you want to pay requires familiarity with what you like and a realistic appraisal of what we talk about when we talk about wine price. I've given you the second part; now all you have to do is discover the first part.

Party Tips for Thrifty Hipsters

Champagne Cocktails

Buying wine for a party can be very expensive, but there are a couple of tricks for cutting back on cost stylishly. The best is to serve Champagne cocktails, because once you're adding any sort of sugar syrup or juice to Champagne you no longer have to buy anything French—the cheapest Australian bubbly or Spanish Cava you can find will now do nicely.

1. Kir Royales: This classic French budget stretcher is made by adding a splash of Cassis liqueur to Champagne. My favorite brand of Cassis comes from a French maker called Mathilde; the stuff is just a heavenly thunderbolt of sweet black currants.
2. Candied hibiscus flowers: You can find these sometimes at Trader Joe's. Soak them in advance in some bubbly to soften, then serve one per flute of Champagne. They look like beautiful undersea flowers.
3. Canned lychee fruits: Like the hibiscus flowers, but even easier. Drop one or two into each glass, with a bit of the canned juice.
4. Exotic simple syrups: To make a simple syrup you simply cook equal parts sugar and water until the sugar dissolves. You can make a flavored simple syrup out of just about anything you can think of—thyme and lemon zest, cardamom pods, apricots and ginger, lemongrass and basil, rosemary and black pepper, cinnamon and chili peppers—and once you do, you are a creative garnish away from having a cocktail you can claim as your own.

Sangria, Punch, and Mulled Wine

I always read magazine stories advising that you shouldn't use bad wine to make sangria, punch, or mulled wine, and when I read them I think these magazines are edited by the soft-headed. Why do you think these wine drinks were invented? What do you think remains of the winemaker's art and the vineyard's *terroir* once you've simmered something with raisins, cloves, and brown sugar? If you use anything but the cheapest non-toxic wine you can find for sangria, punch, or mulled wine, you're doing it wrong.

1. Sangria: Wine stretched with brandy and fruit, or just fruit juice and fruit, has been the stylish bohemian's way of stretching the party dollar ever since there were stylish bohemians. Your best bet is to hit the grocery store before the wine shop and look for the ripest fruit that's on sale. Kiwis, blueberries, pears, grapes, oranges, tangerines, or mangoes will go best with a white wine; oranges, apples, and pears are most commonly used with reds, along with cinnamon sticks. If your red-wine-based sangria doesn't taste right, add brown sugar cooked and dissolved in a little red wine, or finely milled quick-dissolving sugar (called castor sugar or superfine sugar; don't use confectioner's sugar, it contains an anti-caking agent that when dissolved tastes like talcum powder).

2. Claret Cup: The classic British way of making a cold red-wine cocktail for drinking on the lawn. For this you'll combine red wine, sugar, and sherry or an orange liqueur such as Grand Marnier in a punch bowl, stir till dissolved, add bubbly water, and garnish each punch cup with orange and lemon slices and perhaps an herb leaf of your choice, like borage, basil, or mint.

3. Mulled Wine: There are as many mulled wine recipes on earth as there are people who have tried to save money when throwing a party. All I can add to the conversation is that too many cloves can turn mulled wine into a mouth-numbing potion, so be careful with them, and if you happen to have a thermal carafe that you ordinarily use for coffee it makes serving mulled wine a labor-free experience for the host.

Cooking with Wine?

Food magazines and cookbooks invariably warn against using "cheap" wine for cooking, for beef Bourgignon and so on. This is a load of hooey; wine is so profoundly changed by cooking it for six hours with beef that if you waste a half bottle of premiere cru Bordeaux on the experience you better have started out your cooking by using a $100 bill to light the stove.

Here's better advice: Use any wine that you *would* drink for cooking. Supermarket "cooking wine" is poisonous-tasting—they make it that way on purpose, to prevent teenagers from guzzling it. If you use it, it will ruin your food. Likewise, skip any wine with off flavors—anything skunky that's been open on your counter for six weeks, anything corked, anything that's so cheap it's noxious. (Use a sour bottom-shelf Chardonnay that reeks of ground-up wood products in your lobster with Chardonnay sauce and you will regret it.) That said, there are hundreds of good $8 and $10 wines out there that will give your tomato sauce depth and your beef Bourgignon flavor without pouring money down the drain. A good rule is that if you're using half a cup of wine or less, simply use what you're drinking for dinner; if you need half a bottle, find a reliable bottom-shelf wine.

Thrifty enough for you? I'll take it a step further: If you find yourself with half a bottle of wine that you have no likelihood of drinking, decant it into a plastic tub and freeze it. Doing so will destroy the wine, but it will still be fine to cook with. This is the general equivalent of using wilted old basil in a recipe instead of fresh—it's not ideal, but it's a good way to use up old basil, and it's better than no basil. If your wine-snob neighbor catches you defrosting wine for your favorite chili recipe and looks askance, tell him it's a trick you learned from a wine critic.

The Inside Scoop for Would-be
Wine Bargain Hunters

Getting good, cheap wine is hard, and should be treated like
a sport: Sometimes knees will get skinned, but it's only a
game. Because you find more reliable wine above $15 than
under $10, a lot of people conclude it's more cost-effective to
simply buy more expensive stuff. But doing this can put you
right in the heart of the dullest wines of all, the $12- to-$18-
dollar mass market ones. There are strategies to maximize
your chance of winning the cheap-wine sweepstakes.

1. The less Americans understand it, the cheaper it will
   be. This is the cardinal rule of the wine store, and it's
   why Riesling and Chablis are vastly underpriced. People find them head-scratchers and regard them with
   vague suspicion. Use this to your advantage: Take a
   notepad with you to wine shops and jot down the
   names you've never heard of. A quick Internet search
   can usually tell you what you're looking at, and all of a
   sudden you're the only person in your city who knows
   what Bonarda is.

   Whether you'll *like* Bonarda is another story, which
   is why you should never buy a case of wine you haven't
   tried, no matter how good the price. Seriously, if you
   feel tempted to do this, take a bottle out to the parking
   lot and try it first, then reenter the store. Don't buy
   cases blind.

2. A $6 white is always better than a $6 red, and a $12
   white is always better than a $12 red, for two reasons.
   One, 99 percent of whites are meant to be drunk
   young, and typically aren't oaked, which eliminates
   two of winemaking's biggest expenses. Two, whites are
   less popular than reds. Fresh little European whites
   are the biggest bargain in wine.

3. Old Europe is drowning in wine. The same thing that Americans find bewildering about French and Spanish wine—there's so much of it!—is the same thing that makes the French and Spanish aisles so full of true bargains. In France and Spain they have wine the way Iowa has corn: It's everywhere, it's what they do, in order to do something else they'd have to invest billions, and more of it is coming next year so they've got to move it out.

They also find their labels self-evident, while Americans find them indecipherable. Learn one thing about the wines of European regions such as Languedoc, Beaujolais, or Penedès (in Spain) and you'll have bargains forevermore.

4. The best cheap American wines come from Washington State. Columbia Crest, Hogue, and Snoqualmie are the most reliable inexpensive wines in America. Why? Massive production, low prestige. Wine critics don't like them because they have no snob or surprise factor. Asking a wine critic about Hogue is like asking a car critic about Toyotas—there's just no news there. However, you could be a happy budget drinker if you drank only big-production Washington State wines. At least until you got bored and went looking for some surprises.

5. If you like rustic French reds you'll like South American reds. South American whites are as underpriced as most whites from unknown regions.

6. All European non-Champagne sparklers are very good, and excellent bargains. Cava, Prosecco, Crémant de Loire—if you find a European sparkler it will be better than any still wine at a comparable price in the store. Why? Sparklers are, as a rule, made with not-too-ripe grapes blended from many sites that are given

that final shot of sparkle with extra sugar and yeast (the classic Champagne method called the Charmoit method when done in big tanks instead of individual bottles). This fixes any unevenness in the wine, like the difference between someone singing into a microphone in a recording studio and what that vocal track sounds like after producers have cleaned it up and mixed it.

7. Never, ever, *ever* shop for wine the day before Thanksgiving. Or the day before New Year's or Christmas. Those are the three killer days that all wine workers dread, and if you want individualized attention, a happy employee, and someone who cares about you as a person, don't even think of going into a wine shop 36 hours before a major holiday. If you do, please don't hold it against them.

8. There's a reason every wine critic tells people to find a good shop. The world wine market is so big—millions of producers, hundreds of grapes, hundreds of wine styles—that there are tens of thousands of bargains available to anyone savvy enough to sniff them out. That's all specialty wine shops do, all day long.

   Build a relationship with a wine clerk, that is, build a common language between the two of you of things you have both tasted, and what you personally thought of them, and you will have made your life much easier. As soon as you can stand in front of a wall of wine and say: I liked this, I thought this was too tannic, I thought this was over-oaked, I loved this—you will now have a personal shopper. This is the fastest, easiest way to increase your odds of getting wine you like, and it's one that every wine critic uses themselves.

9. Wine shop employees are people too. They are slammed in the hour before dinner and all of Friday and Satur-

day evening, and more or less completely relaxed the other thirty hours of the week. And most work on the same seniority system as everyone else, and the most senior, most knowledgeable employees are going to have worked their tails off *not* to be on the floor during the beer frenzy of Friday night. You can usually get a personalized wine class if you go to a good wine shop, at, say, 2:00 P.M. on a Wednesday, and approach the clerk in the spirit of a seeker of wisdom.

10. If you can put your taste into words, you can get all the help in the world. Putting your taste into words is incredibly hard. First you have to know your taste, which means you have to taste a lot, and then you have to have the vocabulary for it. Once you do, though, you'll be amazed at how helpful wine store workers are. And when they're not, you'll be amazed at how little it bothers you.

What's your takeaway for wine and price? The way I see it, the key to all wine is simply this: finding the wine you like, at the price you want to pay. The nine chapters of this book covering various wine varieties were meant to help you with the first part, but the question of the price you want to pay can be absorbing as well. For instance, did you ever wonder why all the cheap wine is Australian? Did you ever wonder where Yellow Tail came from? Did you ever wonder how Australia could make so much cheap wine? If you never did, you should.

Yellow Tail, and all the cheap "critter" wines, came from a bright idea the Australian government had back in the 1960s. The idea was that Australia no longer wanted to have a dry, rocky, desert interior but instead a green and verdant one—like England's. So they started building dams like crazy, and today three quarters of the water in Aus-

---

Grocery Stores vs. Wine Shops vs. Costco

What kind of store offers the best value; grocery stores, wine shops, or big box stores like Costco and Sam's Club? The answer is an annoying: It depends. For the biggest international big brands—Kendall-Jackson, Yellow Tail, Kim Crawford, and so on—big stores have the best prices because they cut big deals at the top levels. That said, I think, and just about every critic on earth agrees with me, that the biggest bargains—that is, best value for price— tend to be found in independent wine shops. This is because the biggest bargains in the world are wines that are unknown or unpopular, or, as critics prefer to call them, *underappreciated.*

---

tralia goes to irrigated agriculture. Wine grapes need *a lot* of water.

In 1993, to speed up the process of turning their desert interior into a green and verdant vine land, the Australians instituted a tax shelter that, literally, has daily ramifications in the liquor stores of London, Los Angeles, and all places in between. Australian growers would be allowed to write off the expense of buying and planting grape vines over the course of four years, instead of in the ordinary way, over the lifetime of the vines. Since they would be writing off the cost of this buying and planting before the grapes bore fruit, it became a loss for tax purposes—a loss that would presumably turn into a profit a few years down the line—and thus it was a perfect tax shelter to protect other income. Between 1997 and 2001, Australia's wine plantings almost doubled.

Meanwhile, the Australian dollar sank. It was worth 80 of our cents in 1996 and sank to 50 cents five years later. So when all those new vines started coming to maturity and bearing fruit, they did so in a period of both cheap gasoline and cheap Australian dollars, which meant they could flood the United States and the United Kingdom with inexpensive, expertly engineered wine.

And I do mean engineered. Australian mega-producers formed by the cheap capital that was sloshing around the globe in the 2000s also have massive state-of-the-art winemaking facilities (which they had to build once their grape supply doubled), and some engage in what wine traditionalists call "better winemaking through chemistry": manipulations such as using acid or enzymes to enhance fermentations and get deeper fruit extracts, adding sugar to boost alcohol levels, concentrating fruit musts, using micro-oxygenation to essentially pre-age the wine, adding color additives like Mega Purple, and various tricks to get the acid in a wine lowered and the pH raised. In 2005, Australia produced 2 million cubic tons of wine grapes.

Then they put them in affordable bottles with critter labels. In 2007 Australia exported three billion dollars' worth of wine, much of it "critter wine." So government irrigation projects plus tax shelters plus cute animals equals you spending the Bush years drowning in affordable, likable Australian critter wine. However, the party came to a crashing halt in the summer of 2008, when the Australian dollar reached an all-time high of 98 cents to the U.S. dollar and Australia was hit by a devastating drought. Demand for Australian wine fell a whopping 26.5 percent that year, as people got bored with critter wine just as it got more expensive. Meanwhile, Australian environmentalists fret about Australia's "inland salinity" problem, which has resulted from irrigating areas that had a lot of salt underground, and the salt traveling upward through newly moist soil.

So should you drink Yellow Tail? Hell if I know. When I

was talking to Robert Parker, the most important wine
critic in the world, the subject of Yellow Tail came up: "Of
course, the popular taste is what it is," Parker told me. "The
most successful restaurant in the world is McDonald's, and
I think they make awful food, and the most successful wine
is Yellow Tail. Now, Yellow Tail doesn't make as bad a wine
as McDonald's makes bad food, but popular taste is what it
is." Now, am I going to tell you not to go to McDonald's? Of
course not. If there's one thing a career as a restaurant
critic has taught me it's that taste is above all personal. To
some people McDonald's is the taste of home. On the
fourth—or is it fifth?—hand, I heard rumors about a movie
star once who was said to drink nothing but the Napa Valley cult Cabernet Opus One, and that made me really sad.
It would be like walking into the grocery store, noticing
that the costliest item in there was foie gras, and deciding
to eat nothing but that, ever again. Really, no tangerines, no
cinnamon toast, no steak? But then, who am I to judge
someone's taste, even a movie star's?

I was talking about wine once with Eric Ripert, the chef
of Le Bernardin in New York City, a restaurant which is either one of the top five or top ten in the United States, depending on whom you ask. "I'm the nightmare of the
sommelier here at Le Bernardin," he told me. "I guess my
palate is not that refined."

You, I asked, your palate? Not refined? You have one of
the most revered palates in the world.

"Yeah," he laughed. "But they think I'm the anti-Christ. I
drink red Bordeaux with everything, oysters, fish, everything. I'm not right, I know it. I'm strongly, wrongly opin-
ionated. The sommeliers shake their head and say, 'Oh, he's
a lost cause.' "

No palate. Of course.

There's a white wine called Picpoul de Pinet, from the

Languedoc. It's very lemony and brisk, not very sophisticated, but every summer I get a bottle or two and drink it well chilled on a hot day while sitting in the shade of a maple tree in my backyard. It costs a little more than it should, probably because of the euro, $10 or $14 for a simple quaffer—but it will always be worth it to me. It's as important to my own personal sense of seasonality as asparagus in May and heirloom tomatoes in August.

I have friends who throw a Beaujolais Nouveau party every year, Beaujolais Nouveau being the youngest possible wine, the one that is released to great fanfare the third Thursday of every November. For this party everyone brings a bottle of the newly released wine and then sits around in the yard around a fire pit drinking the new wine, eating baguettes and butter and paté—it's a blast. Is Beaujolais Nouveau worth it? Certainly you could find a better-scoring wine at a lower price, certainly there are nobler wines—but I love those parties. (If you can, I encourage you to throw one of your own. They're a great way to mark the coming winter, and see friends who might not be around for Thanksgiving.) Is Beaujolais Nouveau worth it? Nothing's more personal than money, so that's a question you'll have to answer for yourself. If you haven't done the tastings in this book yet, you'll find that when you do them you'll try wines at many price points, and you should walk away knowing not just the most important thing—what you like—but also the second most important thing: What the price, cost, and value of wine means to you.

12

RESTAURANT CONFIDENTIAL

Dear Dara,

Okay, I'll give you this; I feel mildly informed. I had some tastings, and even this dude I went to college with who has Grateful Dead tattoos all over his body could tell the difference between the fruity Sauvignon Blanc and the mineral one. So thanks for that. However, I'm still completely baffled by lots of other stuff about wine. Like, why are restaurant wine lists two inches thick?

And another thing: What about corks? I sit down, I finally pick a wine, and then when it arrives, stuff gets weird. The server whips out a corkscrew with a little knife, peels off some junk, sticks it in her apron pocket. Then she pulls out the cork. Fine, I heartily endorse this action. I don't see any other way I'm going to get a drink short of someone shooting off the neck of the bottle.

But then she puts the cork down in front of me. What on earth am I supposed to do with this thing? I've seen other people sniff corks, but when I do it, they just smell like . . . well . . . cork.

Frankly, I can think of a hundred things that handing someone a cork might mean. Like, "Put a cork in it." Or "Stick this where the sun don't shine," or "I hereby demonstrate my contempt for you by handing you a useless stub of wet bark . . ." Seriously, what's the point?

Oh, and while I got you on the line: What's the best wine to order at my favorite Thai place, the cheap one by the park?

—Still Kind of Baffled

So many good questions. I'll pick off the easy one first: I'm guessing the best wine in that Thai place is a bottom-shelf Riesling or Sauvignon Blanc from an American producer like Hogue or Columbia Crest, or a bottom-shelf Syrah from Australia, like one from Alice White or Yellow Tail. Either of those should have enough sweetness and acidity to hold their own against something spicy like a coconut curry, and they're widely distributed enough that you can find them anywhere.

Of course, those are the best choices *unless* the place doesn't sell a lot of wine and the half-empty bottle has been sitting on top of their refrigerator for a week, in which case the best wine is going to be a cold beer. You have to know when to hold 'em, know when to fold 'em.

Wine in restaurants is a subject big enough for a book on its own. Some fun facts: About one-fourth of the wine sold in this country is sold at "on-premise" establishments, that is, restaurants, bars, wine bars, bowling alleys, and so forth. For high-end wine, that number is going to be even higher, and many wines are distributed *only* through restaurants. In fact, there are four distinct situations in which the restaurant you find yourself in will have completely different wines than you will find in local shops.

First, there are the exclusive upscale restaurants. Wineries see a high-end restaurant wine list as a marketing opportunity. If you see Snickerdoodle Cinnamon Vineyard Pinot Noir during a fancy expense account dinner at $200 a bottle, and then one day you walk into a store and see Snickerdoodle Plain Old Pinot Noir for $40 a bottle, you might think, "What a bargain!" Even if it was sitting next to a better $30 wine.

These wines that only get distributed through restaurants are called "restaurant-only allocations." Of course, the world of good restaurant-only allocations brought in a secondary universe of what I call fake restaurant-only allocations. Restaurants hate it when you know that their $8-a-glass Chardonnay retails for $8 a bottle, so some really big chains have found a way around this. They'll get a winery to make them a special "restaurant-only" wine for, oh, four bucks a bottle, and sell it for $8 a glass or $40 a bottle. And unless you're inside the company you'll never be the wiser. The wine is not reviewed by critics and generally spends its life in a dark, happy, profitable place.

In addition to real and faux restaurant-only allocations, small, independent bargain-hunting restaurants actually go to Europe, find wines they want, and arrange for a local importer to bring them in exclusively for them. They do this not only because they love wine, but also because if you're a fellow wine nut you're more likely to return to their restaurant for their rare finds.

Then there are the established restaurants that have a $500,000 annual wine budget. They buy their '96 Cabernets in '99 and put them on their wine lists in '05, and if you go to one and fall in love with something old and wonderful, too bad for you. Unless you can time-travel in your wayback machine to buy some. And that's why every store in the universe carries the same brands of potato chips, but you can go to four restaurants in a week and never see the same wine.

So as you ricochet through restaurants there's no great way to tell whether the wines you run across are fabulous bargains, fair and wonderful, or giant rip-offs unless you rely on your very own taste.

Speaking of individual taste, the reason sommeliers with those overwhelming thousand-bottle wine lists usually give for having such long lists is that they need to have something to satisfy every taste. However, please know that if you're confounded by those mega-lists, and see people at other tables blithely ordering from them as if they're in full knowledge of every winemaker and every vintage and are simply riffing through the names as easily as a fourth-grader rips through his own baseball card collection, this is not so! A good number of people just know their taste and don't even look at nine hundred of those thousand bottles, simply zeroing in on Pinot Noir or what have you.

More important, there's an argument to be made that any list with that many wines on it is lazy and bad. The co-owner and wine director of two of Los Angeles's best restaurants, Lucques and the wine bar A.O.C., Caroline Styne has been named one of the hundred most powerful people in Los Angeles by *L.A. Magazine;* she was on the list right after Arnold Schwarzenegger and Steven Spielberg. I asked her about that nagging fear that the happy people at the next table know what they're looking at.

"People always think that," Styne told me. "They think, you're a celebrity, you're rich, you're powerful, so magically you know everything about wine. A lot of time it's just the opposite, if you're a really powerful celebrity maybe you haven't had any time to devote to wine. I got a call this summer from somebody who said, 'I want to buy my brother-in-law wine lessons, would you be interested in teaching him? His name is Dustin Hoffman. He's had private chefs for years, whoever has been cooking for him has told him what wine to buy, but we go to a restaurant now and he looks at a wine list and doesn't know where to start.' "

Beautiful people like Hollywood celebrities and the people around them feel the same pressure as people in wine bars in Brooklyn or Seattle, Styne told me, if not worse. "Imagine you're an agent and you're trying to woo an actor, then the pressure really mounts: What if it gets here and it's a horrible wine? Especially in L.A. there's so much pretense and façade, sometimes you walk up to a table and there's this palpable element of 'Oh my God, it's time to order the wine, please don't make me do this.' "

When Styne finds a table on the verge of a wine-ordering breakdown she'll step in. "Let's just find something you're going to enjoy, and forget about everything else," she'll say.

What most customers fail to understand, Styne told me, is that the only people who are really expected to know the wine list at A.O.C. or Lucques are the people who work at A.O.C. or Lucques. "I taste twenty, thirty wines a week, and, at various periods in my life, lots more than that," she says. "Add that up over a career"—and add in that Styne has formal sommelier training—"and there's still a lot I don't know about wine. I can't possibly know every wine on every list."

What's more, she doesn't want to. Part of what you are paying the restaurant to do for you, says Styne, is to preselect a limited number of wines for you to choose among. Because a thousand wines is too many words for anyone to read before they get a drink.

Of course, there are people who like an endless brain-boggling list. At Bern's Steak House in Tampa, Florida, for instance, the list is, as of this writing, 6,800 bottles and more than two hundred pages long, and is remarkable to wine people the same way a three-headed duck or the Great Wall of China is: you just don't see that every day, and you'd be silly not to cross the street to get a closer look.

However, sometimes a 2,000- or 3,000-bottle list is a restaurant's version of a Michigan bankroll: a single hundred-dollar bill wrapped around a wad of singles to dazzle the easily impressed. What's with all those old, not-so-fresh whites and obscure off-vintage reds? Wine has to go somewhere to die.

Part of the reason Los Angeles' beautiful people flood Lucques and A.O.C. is that Styne's wine list is so tight. "My three-hundred-wine list represents years of tasting, years of relationships with winemakers, years of exploring new wine areas, finding new varietals, thinking about different winemaking styles," she says. "People know that when they're coming into one of our restaurants they're coming to choose wine that I've picked out, that I stand behind, and that's tailored to my palate. Our wine list is a continuation of the personality, spirit, and sense of the restaurant."

So you can think of the thousand-bottle wine list as a coward's defense against the criticism that he hasn't provided something for everyone. They're lazy efforts built on the idea that if you alienate no one, you please everyone.

Speaking of alienating no one, that's where the whole ritual of uncorking wine at your table got started. Once upon a time restaurants often bottled their own wine, meaning they had a barrel of wine in the basement and a load of bottles they washed and reused.

Meanwhile, there were also expensive premium wines, wines bottled at a château and shipped out wearing their own labels, corks, and foil. If you showed up at a restaurant and splashed out for the super-premium wine, how would you know you were getting what you asked for and not wine from the basement barrel? Thus was born the whole uncorking-at-table ritual. All that stuff your server is doing is an elaborate pantomime meant to prove she is not defrauding you.

First she shows you the bottle so you can see it's the bottle you've ordered, and the vintage you've ordered. Look carefully! I've had servers grab wines from the wrong bin, or the restaurant switch vintages without noting it on the wine list. This display of the bottle is your time to say, "Yeah, that's what I ordered," or, "No, wake up, pal!"

Step two, the foil removal, is to show you that the bottle has not been tampered with since it left the winery.

Step three is the cork. This is the big fraud protection device. Most wineries have their name printed on the side of the cork, and expensive wines always do. The corks in most French wines will note the vintage as well. When your server hands you that cork, she's really giving you your chance to match the carpet to the drapes, so to speak. Do they match? Unless it's 1879 and you're in rural France, or you're buying the kind of million-dollar wines that people take the time to make fakes of, they probably match. (Yes, there are faked wines, but don't get too heated up about it; they're mainly premium ultra collectibles. The wine writer Lettie Teague once compiled a list of the most-faked wines—look out for the 1811 Château d'Yquem, the last authenticated bottle of which sold for seventy-five thousand dollars! If someone brings a bottle round with the cheese cart, think twice.) Once you have determined that the label on the front of the bottle you ordered is the wine you wanted, proceed with your wine theater.

Next she'll pour a taste of your wine and wait for you to do something. You are now supposed to sniff the wine to determine whether the cork was infected by something called

TCA (2,4,6-trichloroanisole), a compound that makes wine smell like wet, acrid cardboard. Better known as "cork taint," it ruins anywhere from 2 to 10 percent of wines. (Sniff the wine, not the cork. Corks smell like corks.)

If corks are so fraught with peril, why have them at all? It's actually pretty simple: Wines meant to be aged have to be bottled with cork, because it permits the wine to breathe and grow and live, which is what it is doing in your cellar. Corks are born as a complex ecosystem of bazillions of microorganisms and fungi. No one really understands the totality of what cork is, or how exactly it interacts with wine and helps it to age. In 2008 researchers from the University of Bordeaux proved that real corks allowed tiny amounts of oxygen to enter wine bottles. Still, corks for fresh young whites are going the way of the dodo bird: Wines that are meant to be drunk young are increasingly bottled under screw caps to avoid cork taint losses.

But getting back to the cork your server hands you: They really are just giving you the cork because of tradition. As previously stated, cork taint can only be discovered by smelling the wine, not by smelling the cork.

Sometimes you can't even tell that a wine is "corked" until the bottle has been open for a little while and allowed to breathe. The first few seconds after your server pours is *not* the only chance you have to send the wine back. If at any point you lift your glass and think, "My God, it smells like cardboard rotting in a gutter," it's a good time to send the wine back.

This is not a rude thing to do, it's a normal part of doing business for the restaurant; they return the wine to the distributor and get a credit, so they're not even out any money. If it smells bad, speak up!

In fact, servers and sommeliers will be in a strange, socially awkward place if you *don't* send back your corked wine. "We had a guy bring in this wine that was so corked we could smell it was corked before we took the cork out," Bill Summerville, the sommelier of Minneapolis's white-tablecloth restaurant La Belle Vie, told me once. "But you never cut a guest off at the knees in front of his guests, so we opened it, presented it to him, and he was like, 'It smells like really old wine.' It probably cost him a couple thousand dollars, and if it made him happy to drink it, who are we to get in the way? People bring in their babies that they've been cellaring for eons. Once we pull the cork we're like, 'Argh, you should have drunk this years ago.' But they'll say, 'Oh you guys have to taste this, it's phenomenal.' On the other end of the spectrum, some of these cult Cabernets that people pay thousands of dollars for, they just taste like bubblegum."

So if you want to know what the high rollers at the next table are doing, chances aren't bad that they're lying to themselves, or floundering in a sea of confusion. Like everybody else.

So let me emphasize that you should feel no pressure to decide that a wine is flawed the second that whole bit of presentation theater goes down. "I have sat with a wine and then my wife will pick up the glass: 'Bill, it's corked,' " Summerville says. "I'm 100 percent fine with a guest taking their time with a wine. But you know, if they drink three-quarters of a bottle and then decide it's corked, what am I supposed to do?"

Which brings up a few more wine flaws that are actually pretty innocuous and natural. One is when a cork breaks and bits of it are floating in your glass. This isn't ideal, but it is harmless. There's even a tradition meant to deal with this: When you pour wine you're actually supposed to pour yourself the first glass, not your guests, because it's likely that any cork bits will end up in that first glass.

Another bit of harmless weirdness is tartrate crystals, usually found in white wine. They look like tiny bits of broken glass, or sand; they're yellowish or clear, and I've read that sometimes they can be so big that they look like little shards of window glass. However, as freaky as they look, they're a totally innocuous byproduct of winemaking, and actually point to a quality wine: Highly processed, repeatedly filtered wines have no tartrate crystals, but they also have no flavor because all that processing and filtering removes it. In Germany, the land of white wine, they call them "wine stones," which is much cuter than "tartrate crystals." Tartrate crystals come from tartaric acid, and are naturally found in "tart" foods, like tamarind and unripe grapes.

Sometimes you'll get a glass of wine that has some sediment in it, especially from the bottom of the bottle. It might be a film, like the skin on boiled milk, but purplish. It might look like pieces of long-dead wet leaves stirred up off the bottom of a pond. It might look like goopy wet dust, or wet ash.

Whatever it looks like, this weird muck, this sediment, is not harmful. Again, it's actually a good sign; you're more likely to find it in better, more carefully made wines in which the winemaker chose not to filter the wine with the aim of creating a more fragrant, more texturally complex wine.

Still, remember that if you're in a restaurant with a sommelier, you really shouldn't have to figure any of this out for yourself. You should be able to just hand them your glass of wine and say, "Is there something wrong with this?" Because that is in essence the job of a sommelier: to worry about the wine so you don't have to.

Of course, one is not always blessed by being surrounded by thoughtful and professional sommeliers. I remember one time I was in a wine bar and got a corked bottle, and no one would believe me. "We served the first four glasses in the bottle to people who liked it just fine," my server told me. When you become a wine person, you will get anecdotes like this of your very own. It happens to everyone. Everyone. Bo Barrett, one of the owners of Château Montelena, puts it well: "No matter where you go, you're going to run into a few peckerwoods. I'll be sitting there with Heidi [Peterson Barrett, Bo's wife, a legendary winemaker]. She's got more 100-pointers than anyone, and we'll run into a bottle that's corked, and we'll say: This wine is corked. The snotty sommelier will say, No, it's not. We'll go back and forth like this until finally I pull out my business card and say: Look. Take this back to your manager and say: 'This customer says it's corked.' I overrun their positions. Story of my life."

This is the dark side of wine intelligence. Is it better to be a happy idiot drinking corked wine or a smart wine person fighting with happy idiots? Welcome to paradise.

Speaking of happy idiots, there are also plenty of near-useless sommeliers, like the "wine directors" who buy wine for a chain that doesn't then put anyone on the restaurants' floors who knows anything about the wines on offer. To my mind this is just another example of how chain restaurants cheat their customers. Restaurant wine's hefty markups are justified in part by the idea that you're paying an employee's salary. If there's no sommelier or anyone else who can help you with the wine in a restaurant, they should be charging exactly what liquor stores do, and not a penny more.

Restaurants, like wine shops, buy their wine from distributors and pay wholesale cost, but restaurants typically mark their wine up 300 or 400 percent versus a wine shop's 200 percent. A bottle of wine that leaves the winery at $10 might be $15 or $20 in an average liquor store, and $30 or

$40 in a restaurant. A glass of wine—and there are typi-
cally five glasses in a bottle—is priced anywhere from the
equivalent of a wholesale bottle to a third of the wine list
cost, so a $10 wholesale wine might appear on a wine list
for $10 a glass (meaning the restaurant nets a $40 profit
when they sell the whole bottle). With those kind of profits
I feel they're obligated to provide good wine service. And
you're obligated to tip for it.

One of the perennial questions that comes up for new
wine drinkers is whether they need to tip on the wine portion of the overall restaurant bill. The answer will be obvious when you consider that the IRS calculates servers' tips
as part of their gross table receipts, as much as 18 percent.
So if you buy a $1,000 bottle of wine, your server is proba-
bly paying taxes on $180 of income he or she was assumed
to have received from you on that wine purchase. If you
don't tip them, you're basically taking money out of their
pockets. If you can't afford the tip, you can't afford the wine.
As an added bonus to your fellow diners, if you can afford to
tip the United States has a chance of developing a true culture of service. Restaurant service, of course, is a thing that
everyone complains about—and then they turn around and
insult servers by regarding them as people who couldn't get
better jobs. The first thing all of us could do to encourage
better service is to consider that servers fill one of the most
selfless and generous roles in the culture. They are there to
help, to serve, to elevate your evening. And sommeliers are
essentially the most trained helpers—as surgeons are to
doctors, sommeliers are to servers.

One of the model sommeliers in the United States is
Bobby Stuckey. And I don't just mean that because he looks
like a model—though he does, he's a square-jawed Captain
America with mountain breezes blowing through his spiky
golden hair. Also, he was once a professional bicyclist on

Team America. No kidding. And he walked away from the most prestigious job in all of American restaurant and wine culture—more on that in a moment—no doubt whistling like a cowboy as he went, his titanium bicycle slung over one shoulder, in order to open Frasca Food and Wine, a tiny Italian restaurant in Boulder, Colorado, dedicated to the cuisine of Friuli-Venezia Giulia.

What's that? You know how Italy has the boot, but then at the top of the boot, there's the wide cuff? All the way over to the far right, on the border with Slovenia, is a subalpine region that's only been part of Italy since World War I; before that it was part of the Austro-Hungarian Empire.

I figured the big connection between Boulder and Friuli-Venezia Giulia was that they're both subalpine regions, but when I called up Bobby Stuckey he said no, that's not it; he and his chef business partner, Lachlan Mackinnon-Patterson, just love the area. And once you decide to walk away from big money and the competitive game, you really don't have to do anything but what you love.

Stuckey used to be the sommelier at Napa Valley's French Laundry, arguably the most important restaurant in America. While he was there, he won the prestigious James Beard award for best sommelier in America, and lots of people credit him with much of the restaurant's early excellence.

French Laundry opened some casual sister restaurants called Bouchon, and then got ready to open the other most important restaurant in America, New York City's Per Se. Stuckey was offered the chance to be wine director for all those restaurants, and took it. He even went so far as to work with architects and designers to put together the cellar and such for Per Se. But somewhere along the way he had a realization. "I'm not a corporate wine guy, and I don't want to be on a plane two weeks a month," he says. "I look at myself as a retro service guy. I can't imagine not being on the floor. I have no interest in not touching the guest." So he walked away.

Why? He has an almost religious devotion to the idea of customer service. In fact, he runs a secret, informal wine training school where he helps tutor the next generation of sommeliers.

As of this writing, only 124 people in the entire history of time have passed the Master Sommelier exam given by the Court of Master Sommeliers—Stuckey, of course, being one. But six of the thirteen people who have passed it in the last two years were protégés of Stuckey's, and trained with him at his restaurant.

Sometimes Stuckey has a wine staff four or five people deep on the floor of his small Boulder restaurant, some paid, some volunteering for the chance to be part of this passionate, learned crew. The whole staff, including servers, does wine training every day before service and a one-hour wine class every weekend. Does this tiny, seventeen-table Boulder restaurant have the best wine service in America? Quite probably.

Which is good, because the wine list focuses on the region of Friuli-Venezia Giulia, which means precisely nothing to the vast majority of Americans. "How do you reach a guest when you have a list of crazy Tokais?" Stuckey asks, rhetorically. "Even great sommeliers don't necessarily know anything about some particular Italian region. Wine is like any other genre of art or music. You might know opera inside out, but not rhythm and blues. All kinds of people know wine really well, but don't know Friuli. That's fine. It's not their job to know our wine list. It's our job to know our wine list."

In matters of taste, Stuckey continues, each guest is the expert on his or her own palate. "The foremost thing we're here to do is listen," he says. "The first thing we ask the guest is not 'What are you eating?' but 'What do you like?' If they say, 'I love Australian Shiraz,' we realize we have to take a step back, we can't talk to them about Nebbiolo," one of Italy's great red wines. "Nebbiolo is nervy, high acid, just something very different from an Australian Shiraz, and if the guest loves Australian Shiraz it's our job to find something on our list that makes them say, 'Wow, I love this.'"

But what if the person at his table doesn't even have enough wine vocabulary to be able to pluck a varietal and region out of thin air? In that case, Stuckey starts with "Red or white?" and brings a few samples of different styles.

This may not seem revolutionary, but it's radical. The customer doesn't have to know *anything,* doesn't have to feel any anxiety whatsoever, just has to sit there and say, "I like this, not this." To me this is really the ultimate in customer wine service, the standard to which every other restaurant should aspire.

So why don't other restaurants do this? Mainly because they haven't thought things through, Stuckey says: "If you're a true professional you embrace all the new people you see because you never know who is going to be the person who you see return over the next twenty years. If you try to turn every new customer into a twenty-year customer every night, you'll have quite a following—and you'll have really changed people's wine lives."

I was talking to another of the country's leading wine service people once, John Ragan, the sommelier for New York City's posh restaurant Eleven Madison Park. Ragan told me there were two things he would change about the world of wine in restaurants. First, he would invert the common understanding of the power relationship between customer and sommelier.

Think of a wine list as a haystack, and the perfect wine

you seek as the needle in it. "It's the sommelier's job to dig through this haystack, not yours," Ragan says. "All someone really needs to know is how much they want to spend, and what sort of experience they want to have—something red, something funky and earthy, or what have you. The only concerns a great sommelier should have are making friends, helping you have a good time, and creating an experience so good that people want to come back." If you feel your sommelier is not doing this, it's not the wine that's subpar, it's the sommelier.

Ragan's other idea for revolutionizing wine service in America is that there should be some sort of universal bill of rights for wine drinkers. He gave me a few ideas about what would be in this bill of rights, and, over the course of a few months the concept really took deep root within me. I've talked to other wine folks about it, adding to the list and refining it.

If I do say so myself, it's a brilliant idea. One of the things that makes American restaurant culture work is that we have shared expectations. If we have a seven o'clock reservation we should be seated by 7:15, or 7:30 with an apology and a free drink. If we order a steak rare and it comes well-done, we have a right to a second steak. If we're in a sushi restaurant, there should be a variety of fish offered; if we're in a bistro, there should be salads as well as entrées. Cold things, like ice cream, should be served cold; hot things, like lasagna, should be served hot. An expensive restaurant should have tempting appetizers, entrées, and desserts; a pizza place doesn't need to have anything more than pizza. I could do this all day, but I think you get my sense: Restaurants don't make us anxious because we have a commonly agreed-upon set of rights (to be seated on time, to be fed appropriately cooked foods). When it comes to wine, however, we're a young wine-drinking country and one that's traditionally nervous about class issues. In wine shops, restaurants, and wine bars, we never know what we should be doing, what we're supposed to know, or what's expected of us, and into this vacuum hearsay, rumor, and misperceptions flood in to create a cesspool of social anxiety. The majority of readers I've heard from over the years, for instance, feel certain that their job is to impress sommeliers. However, I've never heard from a single reader who felt it was necessary, or difficult, to impress their plain old server.

"In my opinion, the worst thing that ever happened to American wine, besides Prohibition, was this establishment in the American mind of what a sommelier is," Paul Einbund, the sommelier of Coi (pronounced *kwa*), the leading avant-garde San Francisco restaurant, told me. "Say 'sommelier' and what do people think? A six-foot-tall fat bearded man looking down his nose at you, past a big silver tastevin." (A tastevin is a little bowl that sommeliers used to wear on a chain around their necks to sample things, usually wines, from barrels, back when restaurants used to have barrels in their cellars.)

"If that big bearded fat guy ever existed, he doesn't exist now," Einbund told me. "But he certainly intimidated a couple of generations into sticking to beer and bourbon. Well, now it turns out you can be just as snobby about beer and bourbon if you want to be, but it happened too late to frighten people away from beer. In any event, I'm a sommelier—someone who's there to help make sure the guests have a good time. That's all!"

How can we get Americans, or at least you, to go from that anxious place of feeling that you're supposed to impress the sommelier to the calm place of feeling that you don't need to impress your server? I think it's by identifying, internalizing, and insisting upon your rights as a wine drinker.

A Wine Drinker's Bill of Rights

1. **The Right to Enjoy Your Own Taste:** Your whole life has been one cumulative process adding up to your own taste. No person, critic, wine shop clerk, or anyone else has a right to disparage or discount it. If you want to drink Bordeaux with your oysters, Port with your burger, or Chardonnay with your fried chicken, it is no one's business but your own. No one lives with your taste buds but you, so no one really knows what you are experiencing except you. It's your taste!

2. **The Right to Know Nothing and Get Help:** Whether you're in a wine shop, a grocery store, a big box store, a restaurant, or a wine bar, you have the absolute right to have someone help you navigate the choices the establishment in question has laid out for you. If you can't get that help, it is not your fault, it is their fault. If it's their stated business plan to put out a variety of objects to be sold by a staff that knows nothing about them, it's a lousy and stupid business plan.

3. **The Right to Be Spoken to in Language You Can Understand:** It's useless to be told that Château Snickerdoodle is a classic Pauillac if you don't know what that means. It's useless to be told a wine smells like lychee fruits and Oloroso Sherry if you've had neither. If the people selling wine to you can't find a way to communicate with you in a way you can understand, they're not cut out for customer service and should find other work.

4. **The Right to Have Wine in Restaurants That Matches the Food:** In terms of both flavor profile and price, you have the right to expect that any restaurant has a wine list that will match your expectations for

your evening. This means that high-end restaurants will have something high-end and dazzling, and that little Thai neighborhood joints will have something fresh and crisp.

5. **The Right to Have Someone on Hand in a Restaurant Who Can Talk About the Wine:** The answer to the question "Is there someone here who can help me pick out a wine?" should always, always be yes. If a restaurant is selling wine its staff can't speak about, they are not offering adequate wine service. Period.

6. **The Right to Have Someone Who Recommends Wine Who Also Knows the Restaurant's Food:** Anyone recommending wine to drink with food should have tasted every dish they need to pair wine with. They should be able to tell you if the lemongrass chicken is spicy or sweet, if the turbot with saffron is dusky, creamy, or both, whether the poached grouse is served in a dark *jus* or a white-wine-based cream sauce, and so on. If a restaurant doesn't want to invest time in educating its employees about the food and wine, they should just pack it up and open an Automat.

7. **The Right to Sample Wine in Wine Bars and Restaurants:** If the wine is open in the restaurant, you should be offered a taste.

8. **The Right to Decent Glassware:** Wine should be served in a glass that allows the customer to both see the wine and smell it. Serving great wine in a shallow tumbler is like having a florist deliver a bouquet by dumping the flowers on the floor. Yes, you have your flowers, but not in any way you can enjoy them. Of course, having a $4 glass of serviceable picnic wine in a tumbler is its own sort of pleasure. But as a general rule of thumb, anytime wine costs more than $10 a

glass or $20 a bottle, you should get a decent glass to drink it from.

9. **The Right to Wine Served at the Correct Temperature:** You wouldn't accept lasagna served ice-cold, so why should you have to accept red wine served at 100 degrees? Likewise, wine meant to be served cold, like Champagne, really should not be allowed to warm on the table through several courses. It should be kept on ice.

10. **The Right to Send Back Flawed Wine Without a Fight:** Flawed wine, whether sold in a wine shop, big box store, or restaurant by the bottle or glass, is a basic part of life, and every wine seller should be prepared to deal with it. There should be someone on hand at all times in all venues who can recognize corked wine, just as there should be someone in a restaurant kitchen who can recognize spoiled food. It's just part of doing business.

11. **The Right Not Just to Pursue Happiness, but to Achieve It:** Above all, the reason you have wine is to have a nice, enjoyable, pleasant life—right? The best way to judge a wine shop's or restaurant's service is to reflect upon it the next day. Were the people nice to you? Were they nice to you even if something awkward happened, like getting a corked bottle? Were they able to answer questions you had about the wine? Were they able to answer any questions you had about food and its relationship to the wine? Did the experience make your life better, or worse? If the people you buy wine from aren't making you happier than you would be without them in your life, you're being shortchanged.

Is this Bill of Rights making much ado about nothing? I'd argue no. Downtime, stemware, your dinner tonight—

they all have value, they all deserve dignity, and they are there to make you happy. They don't deserve a SWAT team to descend and silence your neighbor's lawn mower during your barbecue, but these little parts of life do deserve respect. Wine is, after all, something you add to make your life a little nicer, a little more enjoyable, a little more fun, a little more involved with the world and the great heritage of Western culture. It's not mandatory. You could drink beer.

If wine can't provide happiness, it should get out of the way and let something else do it, like chocolate. And if the people taking your money when you get wine, no matter where you get it, are not working to make you happier than you'd be if you were drinking a beer on your porch, that's bad service, that's bad manners, that's not nice. Sure, I know that there are big box stores whose unspoken business plan is "We have bad service so you get low prices!" But it's still bad service. And you still deserve better. You may not choose to pay for better, but you still deserve it.

As my parting words, I'll offer you an anecdote. Have you heard the one about the finger bowls, the queen, and the foreigner? Finger bowls are little bowls of water that might appear at your place setting during an exceptionally formal dinner party; they were really big in the nineteenth century. To use a finger bowl properly you dip your fingers in the water, dry your wet fingers on your napkin, and get on with your meal.

Legend holds that one day an esteemed foreigner was dining at the palace. When the finger bowls appeared, the foreigner, not knowing any better, drank the contents. Seeing this and not wanting to embarrass her guest, the queen immediately downed her finger bowl as well. Seeing her lead, so then did all the other guests.

That's manners. That's hospitality.

I know you won't be treated like that everywhere you go, but still that's what I want for you.

Because if you would discover your taste, and greet the world with openness and a firm understanding of your rights, and the world responded with manners and hospitality, we'd have a wine-drinker's paradise.

ACKNOWLEDGMENTS

The thank-yous and indebtedness of a writer's first book could fill pages, and this one is no different. First, I'd like to thank all who took the time to ask questions. There's much made these days about "crowd-sourced" journalism; this book is an exercise in "crowd-asked" journalism.

To my husband, Nathan, my thanks are infinite; behind every woman with a toddler and a newborn and a full-time job who meets a book deadline is a dad doing some serious heavy lifting. Thanks for believing in me well past the point of self-sacrifice. (Thanks too to grandma and grandpa Grumdahl, hosts of lifesaving sleepover weekends.)

Thanks to my longtime editor Beth Hawkins for helping me in every way imaginable, and also for assisting me over the course of a decade in developing my idea that speaking truth to power applies in restaurants and wine shops too.

Thanks to my secret-agent Dennis Cass, a friend and fellow writer who has put more energy into my work, and its natural sidekicks, complaint and self-doubt, than you'd ever believe.

Thanks to all the winemakers, critics, chefs, sommeliers, and others who gave so freely of their time and energy; obviously this book wouldn't exist without you, but only you and I know the importance of the things you told me that ended up on the cutting-room floor, so thanks for those too.

Thanks to Tim Teichgraeber and Tara Q. Thomas, bona fide wine critics and even more bona fide friends who each devoted vast energies to helping me understand what I didn't. Thanks to cover designer Brian Johnson, who is awfully good at putting a writer's poorly expressed aspirations into striking visual form.

Thanks to Evan Camfield, a production editor of great and unflagging insight who battled accents and winery names in five languages with aplomb.

Thanks to my agent Scott Moyers for being an ever poised and insightful spot of calm in a storm, for believing in my voice, and for believing in a world of readers who want to be met as peers, not schoolchildren.

Deep thanks to my book editor Pamela Cannon, whose instincts for this book have been inerrant, and even, as much as it pains a writer to admit, better than mine. I thank you for your vision; if wine culture in this country gets nudged a few degrees out of confusion and into clarity the world will largely have you to thank.

Finally, thanks to my mom for raising kids who believed they could do anything—including something as foolhardy as trying to make wine simple.

INDEX

===

ABOUT THE AUTHOR

Dara Moskowitz Grumdahl is senior editor of *Minnesota Monthly,* editor in chief of *Real Food,* and a regular contributor to *Gourmet, Bon Appétit, Condé Nast Traveler, USA Today,* and other national publications. She also appears regularly on local Minnesota television and radio. She has won four James Beard awards for wine writing and restaurant criticism, and lives in Minneapolis with her husband and two children.

ABOUT THE TYPE

This book was set in Century Schoolbook, a member of the Century family of typefaces. It was designed in the 1890s by Theodore Low DeVinne of the American Type Founders Company, in collaboration with Linn Boyd Benton. It was one of the earliest types designed for a specific purpose: the *Century* magazine, maintaining the economies of a narrower typeface while using stronger serifs and thickened verticals.